CREATING ETHNODRAMA

Qualitative Methods "How-To" Guides

Patricia Leavy, Series Editor

This series provides researchers and students with step-by-step, practical instruction on established and emerging qualitative methods. Authors are leaders in their respective areas of expertise who demystify the research process and share innovative practices and invaluable insider advice. The basics of each method are addressed, including philosophical underpinnings, and guidance is offered on designing studies; generating, analyzing, interpreting, and representing data; and evaluating the quality of research. With accessible writing, robust examples, and ample pedagogical features, books in this series are ideal for use in courses or by individual researchers.

Re/Invention: Methods of Social Fiction
Patricia Leavy

Case Study Research: The Art of Studying the Singular
Helen Simons

Creating Ethnodrama: A Theatrical Approach to Research
Joe Salvatore

Creating Ethnodrama

A THEATRICAL APPROACH TO RESEARCH

Joe Salvatore

gp

THE GUILFORD PRESS
New York   London

For product and safety concerns within the EU, please contact *GPSR@taylorandfrancis.com*,
Taylor & Francis Verlag GmbH, Kaufingerstraße 24, 80331 München, Germany.

Last digit is print number: 9   8   7   6   5   4   3   2   1

Library of Congress Cataloging-in-Publication Data

Names: Salvatore, Joe (Artist-researcher) author.
Title: Creating ethnodrama : a theatrical approach to research / Joe
    Salvatore.
Description: New York : The Guilford Press, 2025. | Series: Qualitative
    methods "how-to" guides | Includes bibliographical references and index.
Identifiers: LCCN 2024058357 | ISBN 9781462557707 (cloth) |
    ISBN 9781462549856 (paperback)
Subjects: LCSH: Playwriting. | Qualitative research. | Social
    sciences—Research—Methodology. | Drama—Technique. |
    Theater—Technique. | Ethnology.
Classification: LCC PN1661 .S325 2025 | DDC 808.2—dc23/eng/20250314
LC record available at *https://lccn.loc.gov/2024058357*

To Harley Erdman and Roberta Uno,
thank you for the introduction

To Johnny Saldaña and Anna Deavere Smith,
thank you for the inspiration

Preface

My relationship with ethnodrama grew out of making interview theatre at the beginning of my career. The early works of actress, playwright, and professor Anna Deavere Smith inspired me to think about topics I was interested in and then interview people who had thoughts and opinions about those topics. I considered this process theatre making, not research. In retrospect, I now understand I was conducting qualitative research in a way that mirrors the work of ethnographers: interviewing participants about a topic or experience to help describe or explain a particular phenomenon. Initially, I might not have worked from a clearly articulated research question, but I was trying to understand something confusing, unsettling, or curious about the world. Sometimes, the topic was personal, while other times, the topic came from a news article or current event. Or a collaborator approached me with a topic they had questions about and asked me to help them explore it through my interview theatre process. The common element across these starting places was that I knew I would share my discoveries through a theatrical performance for an audience.

I hoped that my interview theatre play would leave the audience with questions about what they had just experienced. I wanted to avoid solving problems for them or dictating how they should think. Instead, I wanted the audience to think for themselves. My goal was for them to leave the performance engaged in meaningful conversations with one another—not about where to grab a drink, but about their feelings regarding specific moments or characters in the play. If the audience left the theatre with more questions than answers, they would be were more likely to take action to change the circumstances portrayed in the play, whether that meant asking critical questions, seeking answers, or working toward solutions to the problems presented.

In most cases, I made these theatrical works as an attempt to understand something more complicated than I could work out on my own. I needed to engage with the thoughts and opinions of others to arrive at a deeper understanding of the topic. Sometimes, I sought external validation for my own experience. Other times, I wanted an explanation for something that made me angry, frustrated, or confused. Through each project, I learned invaluable lessons through interactions with participants, fellow artists, and audiences. Creating an ethnodrama is an iterative process from start to finish, and the possibilities for learning and discovery exist at each step along the way.

Organization of This Book

This book introduces ethnodrama as a qualitative, arts-based research methodology and then outlines a unique and specific step-by-step process that I have refined over nearly 30 years of experience. Reading this book will not make you an overnight expert, but it provides a solid foundation for beginning your journey with ethnodrama. I also offer multiple examples from my projects that use interview-based data throughout the book. Ethnodrama and ethnotheatre can incorporate various textual data, but I have chosen to focus on a creation process using interview-based data, as that is where I have most clearly defined and articulated the steps of my methodology. I encourage readers interested in applying these steps to other kinds of textual data to explore, experiment, take risks, and then report back!

How you encounter and use this book will inform how you read it. I've organized the chapters to reflect moving through the steps in my process in a particular order. The book also emulates how I teach my ethnodrama course, so students move through these steps over a semester of study. I am a big fan of scaffolded experiences that allow steps to build upon each other to arrive at a tangible outcome. I also don't like to give away the end at the beginning. I recommend moving through the chapters in order so that you understand the overall process. Then, you can revisit whatever chapters you need as you work on your own ethnodrama.

To be clear, the approach I outline in this book is only one way of using ethnodrama as an arts-based research methodology. Other researchers and practitioners have different and valid ways of working with the form, and I encourage you to seek those out as well. I focus on one specific method that I have found effective because I believe learning a methodology, applying it, and experiencing the results can allow for greater experimentation and innovation. Learn the rules, understand how they work, then break them. Additionally, the years of working with this particular step-by-step approach have allowed me to continually refine and deepen my intentions related to the ethics of working with participants, gathering their personal stories, thoughts, and opinions, and then disseminating them to an audience. Throughout this book, I continually emphasize the need for care when working with participants and how care must inform the relational and procedural ethics at play in every step of an ethnodrama's process.

Chapter 1 establishes ethnodrama as a qualitative, arts-based research method and identifies connections to other forms of qualitative research and styles of theatre. The chapter also identifies reasons to use ethnodrama for a particular study or project and articulates how a person interested in using ethnodrama can best prepare for the experience. That preparation includes understanding their relationship and experience with theatre as an art form and becoming familiar with ethnodramas as dramatic literature and research projects.

In Chapter 2, readers learn how to conceive and design a project that leverages the power of ethnodrama as an arts-based form, while maintaining the rigor needed to legitimize the research within more traditionally minded academic environments. The chapter emphasizes the importance of a central research question that drives the creation of the ethnodrama. It also outlines how to develop a set of interview prompts that generate data to answer the ethnodrama's central research question. The chapter also highlights the importance of the literature review, the ethnodramatist's point of view or stance, and an ethics committee and its review process.

Chapter 3 discusses ways to recruit interview participants for a data collection process and shares a template for an interviewing protocol that prioritizes the interview participant's experience first and foremost. I emphasize the importance of procedural and relational ethics within the process and how they must be monitored and maintained throughout data collection, analysis, and dissemination. The chapter also establishes best practices for recording interviews and gathering field notes.

Following the data collection process, Chapter 4 provides guidance for presenting interview data as transcripts and then coding those transcripts for recurring themes that answer the project's central research question(s). I give special attention to organizing the dataset, identifying emergent themes through individual and group analysis techniques, and considering how the proposed dramaturgical structure of the ethnodrama may affect the analysis process.

Upon completion of data analysis, Chapters 5 and 6 shift to disseminating the findings via the ethnodramatic scripting process. Structures of scripting take central focus in both chapters, with emphasis on creating a clearly defined script that translates easily to an ethnotheatrical production. The chapters include multiple examples of scripting structures from various projects demonstrating how to arrange interview material to disseminate research findings most effectively. Chapter 5 begins by addressing how best to begin a script, alongside some of the struggles associated with getting started. Chapter 6 concludes with advice about drafting and revising a script, so that the ethnodrama is in the strongest shape possible to enter a rehearsal process.

Once the script is complete, Chapter 7 explores moving an ethnodramatic script into rehearsal and production as a piece of ethnotheatre. The chapter includes information about performance phenomenology, including the difference between a performance triad and a performance pentagon, and discusses the approach an actor should take when performing in an ethnotheatrical production. I also share how the writings of Bertolt Brecht and Anna Deavere Smith inform and inspire my approach to ethnodrama and ethnotheatre. The chapter also addresses ways to rehearse for production and incorporate other textures, such as staging, movement, and various design elements, to help differentiate the dissemination for multiple audiences.

Chapter 8 concludes the process with a discussion of evaluating the research project based on how audiences who experience the ethnodrama in performance respond to the presentation of the research findings, how research participants in the data collection process react to the sharing of their stories via the ethnodrama, and what artists engaging in the creation and performance of the ethnodrama discover through their work. Techniques include surveying, facilitated discussions and focus groups, and postperformance data collection and analysis.

Each chapter concludes with activities to help you build the skills needed to create ethnodrama. Some activities focus on specific techniques, while others encourage you to consider the mindset necessary to work with ethnodrama as a research methodology. I also include a glossary of terms, all of which are **bolded** when they appear in the chapters, as well as additional resources that I hope you will find helpful.

Audience for This Book

As I discuss more in Chapter 1, ethnodrama has its origins in anthropology and psychodrama, but the methodology also shares a close relationship with documentary and verbatim theatre. Depending on how you identify as an artist or a researcher, you may find that these forms substantially overlap in source material, structure, and format. As I've written the book, I've imagined two kinds of readers. One might be a researcher who has recognized the potential for ethnodrama as a methodology, beginning with the start of a research process and carrying it through to the dissemination of the findings via performance. Another might be a theatre artist who wants to understand better how their creative work relates to qualitative research and thus can contribute to academic scholarship. Because I also teach master's and doctoral students, I have framed much of my articulation of the method for that audience; however, undergraduate students engaging in qualitative, arts-based research for the first time will find the book accessible. The book is also a valuable resource for scholars with experience in other qualitative research methods who wish to expand their understanding to include arts-based research, particularly ethnodrama. The book can support courses devoted to arts-based research, qualitative research, data analysis, research design, emergent research methods, and public scholarship. Instructors and faculty advisors will also find the book useful for guiding arts-based research projects in sociology, applied health sciences, creative arts therapies, education and curriculum studies, political science, and theatre and performance studies. Additionally, theatre instructors and students interested in documentary and verbatim theatre can use the research process outlined in this book to inform their own creative processes. Whoever you are and however you arrived in these pages, welcome. I'm happy you're here.

Acknowledgments

I begin by expressing immense gratitude to Patricia Leavy for asking me to write this book. Patricia's initial invitation and subsequent encouragement and support helped me accept that I could move through this process and make this book a reality. Thank you, Patricia, for seeing something I couldn't see myself and sticking with me for the long haul.

C. Deborah Laughton has been an extraordinarily patient and understanding editor and guide as I went through the writing and editing process. I'm grateful to have such a generous collaborator for my first attempt at a book. Thanks also to the entire team at The Guilford Press for their work in making the book a published reality, especially Paul Gordon, Jared Greenberg, Samantha Grossman, Katherine Lieber, and Laura Patchkofsky.

I am also thankful for the assistance of Eric Marcus, Julie Golia, and Michelle McCarthy-Behler in securing necessary permissions from Manuscripts, Archives, and Rare Books at the New York Public Library, and Christopher Browne and Stacey Weihe in securing photo permissions from Marketing and Communications at New York University.

Thank you to Joseph D. Sweet, English Education, Department of English, Theatre, and World Languages, University of North Carolina at Pembroke, and Stephen Snow, Department of Creative Arts Therapies, Concordia University, Canada, for their time and energy reviewing the initial draft manuscript and for sharing their knowledge and expertise with me. Their feedback helped the book improve, and I appreciate it.

I am grateful to the many individuals who have agreed to participate in interviews for my projects over the years. The processes outlined in this book have benefited from our real-time interactions, your candor and generosity, and the reflections following our interactions. My learning has continued because of all of you.

To the folks at Colomba Bakery on Waverly Place, NYC, especially Garrett Barrientos and Isidro Loredo: Thank you for keeping me caffeinated and carbohydrated throughout this writing process.

I have had the good fortune to work with a fantastic administrative and artistic assistant, Sammie Taxman. She completed any task I requested efficiently and with a sense of humor. Sammie was also the first to read the initial draft manuscript from start to finish, and her honest responses helped immensely.

Leila Adu-Gilmore read drafts of chapters, provided lots of affirmations, coaxed me through rough patches, and encouraged me to keep going when I wanted to stop. She also created spaces for group and partner writing, and I benefited from her generous facilitation and community building.

Jenny Macdonald and Joanne Durkin read early drafts of sections of this book and, through ongoing conversations and reflections, helped me navigate the subsequent phases of writing.

Lauren Gorelov and Ryan Howland assisted with early research and organizing for this book. They have continued to provide vital insights through our collaborations and sharing their own projects and discoveries with me.

Meghan Drury provided invaluable feedback on later drafts of the manuscript. Her affirmations and suggestions moved me across the finish line, and I'm eternally thankful.

Jonathan Angelilli helped me timeline this project, coached me, and reminded me not to sit at the computer for too long, which was much-needed advice. Stephen Borow has listened with great compassion and care, providing comfort and reality checks when I needed them most. These men supported and guided me on this journey, just as they've done so many other times over the last 20+ years.

Since 2002, I have encountered many generous colleagues at New York University (NYU) who have supported my work, created space for experimentation, and challenged me in ways that broadened and strengthened my ideas. Some continue at NYU, others have moved on, and some have passed on. In all cases, I'm grateful to each of them for their contributions to my personal development and the processes outlined in this book: Jeanne Bannon, Mary Brabeck, Dominic Brewer, Elise Cappella, Patricia Carey, Daniel Choi, Amy Cordileone, Drew Francis, Perry Halkitis, Maria Hodermarska, Jonathan Jones, Jack Knott, Heddy Lahmann, Lorena Llosa, Ted Magder, Joe Mathers, Natasha McLeod, Judith McVarish, Rochelle Mobley, Pamela Morris-Perez, David Montgomery, Marilyn Nonken, Andy Palmer, Kristie Patten, Robert Rowe, Nisha Sajnani, Mauricio Tafur Salgado, Nancy Smithner, Randy Susevich, Philip Taylor, and Toni Urbano and the team at NYU-TV.

I'm especially grateful to three NYU colleagues, Elisabeth King, Lisa Stulberg, and Lindsay Wright. Each of them has provided mentorship when I needed it most, and their good counsel and positive encouragement have kept me moving forward.

I'm also lucky to have colleagues working at other academic institutions and in theatre companies and organizations, nationally and internationally, who have provided guidance and offered opportunities to learn and collaborate: Alex Ates, Selina Busby, Amanda Chas, Ryan Conarro, Katie Dawson, Jack Dod, Mary Filippone, Sarah Fitzgibbon, Freshly Ground Theatre, Declan Gorman, Maria Guadalupe, Jonathan Harden, Kate Harris, Sobha Kavanakudiyil, Phil Kingston, Carmen Meyers, Kate Nugent, Ilana Pergam, Joanna Parkes, Chrissie Poulter, Daphnie Sicre, Smashing Barriers Theatre Collective, SoloSIRENs, Elena Stephenson, Tallaght Community Arts, Wolfgang Vachon, Jennifer Webster, Ryan Weible, Blayne Welsh, and Stuart Young.

George Belliveau has given me many opportunities to engage in fruitful discussions and collaborations through the Research-based Theatre Lab at the University of British Columbia. His mentorship has been a highlight of my time working in academia. Through George, I met and engaged with Christina Cook, Graham Lea, and Testuro

Shigematsu, who have also impacted this book. At George's invitation, I also participated in a week-long residency exploring Research-Based Theatre, pedagogy, and diversity sponsored by Faberlull Olot in March 2023, which helped to inspire and support my work on this book.

Johnny Saldaña has provided direct and indirect mentorship and inspiration throughout my academic career. I would not have written this book without Johnny and his innumerable contributions to the field.

Ashley Hamilton invited me to work with the University of Denver Prison Arts Initiative (DUPAI), and that experience changed me and impacted my understanding of this work's possibilities. Thanks to Matthew LaBonte, Brett Phillips, Terry W. Mosley Jr., George Chavez, Angel Lopez, Andrew Draper, Craig Forbes, and all the folks at Sterling Correctional Facility for welcoming me into your seeing place. Love and light up to Quent Scaggs.

Many teachers taught me invaluable lessons about art making and sense making. I'd especially like to thank Guy Alchon, James Brophy, Andrew Cottle, Harley Erdman, Heinz-Uwe Haus, Kevin Kerrane, Elisabeth Messer, Julian Olf, Lois Potter, Penny Remsen, Sanford Robbins, Virginia Scott, Richard Trousdell, and Roberta Uno.

I've had the privilege to work with many students in courses, projects, and productions, and I've benefited from their questions, insights, talents, and generous spirits. Their contributions have helped me to clarify and deepen the practices outlined in this book. Special appreciation goes to Micaela Blei, Darci Burch, Laura Cabochan, Averil Carr, Morganne Evans, Melanie Harrison-Milton, Derek Herman, Barbara Kaynan, Daniel Kenner, Britnee Kenyon, Rita Liu, Dylan Licastro, Lucy Medeiros, Martina Novakova, Alex Oleksy, Mackie Saylor, Stephanie Schneider, Emily S. L. Silver, Jamila Humphrie Silver, Lilly Stannard, Peter Zerneck, and Rachel Zweig.

I also thank the students enrolled in my ethnodrama course in 2023 and 2024 for providing invaluable feedback on draft chapters of this book.

Many actors, designers, and creative team members have contributed to the projects I discuss throughout this book and others created at NYU and in the Verbatim Performance Lab. I am grateful to them for their time and talents. I'd especially like to thank Sharon Counts, Traci DiGesu, Daryl Embry, Andy Hall, Cassie Holzum, Troy Hourie, Emily Stork, Tammie L. Swopes, Adam J. Thompson, Andy Wagner, Jenni Werner, and Rachel Tuggle Whorton.

Márion Talán de la Rosa has designed nearly every ethnodrama I have created over the last 17 years. She has developed an aesthetic orientation to this work that continues to impact and influence each piece I create. Márion's talent is matched only by her generosity, both of which always far exceed expectations.

Sarah Bellantoni has become my trusted dramaturg and dear friend through our work on many ethnodramas. We have poured over stacks and stacks of data, learned together, laughed a lot, and made some exceptional theatre.

Keith R. Huff, my primary artistic collaborator for nearly a decade, has greatly impacted how I craft ethnodrama, primarily through his work as the Associate Director of the Verbatim Performance Lab. His name appears throughout this book, but his influence goes well beyond those mentions and these pages. Through our work together, Keith has demonstrated ways to make the work more potent and precise, systematized processes, and served as a trusted thought partner through complex and challenging moments. I am beyond grateful to him for his artistry, commitment, questioning, and friendship.

Thank you to my parents, siblings, and in-laws for their love and support. They stand with me, even when I'm the wild card, and I hope they know I've also got their backs.

Claudia and Elena, thank you for always being there for me and including me in all the adventures.

Miguel, you have lifted my spirits many times in this process, and I know that's not been easy. At one point, you said, "This is going better than we expected," and you were right. Another time, I was lamenting about some section of the book, and you chuckled and offered an insightful observation. You saw something I couldn't see, and once you said it, I realized I could finish. Thank you for helping me understand what I could offer. I learn from you every day. #grateful

Contents

4 Data Analysis and Interpretation

5 Scripting: Getting Started and Basic Scripting Conventions

6 Scripting: Complex Scripting Conventions, Finding an Ending, and Drafting

7 Production: Moving from Ethnodrama to Ethnotheatre

1

Definitions, Contexts, and Preparations

My understanding of ethnodrama emerged over time and via an indirect path. I earned an undergraduate degree in history, which included conducting historical research using primary and secondary source materials and even a bit of oral history, an early encounter with initial connections to ethnodrama. During my undergraduate studies, I saw a play called *The Caucasian Chalk Circle* by 20th-century German playwright Bertolt Brecht. I had already developed a love for theatre, mainly as an audience member and a performer, but the production of Brecht's play demonstrated new possibilities. After that production, I better understood how plays could prompt audiences to ask questions about the world around them, and I turned to Brecht and his writings to learn how to do that. I completed an undergraduate thesis about Brecht, and what I learned in that process continues to inform my work to this day. More on this in Chapter 7!

After those years studying history, I pursued advanced studies in theatre and earned a Master of Fine Arts degree, concentrating on dramaturgy and directing. I wanted to direct plays like Brecht's that could impact audiences, and I knew that, to achieve that goal, I needed to study dramaturgy to learn more about dramatic literature and play structure. During my graduate studies, I served as a teaching assistant for an introductory theatre course taught by my professor and mentor, Harley Erdman. In 1995, I was introduced to the work of actress, playwright, and professor Anna Deavere Smith through Erdman's course. It was a teleplay version of *Fires in the Mirror*, and I was dumbstruck. The analytical part of my brain fired throughout the screening. I found myself questioning the circumstances and events covered by the play and made immediate connections to my undergraduate work on Brecht.

Fires in the Mirror (1992) explores the events that unfolded in the Crown Heights neighborhood of Brooklyn, New York, following the deaths of Gavin Cato and Yankel Rosenbaum in August 1991. Smith created the play from interviews with participants directly and indirectly affected by the event. She transcribed sections of those interviews and arranged them into a performance script. Smith then learned each interview excerpt verbatim and portrayed all the characters in the play. As I watched Smith embody the various people she had interviewed, I appreciated that her arrangement of the interviews complicated my perceptions of the event rather than simplifying them. Smith presented many different viewpoints within the time constraints of the play and did not draw an easy conclusion for the audience to think, "Oh, that's what happened, and that's who's at fault." And I loved that. I loved that I agreed with one person at one moment and then someone with an opposing viewpoint at another. Smith's play and performance captured the realities and complexities of an issue in a way that I had never experienced before in the theatre. The impact on me was profound, and I wanted to learn how to have that same kind of impact. Luckily, another professor and mentor, Roberta Uno, included Smith's work in her course "World Drama: Contemporary Movements." Uno assigned us to interview someone and transcribe it in the style of Smith's early published plays, reflecting the speech pattern of the interview participant. The resulting monologue appeared like poetry on the page rather than typical prose.

That first interviewing assignment for that graduate course in the Spring of 1996 began my journey with "**interview theatre**," the term I used as I began working with interview data as source material for plays. I loved everything about that assignment. I loved the interviewing process, the transcribing, and the careful listening and documenting that the transcribing style required. As I continued my graduate studies, my interest in creating original plays began to overtake my interest in already published and produced works, so my focus as a dramaturg and director shifted to new play development. Another of my professors, Julian Olf, stopped me in the hallway one day after class and said, "You know, Joe, I think you're really a playwright." To which I just laughed and walked away. No, I did not publicly identify as a playwright, but Olf sensed something else. Yes, secretly, I did want to write plays, but I had tried, and at that particular time, I had very little confidence in my ability to write authentic-sounding dialogue.

Not long after that hallway conversation, I had a second opportunity to work on an interview theatre project in another of Uno's courses, and a lightbulb went off for me. Maybe I wasn't a playwright in the traditional sense, sitting alone in a room and crafting dialogue for fictional characters to say. However, I discovered an affinity for listening carefully to what real people had to say about a topic, identifying their most salient points, transcribing those moments, and arranging them, so an audience could better understand something new about the topic. Eureka! And the rest, as they say, is history.

In 1999, I made my first interview theatre play with my then–performance partner, Kate Nugent, and since then, I have continued making interview-based plays and performances across scores of projects. I have created plays about all sorts of topics: childhood bullying, nonromantic relationships between gay men and heterosexual and bisexual women, understandings of borders in the Republic of Ireland, COVID-19, and the list goes on. At times, my work has expanded to include various types of source material beyond interviews, such as letters, journal entries, and audio and video artifacts. That said, my primary mode of investigation and creation still relies mainly on data gathered from interviews.

Now, all these years later, I categorize my work as ethnodrama. I identify as an **artist-researcher**, a dual identity that I embrace as someone trained as an artist, who creates theatre and conducts arts-based research using ethnodrama. I recognize and understand that, over the last three decades, my creative output has lived at this hyphen between two identities, bridging *artist* and *researcher*. I have also developed methods and techniques for teaching others how to create work in a similar style. Over the past 15 years, I've taught scores of students how to use this methodology, from secondary school to doctoral students, through university courses, school residencies, and professional development workshops. I've guided numerous group projects, independent studies, theses, and dissertations, and have had the privilege of seeing many of these projects scripted and performed.

In 2017, I founded the **Verbatim Performance Lab** (VPL), a project of the Program in Educational Theatre in the Department of Music and Performing Arts Professions at New York University's (NYU) Steinhardt School of Culture, Education, and Human Development. VPL creates ethnodrama and verbatim documentary theatre performances and investigates the results with actors and audiences. We perform words and gestures collected from found media artifacts and interview-based data. Through these investigations and performances, VPL aims to disrupt assumptions, biases, and intolerances across a spectrum of political, cultural, and social narratives. Since its inception, VPL has provided a platform to explore ethnodrama and related methods, emphasizing research and audience engagement to address societal challenges such as media literacy, implicit bias, and political polarization (Salvatore, 2023).

Throughout this book, you will encounter examples from plays and performances I have created as an ethnodramatist and with VPL. These examples will help illuminate my unique, step-by-step approach to building an ethnodrama. Before we get to those examples and my approach, let's define terms, establish context, and engage in some preparation to use this dynamic research method.

Defining Terms: Ethnodrama and Ethnotheatre

Ethnodrama and **ethnotheatre** are constructed academic terms that establish the legitimacy of form and process for scholars and researchers working within certain paradigms (Ackroyd & O'Toole, 2010). The root of both words—*ethno*—links them to ethnography, a research technique with origins in anthropology. **Ethnography** is a particular kind of qualitative inquiry that includes studying, describing, and interpreting culture and cultural behavior. Ethnography often contributes to naming and describing a culture or community. It has expanded beyond anthropology to other fields in the social sciences, applied health sciences, education, and cultural studies (Saldaña, 2005). When "drama" and "theatre" combine with the *ethno* root, a specialized form of ethnographic research emerges that uses theatre making in the process of meaning making. As an artist, I find these word combinations to make natural sense. In the same way that an **ethnographer** studies, describes, and interprets culture and cultural behavior, artists observe the world around them and then find ways to express an analysis of their observations. The artist's expression can be literal or abstract and illustrates their new understanding through some artistic presentation, be it a painting, a song, a novel, a dance, or a play. In both cases, artists and researchers working ethnographically use their heightened sensitivities as human beings to guide their process.

Drama therapist Stephen Snow (2022) asserts a clear etymology for the term "ethnodrama." He identified its earliest use in a published paper delivered at a meeting of the New York Academy of Sciences in 1953 by NYU professor of sociology and anthropology Joseph Bram, who had experienced the psychodramatic work of psychiatrist Jacob L. Moreno. Bram (1953) offered that there might be uses for elements of Moreno's psychodramatic approach in anthropological research but "identified under a separate name, such as ethnodrama" (p. 255). Snow unearthed a subsequent use of the term in an article by Jerry M. Rosenberg (1962) titled "Ethnodrama as a Research Method in Anthropology." Rosenberg focused his writings on "the methodology and suggested application of ethnodrama to the field of cultural anthropology" (p. 236) and noted that "ethnodrama can become a valuable source of information about a culture, in respect of speechways, motor habits, attitudes, and the specific content of culture, the customs that are transmitted from generation to generation" (p. 237).

Beyond these 1953 and 1962 references, the term seemed to disappear from academic writing until the mid-1990s when Jim Mienczakowski (1995) used "ethnodrama" to name his ethnographic research practice within health education and health promotion. Snow (2022) identified Mienczakowski as "the creator of the performance-based method of ethnographic research, known as ethnodrama" (p. 5), linking the form to the field of performance ethnography (Denzin, 2003, 2018). Mienczakowski described his ethnodrama as a form of "public-voice ethnography that has emancipatory and educational potential" (p. 364). He cultivated emancipation and education through "informant validation" (p. 361), a process of working closely with interview participants ("informants") at each step of the research, from data collection to analysis to dissemination. Participants provided feedback to Mienczakowski and his collaborators during the scripting and rehearsal processes. They then previewed and fed back on the performance before researchers shared it with a public audience. Upon viewing the performance, audiences could respond with their own feedback, including through forum theatre scenes that investigated alternatives to the original scenarios shared in the performance (Boal, 1985). The audience's responses to and experiences with these alternatives then impacted subsequent performances of the ethnodrama. The sharing of the findings was not the end of the process but rather a step along the way. Informant validation and direct audience engagement with the research findings seeded the "emancipatory potential" that Mienczakowski (1995, 2001) identified as one of the hallmarks of ethnodrama.

Mienczakowski (2001) aligned ethnodrama with ethnography, anthropology, and theatre, as it is "explicitly concerned with decoding and rendering accessible the culturally specific signs, symbols, aesthetics, [behaviors], language and experiences of [participants] using accepted theatrical practices" (p. 468). In more recent writing on ethnodrama, Mienczakowski (2019) noted that the term is now "often applied to all forms of ethnography presented through drama or performance" (p. 3). His use of the phrase "applied to" acknowledges that scholars often assign the term to work created by theatre artists who would not refer to their creative processes or plays as academic research. Mienczakowski also distinguished between ethnodramas that primarily entertain and explain, ethnodramas that inform and report in nonwritten ways, and "critical ethnodramas [that] seek to deliver potential social and cultural change on behalf of [research participants]" (p. 3). Common throughout Mienczakowski's writings is an emphasis on ethnodrama's ability to share "research findings in a language and code accessible to its wide audiences" (2001, p. 468), a primary strength of ethnodrama as a research modality that connects it to the broader possibilities of public scholarship (Adams & Boylorn, 2019).

In *Ethnodrama: An Anthology of Reality Theatre*, Johnny Saldaña (2005) asserted, "All playwrights are ethnodramatists," indicating that playwrights have told the stories of human beings and their social conditions for thousands of years (p. 4). In his followup, *Ethnotheatre: Research from Page to Stage* (2011a), he further broadened the scope of ethnodrama and ethnotheare by identifying 80 unique terms that refer to plays and performances that could fall under their umbrella (pp. 13–14). Saldaña defined ethnodrama as "a written play script consisting of dramatized, significant selections of narrative collected from interview transcripts, participant observation field notes, journal entries, personal memories/experiences, and/or print and media artifacts" (p. 13), while ethnotheatre "employs the traditional craft and artistic techniques of theatre or media production to mount for an audience a live or mediated performance event of research participants' experiences and/or the researcher's interpretations of data" (p. 12). In the simplest of terms, "ethnodrama" refers to the script and "ethnotheatre" refers to the performance of a script. Saldaña's definitions followed 16 years after Mienczakowski's (1995) and marked a significant moment in the form's history. By articulating these definitions, Saldaña invited works created by theatre artists to be identified as ethnodrama and ethnotheatre, even when those artists had no stated intentions of conducting research in a formal academic sense. Saldaña's strong assertions expanded the possibilities for the term, allowing scholars and artists to categorize more plays and performances as ethnodrama and ethnotheatre.

Around the same time as Saldaña's second text, Judith Ackroyd and John O'Toole (2010) identified the importance of "ethnodrama" as a compound term of "ethno" and "drama." They emphasized their use of it to acknowledge the connections between ethnography and drama inherent in the term, while simultaneously avoiding privileging one term over the other. Ackroyd and O'Toole also noted that "dialogic" appeared more often in descriptions of ethnodrama and related research forms and less frequently in descriptions of artist-driven forms such as documentary theatre and verbatim theatre. This higher frequency of appearance indicates more specificity around the intentions of ethnodrama as a form of research and the importance of audience engagement with the research's findings following a performance. This acknowledgment of intention complicates the broader approach to categorizing plays and performances as ethnodrama and ethnotheatre, suggesting that creators should have clear intentions for how they use the methodology and form.

In considering the writings of Bram, Rosenberg, Snow, Mienczakowski, Saldaña, Ackroyd, and O'Toole, alongside my own experiences, I think it is important to distinguish that ethnodrama and ethnotheatre require two key attributes: (1) the presence of a research question to drive the creative process *from a project's inception* and (2) the dissemination of research findings through a two-part process of scripting and performance that catalyzes further data collection and analysis. I offer these distinctions to highlight the importance of the creator's *intention*. A theatre artist may use **textual data** to construct a play with *ethnodramatic qualities*. However, if an overarching question did not drive the creative process and the audience does not somehow explore what they learned as part of the performed dissemination, I would not categorize that artist's work as ethnodrama or ethnotheatre.

For this book and the process I outline within, an **ethnodrama** is *a script created from textual data gathered and/or analyzed by an artist-researcher with the explicit purpose of investigating a research question, performing the investigation's findings for an audience, and collecting and analyzing their responses to those findings.* **Ethnotheatre** refers to *the theatrical production of an ethnodrama that disseminates the investigation's findings to an audience and then engages them in an additional data collection process to further explore the ethnodrama's research question and assess its impact.*

TABLE 1.1. Examples of Textual Data

- Interview transcripts
- Field notes
- Written and electronic correspondence
- Personal narratives culled from
  - Written journal entries
  - Social media posts
- Publicly available print and media artifacts, such as written transcripts and audio/video recordings
  - Court proceedings
  - Political speeches and debates
  - Media interviews
  - Sporting events
  - Testimonials
- Visual materials
  - Photographs
  - Video recordings
  - Films
  - Paintings
  - Drawings

Given the proliferation of easily accessible media, the textual data available as source material for ethnodrama and ethnotheatre have grown in recent years. Table 1.1 presents various examples of textual data.

Ethnodrama and ethnotheatre creation rely on skills and expertise linked to playwrights, actors, directors, designers, dramaturgs, and other theatre artists and professionals trained in theatre making (Saldaña, 2005, 2011a; Salvatore, 2025). However, they also require a clear research intention and sound methodology. An artist-researcher must combine the skills and methods of a theatre artist and a qualitative researcher to create effective ethnodrama and ethnotheatre. Given the necessity of theatre technique and research methodology, it is helpful to situate ethnodrama within some broader contexts in both areas.

Context: Theatre

Ethnodrama draws inspiration from theatre artists working in documentary theatre and verbatim theatre, particularly those working in community-engaged and social justice-oriented practices (Mienczakowski, 2019; Saldaña, 2005). Documentary theatre and verbatim theatre are debated and contested terms and, depending on whose writing you read and where that person is from, you will encounter these same terms used to describe similar kinds of performances (Fisher, 2020; Parenteau, 2017). In my own experience, I have found that "documentary theatre" generally appears more often in writings originating from the United States, whereas "verbatim theatre" tends to occur more in writings originating from Canada, Australia, Ireland, and the United Kingdom.

Documentary theatre traces its origins to the German agitprop theatre maker Erwin Piscator, who is often credited with creating the form in the 1920s (Fisher, 2020; Irmer, 2006; Watt, 2009). Piscator used recent political and historical events as source material for his large-scale performances, including film footage (Irmer, 2006). The documentary form based on current events also emerged in other parts of the world, most notably in the United States, through the Living Newspaper productions staged by the Federal Theatre Project in the 1930s (Watt, 2009). The form expanded in Germany in the 1960s through the plays of Rolf Hochhuth, Peter Weiss, and Heinar Kipphardt. All three playwrights used historical documents as source material to create plays that explored and reexamined significant events from the first half of the 20th century (Fisher, 2020; Irmer, 2006). Weiss (1971) identified that the sources for a documentary theatre performance could include various kinds of materials, such as "records, documents, letters, statistics, market-reports, statements by banks and companies, government statements, speeches, interviews, statements by well-known personalities, newspaper and broadcast reports, photos, documentary films, and other contemporary documents" (as cited in Paget, 1987, p. 335).

Using Weiss's list of source material as a starting place, scholars also break down documentary theatre into subgenres, notably tribunal theatre and verbatim theatre. **Tribunal theatre** uses "edited transcripts . . . of trials, tribunals, and public inquiries" as its source material, whereas **verbatim theatre** uses recordings of "edited . . . interviews with individuals." When preparing to perform these interviews, actors may use transcripts generated from the recordings, the actual recordings themselves (Paget, 2011, pp. 233–234), or a combination of both (Salvatore, 2023). To further clarify the distinction between documentary theatre and verbatim theatre, Ackroyd and O'Toole (2010) note that "it is often assumed that documentary theatre uses more than voices as its source materials, whereas verbatim is based solely on voices" (p. 25), while acknowledging that this assumption may not always play out in practice.

In his often-cited article "'Verbatim Theatre': Oral History and Documentary Techniques," Derek Paget (1987) traces the emergence of verbatim theatre in England, beginning with the work of Peter Cheeseman at the Victoria Theatre in Stoke-on-Kent in the 1960s and continuing through the late 1970s with the work of Chris Honer, Rony Robinson, David Thacker, and Ron Rose at the Gateway Theatre in Chester. In an interview conducted by Paget in 1986, Robinson describes verbatim theatre as

> a form of theatre firmly predicated upon the taping and subsequent transcription of interviews with "ordinary" people, done in the context of research into a particular region, subject area, issue, event, or combination of these things. This primary source is then transformed into a text which is acted, usually by the performers who collected the material in the first place. (Paget, 1987, p. 317)

Paget (1987) identified that these early creators "found themselves in contact with an essentially *non*-theatrical tradition of social observation and oral documentation" (p. 318). These early verbatim theatre plays focused on issues within a specific community and prioritized performing the play in that community for the members who had participated in the interview process. The actors for these performances also embraced the vernacular of the particular community (Paget, 1987), meaning that they focused their performances on the language and dialect of the interview participants. As practitioners have continued to create verbatim theatre in the 40 years since Robinson's description appeared in Paget's writing, some now consider verbatim to be a technique rather than a form (Hammond & Steward, 2008), which contributes to the complexity of defining verbatim theatre because the meaning is ultimately determined by the practitioner engaging it in practice (Garson, 2021). Most importantly, with Paget's identification of "social observation and oral documentation" within the theatrical art form of verbatim theatre, we see the origins of ethnodrama as a qualitative, arts-based research methodology. We also see a precursor to Saldaña's (2005) later assertion that "all playwrights are ethnodramatists."

Context: Research

While strongly connected to art making, ethnodrama falls squarely within a qualitative **research paradigm** because it uses textual data as source material for the research process. Saldaña (2011b) defines **qualitative research** as "an umbrella term for a wide variety of approaches to and methods for the study of natural social life. The information or data collected and analyzed is primarily (but not exclusively) nonquantitative in character" (p. 3), meaning that the majority of the data are textual rather than numerical. This difference between numerical and textual data constitutes one of the main distinctions between quantitative and qualitative research paradigms. Other differences between the two have to do with approach and purpose.

Quantitative research is "characterized by deductive approaches to the research process aimed at proving, disproving, or lending credence to existing theories," while qualitative research is "generally characterized by inductive approaches to knowledge aimed at generating meaning" (Leavy, 2023, p. 9). Quantitative research uses numerical data to draw positivist conclusions that are more definitive and not as easily questioned. In contrast, qualitative research uses textual data to describe a situation or phenomenon that is more open to interpretation. While some like to place a value judgment on these approaches, saying one is "better" or "valid" or "trustworthy" compared with the other, the more useful distinction comes from understanding when to embrace which paradigm, why to use it, how to do it with rigor, and when to know that a combination of approaches might be the best option.

Because ethnodrama often relies on qualitative data gathered from participant interviews and field observations, scholars also note ethnodrama's relationship to **performance ethnography** and **performed ethnography** (Denzin, 2018; Madison, 2018). Denzin (2018) identified that an interview is performative in nature, a "site where meaning is created and performed" (p. 163), implying that when a researcher conducts an interview as part of their fieldwork, the interview participant's responses are a performance. Madison (2018) refers to these performances during fieldwork as performance ethnography; however, if a portion of that interview is re-performed by someone else, as it is in an ethnodrama, Madison names this action "perform-*ed* ethnography, to emphasize the dramatic scenarios, public staging, crafted theatricality, and improvisational enactments of fieldwork and ethnographic data that will *be*, that have *been*, and that are *being* performed" (p. xvii, original emphasis).

Vanover and Mihas (2022) characterize qualitative research as "a creative practice as well as an analytical one" (p. 1). As such, qualitative research has also come to include a set of practices known as **arts-based research** (ABR) that leverages various art-making processes to generate and analyze data and disseminate research findings (Barone & Eisner, 2012; Chilton & Leavy, 2020; Kara, 2020; Leavy, 2020b; McNiff, 2014). ABR can use various methodological tools grounded in fiction writing, poetry, music, dance, theatre, film, and the visual arts (Leavy, 2020b). Barone and Eisner (2012) describe ABR as "an approach to research that exploits the capacities of expressive form to capture qualities of life that impact what we know and how we live" (p. 5), and that "arts-based research is the utilization of aesthetic judgment and the application of aesthetic criteria in making judgments about what the character of the intended outcome is to be" (p. 8). Freiband (2023) similarly identifies that when making these judgments, artists are using literacies that are "unique ways of knowing," and as a result "artists know things nobody else knows, and are able to learn in ways nobody else can learn" (Artists' Literacies Institute).

When a researcher combines their unique ways of knowing as an artist with a clearly defined research process, they can then "[consciously pursue their] expressive form in the pursuit of understanding" (Barone & Eisner, 2012, p. 7). ABR also privileges the idea that a research question does not have just one answer. Leavy (2020b) reinforces this idea, writing, "Arts-based [research] practices are able to get at *multiple meanings*, opening up multiplicity in meaning-making instead of pushing authoritative claims" (p. 27, original emphasis). The way to new understandings does not have to take a positivist route that leads to a concretized outcome on a particular topic, but rather ABR, via art making, can present an audience with research findings and encourage them to make their own interpretation of what they have experienced. In this way, ABR promotes participation, dialogue, and access, and democratizes how knowledge is constructed by and with an audience (Chilton & Leavy, 2020; Leavy, 2020b).

Since ethnodrama relies on theatre making as its arts-based mode of inquiry and can embrace multiple meanings and reach a broad audience, it also has connections with **research-based theatre** (RbT) (Belliveau & Lea, 2016; Shigematsu, Cook, Belliveau, & Lea, 2021). Belliveau and Lea (2016) recognize RbT's relationship to theatre making, arts-based, and qualitative research methodologies, while also identifying it as "a more inclusive term to describe the multiple ways of integrating theatre throughout the research process" (p. 6). Researchers often use ethnodrama and ethnotheatre only to disseminate research findings, rather than integrating the methodology throughout the research process. In identifying this limitation, Belliveau and Lea inspired me to articulate why an artist-researcher should name ethnodrama as their research methodology from their project's inception and then use its various techniques in the step-by-step research process outlined in this book.

An artist-researcher using ethnodrama must think carefully about the intended audience for the research, as this affects all stages of a project's development. The audience for an ethnodrama can include stakeholders with a particular interest or investment in the topic of exploration, participants who shared their ideas and insights during the data collection, or members of the general public who happened upon the project by chance. Suppose that the intended audience has a vested interest in the project's topic. In that case, the research question may use more specific language related to the audience's particular discipline of study, shared experiences, and/or relationships. If the intended audience is more general, the artist-researcher would need to frame the research question and the interview prompts through a different lens that does not assume inside knowledge of a particular subject area or experience. Regardless of the audience's makeup, the ethnodrama must present its findings, so all can understand (Salvatore, 2025).

Why Ethnodrama?

Since ethnodrama relies on textual data as its source material, the form works best with projects that gather multiple perspectives on a given topic through personal interviews and field observations or utilize archival data such as letters, journals, images, and artifacts (Salvatore, 2025). As with most interview-based, qualitative research, ethnodrama should be used for projects focused on "exploring, describing, and explaining a complex situation" or phenomenon (Rubin & Rubin, 2012, p. 49). An artist-researcher should not use ethnodrama when a study relies on positivist outcomes. An ethnodramatic script may be included as a chapter in a dissertation or as part of a journal article, but the script is the first part of a two-part dissemination process. Playwrights write scripts to be performed, and an artist-researcher should create an ethnodrama for performance.

When an artist-researcher chooses ethnodrama as their research methodology, they should understand and accept that they will disseminate their data and resulting analysis to an audience as a script *and* a piece of ethnotheatre. I have encountered ethnodramas that read like a book chapter or an academic journal article because they lack any sense of theatricality and demonstrate a limited understanding of how a script serves as a precursor to performance. Whenever that happens, I find myself asking, "Why ethnodrama?" If a researcher chooses ethnodrama only as a clever dissemination strategy, they are making a mistake. Qualitative researchers choosing ethnodrama must recognize from their project's inception that they are creating a script for performance. If published, that script will also be read, but the researcher should fully commit to the performative nature of the form or choose a different research methodology. An ethnodramatic process should not prioritize academic research skills or content knowledge over aesthetic and theatrical sensibilities, as doing so likely results in a disservice to the form, the data, and the audience (Belliveau & Lea, 2016; Leavy, 2020b; Saldaña, 2005, 2010; Salvatore, 2020b, 2025).

So why, then, do we choose to use ethnodrama? Here are four main reasons to consider.

Ethnodrama dynamically disseminates research findings. A few years ago, during a meeting about my work in VPL, a member of my school's leadership team said, "Joe, we're interested in what you do because it's not sitting on a shelf somewhere collecting dust." While I have been lucky that my school has consistently supported my work in ABR and ethnodrama, that comment marked the first time anyone acknowledged the work's dynamism and ability to reach a wider audience. Leavy (2020b) encapsulates this idea with her emphasis on the capacity of ABR to serve as public scholarship, reaching wider audiences and, therefore, being "useful" (p. 32). Researchers do not always have the most accessible methods of sharing the story of their research with a broad audience, and ethnodrama offers one way to combat that shortcoming. When audience members gather to watch a play, they experience the performance together versus when a person reads an academic article alone. The performance dissemination creates the opportunity for a collective experience that can lead to immediate conversation. Dissemination through an academic journal creates a lag in that conversation happening. Yes, researchers present their findings at academic conferences, but that presentation style relies less on theatricality and metaphor and more on straightforward dissemination. Ethnodrama increases the usefulness of research by expanding its reach and disseminating findings in ways that can be understood and processed by a wider audience, what Derek Paget (2011) calls "pleasurable learning" (p. 228).

As an artist-researcher, I typically choose ethnodrama when conceiving a project and then implement a step-by-step process (see Table 1.2) that includes dissemination as two integrated steps, not add-ons. Each step requires an awareness of the scripting and performance as the two-step dissemination strategy. An interested person can read my script and learn something, but its full impact only emerges through the performance of my data analysis. I prefer that the performance happens live, but recorded film and video performances can have a similar effect and often reach even wider audiences.

TABLE 1.2. Steps for Creating an Ethnodrama

- Identify a topic of interest.
- Articulate a research question.
- Develop an interview protocol.
- Recruit participants.
- Conduct interviews.
- Transcribe and code data.
- Analyze the findings.
- Arrange the findings into a script.
- Stage a performance of the script for an audience (ethnotheatre).
- Gather the audience's response to the dissemination.
- Assess the ethnodrama's effectiveness and impact.

As ethnodrama has grown in popularity over the last 20 years, more qualitative researchers have attempted to implement it as a dissemination strategy, but they make this decision later in their process. While possible, this late-stage choice does not create the best circumstances for success. The likelihood of dynamic dissemination increases when the artist-researcher identifies ethnodrama as their preferred research modality at their project's conception. I have had successful experiences using data collected by someone else to create projects, such as an archive of interviews conducted many years ago or personal letters and journals. However, regardless of the origins of the data, I articulate a research question to guide my investigation of that preexisting dataset, and dissemination occurs through performance. I share more about the process of working with a preexisting dataset in subsequent chapters.

Ethnodrama encourages multiple voices and ideas to come together in one space. Because ethnodrama focuses on exploring, describing, and explaining a complex situation or phenomenon, the form offers ample space to include multiple perspectives on a particular topic. Depending on the purpose of the project and the participant recruiting process, interview participants can come from various backgrounds and lived experiences, including those from historically underrepresented communities. An ethnodrama does not "give voice" to participants. Participants already have voices that need to be listened to and heard. Ethnodrama creates a space for participants' voices to gather and for audiences to hear them in an ethnotheatrical performance.

When I interview participants for a project, I do not interview with an agenda. I do not manipulate the interview to extract the answers I want or need from a participant to confirm my own preconceived notions or biases. I interview participants because I want to hear their genuine responses. I also seek out participants who may not otherwise be asked about their thoughts and opinions on a topic. Frequently, we hear from so-called "experts" and high-profile, public-facing individuals about a subject or issue, and they use a particular kind of language. At the 2020 Aspen Ideas Festival, Anna Deavere Smith referenced this way of speaking as the "official language," saying, "I think of the language of politicians and intellectuals as a kind of haute couture of language—very considered, long sentences." Instead, Smith expressed interest in the "unofficial language," saying, "I'm always interested in talking to the people who are not presenting what happened. . . . I'm interested in the people who are still walking around without their verbal clothes on . . . who can't get through a sentence" (The Aspen Institute, 2020). Smith's analogy describes participants working to construct meaning and make sense of their experiences in the moment rather than offering a prepared, practiced response.

Ethnodrama also offers an opportunity to place participants and their ideas in dialogues that might not otherwise happen. For example, I co-created a VPL project about political polarization in the United States that interviewed participants from across the political spectrum and then had actors perform their perspectives and viewpoints sitting alongside one another on stage. In reality, this kind of gathering of viewpoints in the same room might not be possible, but ethnodrama allowed it to happen. Individuals might have refused to enter into a dialogue with someone they disagreed with, but with ethnodrama, I could construct a fictional interaction between participants with opposing viewpoints, using their exact words and gestures as they delivered them. As a result, the audience experienced those fictional conversations, which complicated their understanding of political polarization in the United States. My project drew inspiration from the work of Carmen Meyers (2021), who created an ethnodrama from interviews she conducted with women in New York City and Phoenix, Arizona, following the 2016 presidential election. Meyers interviewed women from across the political spectrum and placed them in dialogue with one another to explore the possibility of what might happen when people with opposing viewpoints come together and attempt to have a conversation. In a follow-up ethnodrama entitled *Two Truths and a Lie*, Meyers (2023) performed a set number of interviews from that same dataset and asked audiences to consider truths and lies about each person she performed as a way to examine how an audience's implicit biases might affect how they receive an individual's story.

Ethnodrama shares this power to gather multiple voices with oral history. Oral historians interview participants to gather stories from various viewpoints and experiences to complicate the understanding of a historical event or moment (Janesick, 2020; Summerskill, 2021). Historical accounts are influenced by point of view, often favoring the experiences of the elite class and those in power. Oral historians work to shift the focus to the testimonials of everyday people as a way to "balance the historical record" (Summerskill, 2021, p. 23). When that shift occurs, a complication arises around truth, as we suddenly become aware of the multiple perspectives and experiences that can exist around a single event. Participants' stories about their experiences are the catalysts for this complication. In considering the complex subject of truth in oral history, Madison (2018) writes, "Stories bind us: 'The shortest distance between two people is a story.' This short distance is where truths meet and gather" (p. 129). Within that quotation, Madison quotes Patti Digh, author, activist, and master storyteller. Madison's use of the plural "truths" reflects the power of oral history and ethnodrama as qualitative research methods, as they acknowledge that a single truth does not exist. Both forms encourage their audiences to embrace the complexity of multiple truths coexisting within one event, experience, or phenomenon.

Ethnodrama can disrupt that which we think we understand. As with all ABR practices, ethnodrama can evoke, provoke, and disrupt our preconceived notions and biases (Leavy, 2020b, 2023), what Mienczakowski (2001) referred to as its "emancipatory and educational potential" (p. 469). I have repeatedly experienced how ethnodrama can disrupt expectations around a particular topic or idea. My work in ethnodrama has confronted my own beliefs about various topics, and I have seen the same hold true for creative team members, audiences, and interview participants. For example, each time I begin a new project, I have some ideas about what I might discover through my investigation of the central research question, but I am consistently surprised by how wrong I am or how much more expansive my findings turn out to be. My exploration through ethnodrama frequently reveals the unexpected. When that unexpected finding goes against my own belief system or preferred way of thinking, the temptation always exists to silence the finding. However, staying open to these discoveries, albeit uncomfortable and unsettling, has helped me learn more than simply pursuing projects that confirm my own beliefs and biases.

Because Mienczakowski (1995, 2001) associated ethnodrama with emancipation and education, scholars often cite it as applicable to projects that explore issues of social justice or intend to instigate social change (Denzin, 2018; Leavy, 2020b; Saldaña, 2005, 2011a; Snow, 2022; Summerskill, 2021). I agree with their assertion and believe in the possibilities of ethnodrama in these areas. However, I also agree with Saldaña's (2011a) reminder for artist-researchers to remain realistic about what ethnodrama and ethnotheatre can achieve regarding social justice and social change. An ethnodrama does not have to disrupt complex systems or change people's minds to be considered relevant or successful.

Over many years of creating ethnodrama and caring deeply about the topics and issues that drove my creations, I have adopted a different goal: *helping participants, creative team members, and audiences to understand what they think and why they think it*. Because I often work on political and socially minded topics, people frequently assume that I intend to change people's minds about their beliefs; those assumptions are incorrect. I make ethnodrama and ethnotheatre so that all who participate in whatever capacity can consider or reconsider their own ways of thinking about a particular topic. If they experience an ethnodrama and its processes and still feel the same way about the topic at hand but have greater clarity about why, I consider that a success. Disruption from an ethnodrama may lead to a moment of cognitive dissonance. However, whether this disruption catalyzes change immediately, in the future, or at all depends entirely on the individual and their perception of the ethnodrama and its findings.

Sociologist Mario L. Small (2019) argues that contemporary society is deficient in qualitative literacy, which he defines as "the ability to understand, handle, and properly interpret qualitative evidence." This deficiency makes it difficult to differentiate between fact and opinion because of how those different forms of information are presented and interpreted. Small and Calarco (2022) also identify how this absence of qualitative literacy impacts polarization, social science, and public discourse. I extend this impact to how we interact with and differentiate our understanding of each other. Working as an arts-based researcher and using ethnodrama can be an antidote to this deficiency. As you will learn, ethnodrama demands careful listening and analysis, and a slowing down of how we consume qualitative data, which increases qualitative literacy, heightens awareness, and calls into question what we think we understand.

Ethnodrama catalyzes meaning-making in an audience and extends the data collection process. As a qualitative, ABR methodology, ethnodrama avoids drawing positivist conclusions for an audience. Rather, ethnodrama invites audiences to consider the various points of view presented and then asks them to draw their own conclusions about what they have experienced through the performance dissemination. One could argue that all art forms offer a similar kind of implicit invitation, asking the audience to interpret a song, novel, painting, or live performance. While I agree with that argument and identify that my artistic impulses come from a similar place, not all art making engenders the deeper analysis and meaning making that ethnodrama can catalyze in an audience. Nor do all artists intend to engage an audience in a complex dialogue through their work. They create art for art's sake rather than with the explicit intention to stimulate further questioning, discovery, and reflection. This difference in intention distinguishes the artist from the artist-researcher and a play created from interviews from ethnodrama.

An ethnodrama emerges from an artist-researcher's investigation of a central research question. Through data collection and multiple forms of analysis, the artist-researcher synthesizes their findings for an audience and then asks them to interpret that synthesis for themselves. The audience should experience a sense of agency during dissemination because the ethnodrama does not tell them what to think or how to feel. The ethnodrama in performance should leave space for an audience to question the findings, draw their own conclusions, and simultaneously pique their interests, so that they pursue their own postperformance investigations. In the same way that reading an academic article might inspire the reader to look at other works cited throughout, an ethnodrama might encourage audiences to consider different perspectives and points of view. This ability to activate curiosity and empathy aligns ethnodrama with other forms of arts-based research as well (Kara, 2020; Leavy, 2020b).

Finally, ethnodrama can extend the research beyond dissemination and catalyze an additional round of data collection during and after the audience experiences the performance event. If the central research question drives the creation and dissemination of the ethnodrama, a subquestion can explore the audience's response to the ethnodrama's findings. For example, an artist-researcher can poll an audience throughout a performance to uncover which viewpoints resonate most with them. Similarly, a postperformance survey or focus group might measure what the audience has learned through their experiences with the data, while simultaneously evaluating the effectiveness of the ethnodrama in delivering the findings. The potential of an ethnodrama to foster further exploration and discovery through its performance offers exciting and unique possibilities for an artist-researcher.

Preparing to Create Ethnodrama

In considering ethnodrama as a research paradigm of choice, the artist-researcher should have the qualifications and the experience to tackle the aesthetic demands of the form: script development, staging conventions, live performance, and presence of an audience. Throughout this book, I intentionally use the language of theatre making because one of the main challenges to ethnodrama and ethnotheatre comes from inexperienced artists and researchers attempting to use the form to generate and report their findings without the necessary theatrical training. The artistry and aesthetics of their work suffer as a result, as does the analysis and dissemination of their research findings.

Given the word "drama" in its name, ethnodrama must engage artistry and aesthetics equally with all other elements of the research practice. Creating a theatrically compelling ethnodrama demands the ability to think critically and aesthetically about dramatic structure and to edit effectively, skills that playwrights and dramaturgs gain through specialized training and years of experience. Simultaneously, ethnodrama demands precise research techniques around data collection, coding, and analysis, skills that develop through training and mentoring in more traditional research methodologies. Ethnodrama requires the artist-researcher to value the ethical standards necessary for research involving human beings as participants. Similarly, staging an ethnotheatrical performance compels an artist-researcher to think like a director, a role that requires an understanding of performance theory and interpersonal skills to engage with actors and other creative team members while maintaining a clarity of vision and awareness of researcher bias and epistemology (Salvatore, 2025).

Without a balance between artistry and research, ethnodrama becomes static, vague, and overly complicated for an audience. Then, research findings get lost because they are never communicated clearly in performance. The movement to recognize ethnodrama as a legitimate form of qualitative, ABR has made significant strides over the last 30 years. However, when we create and present an aesthetically lacking piece of ethnodrama or ethnotheatre, we undermine the progress that arts-based researchers have worked so hard to achieve. To combat this issue, researchers engaging with ethnodrama must have strong skills in their academic disciplines and the craft of making theatre. Accomplished researchers develop their skills over time and are mentored by those who came before them. Accomplished artists are no different (Salvatore, 2025).

If ethnodrama seems like a research modality you would like to use, here are some suggestions to consider:

Identify and catalog your experiences with theatre. If you want to use ethnodrama and ethnotheatre for your research project, take some time to reflect on your past experiences with theatre. Consider whether those experiences provide you with enough background to use a methodology that privileges and centers theatre as its primary mode of expression. Please note that I'm talking about live theatre, not film or television. Some questions to consider:

- What is your primary relationship to theatre as an art form? Audience member, theatre maker, or both?
- If you have previously worked on theatre projects, what role(s) have you played in those processes? Actor? Director? Designer? Playwright? Producer? Stage manager? Other?
- What about these past experiences inspires you to use theatre for your research project?

Consider these questions carefully and honestly. If you have limited theatre experience overall, particularly as a theatre maker, you should reconsider using ethnodrama for your project. I'm being frank here because there is a long and unfortunate history of people deciding that they can work in the theatre (and other art forms, for that matter) with no training or experience. I have also seen aspiring ethnodramatists, with training primarily as actors, encounter significant struggles as they attempted to research and create their projects because they lacked any training or experience in playwriting or directing.

As an artist-researcher using ethnodrama, my work lives squarely in a qualitative realm; therefore, I cannot suddenly decide to do a project that requires me to analyze quantitative data by programming code and running regressions. If I wanted to incorporate quantitative data analysis into a project, I would find a collaborator who has those skills. The same holds for using a methodology as specialized as ethnodrama. If you want to use ethnodrama but have limited theatrical experience, identify a collaborator with the necessary artistic skills and work jointly rather than independently. I cannot overemphasize the importance of theatre skills and techniques when attempting this work. Once you assess your relationship and past experiences with theatre, the choice to use ethnodrama and how to use it most effectively should also be more apparent.

Read other research projects that use ethnodrama. This advice may sound logical and straightforward; if so, you're ahead of the game. However, if you have not read any other research projects using ethnodrama, begin here. I discuss the literature review in Chapter 2, but before solidifying a project idea, I recommend exploring how other researchers, especially those within your academic discipline, have used ethnodrama in their work. Read other research studies to understand how ethnodrama is applied in various contexts. I have included a list of studies and projects in the Additional Resources section of this book for your consideration, but I encourage you to conduct a keyword search in the disciplines that matter to you.

Read plays. Again, this advice also relates to the literature review, but it goes beyond simply reading other ethnodramas. Plays, also called scripts, have a unique way of presenting on the page, and reading a script requires an understanding of formatting. A traditional script includes stage directions that define the play's setting and provide information about how the characters in the play may move around in different settings. The dialogue between the characters in the play also appears in a particular format on the page. These added elements can make reading a script more challenging than reading a novel or journal article. The reader has to imagine how the script moves from the page onto the stage in performance. Researchers interested in using ethnodrama should read plays to become familiar with how writers present plays as scripts. Ethnodramatic scripts may have their own unique qualities, so once you understand how to read a traditional script, you can move on to scripts categorized as ethnodrama. Aspiring artist-researchers aiming to use ethnodrama must understand the repertoire they seek to emulate. This book's Additional Resources section contains a list of plays for your consideration, including documentary and verbatim theatre plays with ethnodramatic qualities. You should seek out others that align with your interests.

My experience with Shakespeare helps to clarify this advice to read plays. As I began college, I had a cursory understanding of Shakespeare's work from the four plays we had to read in high school, where we focused mainly on understanding the plot and analyzing literary devices. We read the plays as part of our English curriculum, and while we had assignments to perform scenes from the plays, we received very little instruction about how to do that. As a result, we gained a limited understanding of the plays as theatrical productions. My best training moment with Shakespeare's plays came during a semester in college where I had to read one play a week for 14 weeks. By the time I finished that semester, the immersion of reading 14 plays helped me to understand how Shakespeare used language to create action for actors to play on stage in performance. The professor for that course, Lois Potter, also encouraged us to watch the plays rather than simply read them because playwrights write plays to be performed—seen and heard by an audience—not read in isolation.

Attend theatre performances. Lois Potter was right. When I watched Shakespeare's plays in performance, either through a campus production or a video recording, I understood much more about the story, the characters, the playwright's technique, and most of all, theatre. I took Professor Potter's class over 30 years ago, and her advice has stayed with me. To work in the theatre, we have to see plays in performance. If you want to use ethnodrama, attend performances of plays. If you can access a script for the play you will see, read it before you go. Then, reread it after you see the play. What did experiencing the play in performance help to clarify for you about the play's content and message? How similar or different was the production that you saw compared to the script that you read? Thinking about these questions helps to illuminate how a director, designers, and actors make choices as they interpret a script.

As an ethnodramatist, you analyze and interpret data to formulate a script, and then a creative team brings that script to life as a piece of ethnotheatre. As I create my work, I draw inspiration from the work of other artists. I shared earlier the impact of Anna Deavere Smith's work on my practice. Through reading, seeing, and studying her work, I found inspiration for my own projects. While I didn't study with Smith, all the exposure to her work taught me invaluable lessons and gave me the courage to give it a go. Then, I gained inspiration from other theatre makers, musicians, choreographers, dancers, photographers, and visual artists. Engaging with these different performances and presentations helped me develop my artistic sensibilities, which all come into play when I create an ethnodrama. Consider attending plays as part of the "literature review" you must complete to use ethnodrama most effectively for your project. And if you can see performances of ethnodramas, that's even better!

Seek out training and experience as a theatre maker. If you aspire to use ethnodrama in your work as a researcher, you should find ways to acquire training and experience as a theatre maker. While acting experience and acting classes can be helpful, experiences with playwriting, directing, and design provide additional skills that more directly help create a script and a production. If you have an affiliation with a college or university, you can contact the theatre department to see what courses they offer and which instructors might welcome you in to audit some of their class sessions. Introductory courses can provide basic skills in these areas and introduce exercises that serve as building blocks for a larger project. If you work outside of an academic setting, a community arts organization might be a source of additional training, as they sometimes offer training courses for a nominal fee. In recent years, following the COVID-19 pandemic, more of these opportunities emerged as online offerings, so you have a variety of ways to gain more experience.

I also suggest looking for opportunities to observe rehearsals of a production in progress. Again, colleges and universities could be great resources, but you could also contact amateur community theatre organizations to see if a director might allow you to observe their rehearsal process. Much of what I learned about directing came from watching other directors work and through trial and error. Same with design. I have some training in lighting design, but I also learned a lot by observing designers working through technical and dress rehearsals. Training in the arts still relies heavily on an apprenticeship model. Early career artists spend much time observing and assisting artists with more experience, absorbing their processes and techniques. Then, the early career artist begins to develop their own unique ways to accomplish their creative goals. They must learn the technique from someone else before making it uniquely their own. Being a fly on the wall in a rehearsal process can provide many opportunities for learning about how a play moves from a script into production and, ultimately, to a performance in front of an audience.

Understand qualitative ABR methods. Similarly, if you aspire to create ethnodrama through your work as an artist, you should gain an understanding of qualitative ABR methods and vocabulary. When I started teaching at a university, I had minimal experience with qualitative research methods. I understood how to conduct historical research, and I knew how to conduct an interview, but I did not have the experience or the vocabulary to articulate how those two skills might come together as a research methodology.

I have spent many hours conversing about qualitative and ABR practices with generous colleagues in the social sciences, education, and theatre education. These mentors helped me gain the necessary vocabulary to situate my creative practice as a research methodology and to write this book. They have suggested books and articles to read, introduced terminology and processes, and offered other ways of naming and describing what I do as an artist. I also learned that researchers who interviewed participants for a project within an academic environment paid much closer attention to the ethical implications of their processes than artists working outside of an academic environment. This increased awareness of ethics has become integral to my process as an artist-researcher and ethno-dramatist, which I illuminate more in the coming chapters.

Similar to my earlier suggestion about theatre courses, if you can find a way to take or audit an introductory course on qualitative or ABR methods, the exposure to terminology alone can help to demystify the idea of "research." Human beings tend to be naturally curious, and research processes satisfy our impulses to investigate and understand. The language of research formalizes our curiosity, which can sometimes inadvertently alienate people who are unfamiliar with that language. As you learn some of the research terminology and processes, you may discover that you are already doing them in your art making and calling them something else.

At one point, a colleague suggested that I teach a graduate-level research methods course focused on the process I used to create my interview theatre work. I remember feeling excited by the opportunity, while worrying about navigating the research language. I accepted the offer anyway and began to prepare for the course. Through preparation and teaching, I adopted research language that helped to explain my process and began to embrace my artistic work as valid research. Teaching others how to do what I do allowed me to step into the role of artist-researcher, and once I realized that role suited me, I didn't look back.

Practice! If you plan to use ethnodrama for your thesis or dissertation project or want to make an ethnodrama the showpiece of your tenure or promotion portfolio, make sure it's not your first time making one. When inviting guests over for dinner, most people don't try a recipe for a new dish for the first time. They've made the recipe before, tested it, worked out the kinks, balanced the seasonings, and then considered serving the dish to their guests. Similarly, I don't suggest testing your skills with ethnodrama for the first time on a high-stakes project.

Because ethnodrama is still considered an innovative form of dissemination, audiences tend to be wowed by it, which might make it tempting to use for a project that you hope leaves a mark. I've seen ethnodramas that were mediocre theatre pieces, including ones I created, but audiences loved them. However, just because an audience loved something doesn't necessarily mean it was a sound demonstration of technique. If a panel of experts in your academic field reviews the same project, they might see something different than an audience sees. Questions about your research design, coding process, ethical orientation, and analysis might arise. You must be able to answer those questions; more experience with the form makes that easier. When your academic career rests on a project, I recommend practicing with a smaller project before tackling a larger, more high-profile one. Practice, make mistakes, and learn from them. Repetition and self-reflection lead to a better understanding of a method. Allow yourself enough time to develop your technique before asking others to evaluate it.

In this first chapter, I've shared some terminology, context, and recommendations for proceeding. The following chapters guide you through my unique, step-by-step process for creating ethnodrama. Other valid approaches exist; I encourage you to explore those as well. Stay open to your questions and ideas as they emerge, but allow yourself to absorb what's on these pages. Learn this process, and your own unique approach to creating ethnodrama will follow.

ACTIVITIES

Keyword Search

Go to your favorite web browser and type "ethnodrama" into the search bar. Look at the entries that pop up and see if you can identify any commonalities and differences in how scholars and practitioners talk about the form and use the vocabulary. If you are affiliated with or have access to an academic institution's library, try the same exercise with its online library search. Try the keyword search for published books, but then also try a similar search with journal articles and databases. Notice the kinds of subjects in which researchers have used ethnodrama as their methodology. Take note of anything that surprises you about the emerging topics and keep those in mind as you read Chapter 2 of this book and beyond.

Theatrical Experience Checklist

Make a list of your past experiences with creating a theatrical production. If they were primarily acting experiences, identify what style of performance. Were they realistic plays? Do you have experience with more presentational performances? If your experiences are more varied, in what other areas do you have experience? Have you directed? Designed? Produced? Stage managed? Once you have your list, consider whether you have any gaps in your knowledge and how you might fill those gaps. Do you need to acquire more training? Do you need to build out your team of collaborators? Identify what steps you can take so your ethnodrama can move smoothly from script to production.

Eavesdrop to Start a Scene

As you'll soon discover, creating an ethnodrama relies on listening carefully and understanding how dialogue works between characters in a play. Try this basic exercise you might encounter in an introductory playwriting class to practice these two skills. Go to a public setting like a park or a coffee shop. Bring a notebook and find an open seat close to other people engaged in a conversation. Without being obtrusive, see if you can pick up a few lines of continuous dialogue from each person. Jot those lines down in your notebook, then use those initial lines to begin a conversation between two characters. Use your imagination from there to create an exchange between two fictional characters that go back and forth 20 times (10 lines of dialogue for each character). When you get close to the end of the exchange, somehow bring the conversation to an end. You've written a simple scene between two fictional characters. Now, ethnodrama works differently, but this exercise gives you a simple introduction to constructing a short conversation between two characters. You've explored a basic building block of playwriting, and from there, you can build a series of scenes into a play. While the source material differs, an ethnodrama still utilizes the basic building blocks of playwriting.

Designing a Project

During a semester of my ethnodrama course at NYU, I had a playwriting student from the Master of Fine Arts program take the class. At our first meeting, everyone introduced themselves, and I asked each student to share why they had registered for the course. This particular student humbly admitted that they had tried to write a play based on interviews in the past but felt that they had failed. They hoped the course would inspire them to try the form again if they learned to do it "correctly." While there is no single "correct" way to create an ethnodrama, the form can easily go awry without a clear set of steps to follow. What I offer in my class and this book is *one way* to create an ethnodrama. It is certainly not the only way, but it is a way that has proved successful across several of my ABR projects and the projects of others who have learned and implemented my methodology. As students move through my course, I ask them to embrace the method I teach, follow the steps, and adhere to the guidelines I provide. Then, once they exit the classroom at the end of the semester, they can research and create however they see fit.

Ethnodrama, as a form, asks an audience to participate in constructing meaning as they experience the performance of collected data. It is not a pedestrian experience for the audience; it is about more than entertainment. An artist-researcher interested in using ethnodrama as a research methodology should also consider how they want an audience to engage in dialogue around the material presented in the performance. When I create an ethnodrama, I think about what an audience could do after the performance finishes. I want the audience to ask questions about what they just experienced, so that the impact of the performance of the data continues beyond the performance event itself. When I think about topics for my projects, I often look at current events and consider my questions about them. Most importantly, these are questions to which I still need to learn the answer. I don't need to do the project if I already know the answer to the question.

This chapter focuses on building a solid foundation for an ethnodrama by ensuring that the artist-researcher knows what they are doing and why they are doing it. We explore how to identify a viable topic, how to conduct a literature review for an ethnodrama, how to state a point of view and why it is important, how to articulate a research question, and how to generate a bank of interview prompts that will help generate responses that could answer the research question. We also consider strategies to help move an ethnodrama through an ethics committee review process, a dissertation process, and a tenure review.

What's the Topic?

As with any research study, an ethnodrama begins with a topic of interest. I have created ethnodramas about various topics, including class and socioeconomic status, nonmonogamous gay relationships, a particular county in the Republic of Ireland, LGBTQIA+ (lesbian, gay, bisexual, transgender, queer or questioning, intersex, asexual, and more) history, and political polarization. Sometimes, the topic emerged from my interests; other times, a collaborator approached me to create an ethnodrama based on their interests.

The topic provides a general starting point for the artist-researcher to explore the need for a particular study in the first place and why ethnodrama is the appropriate form for an arts-based, qualitative research study. For example, past research, a current event or trend, or a problem facing a particular individual or community might inform a topic. When a student interested in creating an ethnodrama around a specific topic approaches me, I ask a straightforward question: Why? After their initial response, I follow up with additional questions that I ask myself as I begin any project:

- Why is this topic of interest to you?
- Why is this topic important? For whom is it important?
- Why do you want to use ethnodrama to explore this topic?
- Who makes up the participant population, the people you are going to speak to and interview about this topic?
- Who is the audience you want to reach through an ethnodramatic exploration of this topic?

The answers to these initial questions may change as an artist-researcher gains more knowledge and understanding of their topic and their relationship to it. Still, they should have some ideas about these initial questions. I often see projects that have skipped this early step in the process. For whatever reason, the artist-researcher thinks it is enough to be interested in a topic and that their interest alone will carry the creation of the ethnodrama forward in miraculous ways. Trust me. Miracles rarely happen. I have experienced, far more often than not, a misguided ethnodrama focused on a cursory interest in a topic. That makes for an out-of-focus, indiscernible research project and a deadly time in the theatre.

When considering the feasibility of using ethnodrama with a particular topic, an artist-researcher should also consider the **participant population** they need to engage and the criteria participants must meet to be eligible for an interview. From where will the interview participants be sourced? Is there a large enough sample size for consideration? How will participants be recruited? Sometimes, a topic has excellent potential, but it can be challenging to find enough participants to interview. For example, the topic may require participants to disclose sensitive information about themselves through a preliminary screening process. Or the topic demands that participants have had a certain kind of experience, which is less common than one might think. A topic might also depend on geographical location, which could limit or necessitate gathering interviews through video-conferencing platforms like Skype and Zoom. Potential limitations can be significant and require consideration early in the planning process for an ethnodrama.

From my past experiences, topics for ethnodramas emerged from my own curiosities and needs. I teach in the Program in Educational Theatre at NYU, and we produce a faculty-directed, main stage production each semester. As I searched for a play to direct for a fall 2008 production slot, I could not find any scripts that inspired me, so I considered creating an original play based on interviews. An idea to make a play about class and socioeconomic status emerged from my perceptions about how a person's social class impacted their experiences of living and working in New York City. I was fascinated by people's assumptions about an individual's perceived social class and the differences between those perceptions and that individual's lived experience. Of course, any discussion of this phenomenon is complex and cannot rely on generalizations, so a new play created from multiple perspectives and experiences with class and socioeconomic status seemed to make sense. This topic emerged from my need for a project to direct within an academic theatre season and out of my own curiosities.

In March 2018, Eric Marcus, the author of *Making Gay History*, approached me with an idea. In the late 1980s and early 1990s, Marcus met with over 60 activists and allies who contributed to the LGBTQIA+ civil rights movement throughout the mid-to-late 20th century. He turned his interviews into two books, *Making History* (1992) and *Making Gay History* (2002). Following the second book's publication, Marcus donated all of his transcripts and audio recordings to the New York Public Library, and he moved on to other projects. However, in 2015, he was asked to turn the original audio files from his interviews into a podcast series, and that request led to the release of 13 seasons over 9 years. Eric contacted me and asked me to collaborate on creating a live performance version of some of the interviews from the *Making Gay History* podcast. He hoped that student performances of the play could help teach LGBTQIA+ history in high schools, colleges, and universities.[1] This example demonstrates how an ethnodramatist can work with a collaborator and create from an existing dataset collected by someone else.

In these examples, regardless of whether the topic came from me or someone else, I had to decide whether to engage with it and, if yes, how I would do it. Some topics have immediate resonance, while others grow on me as I learn why they might be relevant to pursue. Before committing to each of these projects, I also made sure that I considered my own list of questions back on page 21. Then, as an artist-researcher, I also wanted to make a tangible contribution, either to knowledge about the topic or by using ethnodrama to explore the topic. In both instances, a literature review becomes an essential next step.

Finding the Gap: The Literature Review

Once the artist-researcher identifies the topic for their inquiry, they should complete a literature review. A **literature review** should uncover what other scholars have discovered and written about the topic in question and adjacent issues related to the project. In the case of an ethnodrama, the literature review should also consider how others have used this particular methodology to explore the topic. If the purpose of research is to unearth new understandings and ways of making meaning of the world, an ethnodrama that considers a topic other scholars have explored may illuminate similar findings differently. A performed ethnodrama can humanize a topic more deeply and impactfully. An audience hears the qualitative data spoken aloud by actors rather than reading in isolation and imagining how they might sound.

Another way to think about a literature review is as a **project need analysis**, which states the importance of a particular project based on understanding what other researchers have discovered about that specific topic (or topics adjacent to it). In less academic terms, it might be most straightforward to say, "So what? Why does this project matter?" Regardless of what we call it, reviewing preexisting literature should establish what has already been discovered about a topic so that the artist-researcher can identify the knowledge gap and work toward filling it as a contribution to their field.

The artist-researcher conducts their investigation into the topic and constructs a written analysis based on their findings to identify the project's need. They generate the analysis from various sources, including books, journal articles, print media, news outlets, interviews, websites, and so on. The purpose of the research project may dictate the types of sources. For example, a literature review for a dissertation project may need to focus more on books and academic journal articles.

Some questions that the review and analysis should consider include the following:

- What have other scholars, journalists, and artists discovered and revealed about this topic?
- Based on other research and information uncovered, what is the specific need for a project like this?
- What gap or void could this project fill in the already-existing knowledge base on this topic?
- How might ethnodrama offer a unique approach to collecting, analyzing, and sharing data and knowledge around this topic?
- What preliminary lines of inquiry are emerging as a result of the analysis?

Consider articulating at least three emerging lines of inquiry supported by your preliminary research. Lines of inquiry represent places of interest for the artist-researcher that arise as they review the preexisting literature. Pay careful attention to these emerging lines of inquiry because they could lead to potential research questions. If the artist-researcher finishes the literature review and they have no more questions, then there's probably no need for another study. If you finish your literature review and have new questions, keep going! You know more about a topic than when you started; you've learned something, and there's a capacity to learn more.

A common error I see in literature reviews for ethnodrama projects is a lack of attention to other arts-based investigations or existing dramatic literature on a particular topic. Researchers who aim to use this form should consider how playwrights and other artists have engaged with the specific topic in question. Consider what other artists may have created around this topic; don't invalidate other artists by ignoring their work. We highlight ABR as a legitimate research modality by including the work of other artists and arts-based researchers in our literature reviews. Have other plays, performances, songs, novels, or visual art pieces explored your topic? Cite all of that work as part of the literature review. However, remember that including a section on ABR in the literature review does not supersede the methodology section of a dissertation manuscript or journal article, but rather demonstrates that the artist-researcher has explored other arts-based investigations. For example, initial research for a project exploring political polarization surfaced Ezra Klein's book *Why We're Polarized* (2020), which cited scores of research projects to consider. I also kept running lists of articles I read from newspapers and magazines, and searched for academic journal articles. A keyword search for other ethnodramas on polarization revealed a project called *Divided We Stand: An Interview-Based Theatre Exploration of the Political Polarization of Women in the Age of Donald Trump* by Carmen Meyers (2021), a project I knew well because I served as Meyers's dissertation chair. In considering other arts-based modalities, a student introduced me to *Violet Protest* by Ann Morton, an art installation featuring 18,000 quilt squares that each used an equal amount of red and blue material. When displayed together at the Phoenix Arts Museum, those squares created the illusion of a wall of violet (Wallace, 2021). Understanding how an investigation of political polarization unfolded in another ethnodrama and a visual art project helped inform the ethnodrama that became *Whatever You Are, Be a Good One* (Salvatore & Huff, 2022).

As a general rule, I suggest that a literature review consider three to five subtopics that further illuminate the overarching topic. By identifying those subtopics to guide the literature review, the artist-researcher establishes a unique perspective on a topic that might have multiple lines of inquiry.

If we continue with political polarization as an example, one artist-researcher might pursue the following subtopics for a literature review:

- Political polarization in educational settings
- The effects of political polarization on the K–12 curriculum
- Pedagogical approaches to civic awareness and engagement in the classroom

Another artist-researcher might pursue these subtopics:

- Immigration as a voting issue
- The effects of political polarization on noncitizens of the United States
- International perspectives on U.S. political polarization

Both examples deal with aspects of political polarization, but each artist-researcher has selected subtopics of inquiry that reflect their curiosities about the overarching topic.

In each case, I would recommend the same two additional subtopics:

- Other ethnodramas and ABR projects investigating political polarization
- Dramatic literature dealing with political polarization

By exploring these two subtopics, artist-researchers can situate their work within a larger field of research and a larger body of dramatic literature. Both perspectives are essential when creating the literature review for an ethnodrama and establishing the need for a particular project.

The literature review does not have to explore a particular topic exhaustively. You can spend months unearthing every journal article that addresses your topic. There might be the temptation to become an expert this way, to keep reading anything and everything accessible. However, be careful about using the literature review to avoid conducting the research. I have seen this happen as a self-defeating avoidance tactic, as a way to steer clear of assuming the role of the expert for a topic. Stay aware of this temptation and avoid it at all costs.

Articulating the Point of View

When a director articulates a concept or point of view to guide the direction of a traditional play, their articulation is informed by a careful analysis of the script combined with personal responses to the play informed by their identity, personal history, and life experiences. Similarly, an artist-researcher should articulate their point of view as a fundamental step in creating an ethnodrama. Identity, personal history, and life experiences also affect how an artist-researcher collects and analyzes data. Even though the ethnodramatist creates from the words and testimonies of real people, they ultimately choose what sections of a dataset to include and how to arrange those sections to illuminate a finding or describe a phenomenon. These choices are influenced by their point of view. Stating a point of view in writing is an important step. The process raises awareness about how the point of view could impact all phases of the research process and raises consciousness about how one's positionality may have ethical implications when working with interview participants and their stories.

A **point-of-view statement** is a written piece in which the artist-researcher takes a *subjective* position in their project. This statement typically dismisses the artist-researcher's neutrality by focusing on their biases, beliefs, and the points of view from which they come at the research. Think of the point-of-view statement as your opportunity to share experiences and prior knowledge contributing to forming your current perspective on the topic. A point-of-view statement is akin to the stance of the researcher statement in more traditional academic research. I use "point of view" intentionally because I find it more artist-friendly and seek to privilege the artist's identity in arts-based, qualitative research.

A point-of-view statement should include the following:

- Some focused information about you
- An exploration of your current relationship with the topic
- An investigation of the lens(es) through which you will examine the data
- An exploration of any problems or tensions you have recognized with the topic and your work with it

As you develop responses to these four bullet points, here are some questions to consider:

Some focused information about you
- What in your background brings you to this particular topic and/or methodology?
- What from your training and experiences qualify you to take on this project?
- What are your values as an artist-researcher?

An exploration of your current relationship with the topic

- Why is the topic of interest to you?
- What do you currently know and understand about the topic?
- What do you expect to discover about the topic? What is your hypothesis about what you might learn?
- What conclusions have you come to from your literature review that may inform your data collection and analysis?

An investigation of the lens(es) through which you will examine the data

- How does your relationship to a particular theoretical school of thought affect how you unpack/question/analyze your data (critical race theory, feminist theory, Indigenous theory, postcolonial theory, queer theory, etc.)?
- How might your personal beliefs about the topic and past related experiences affect how you analyze and interpret data?

An exploration of any problems or tensions you have recognized with the topic and your work with it

- What challenges or controversies are inherent in the topic itself?
- What biases do you have about this topic that could influence your analysis and interpretation of data? Another way to think about this: Where are your gaps in understanding?
- How might your positionality in the world affect your analysis and interpretation?

Traditional academic researchers often cite theoretical schools of thought they subscribe to when conducting research and analyzing data. Some examples include critical race theory, feminist theory, Indigenous theory, postcolonial theory, and queer theory, among others. Often these are referred to as **lenses** through which data are analyzed: "I will analyze these data through a queer lens, which means I'll consider the tenets of queer theory as I interpret the data." Of course, personal lived experience affects analysis and interpretation as well. If your lived experience connects to one of these theories, then there may be more natural synergies as to why the theory would influence your point of view. That said, I do not suggest arbitrarily using one of these theoretical schools of thought to analyze data unless you are well trained and well read in the theory.

I would also suggest that other lenses can affect analysis and interpretation, so it is essential to consider those as part of a point of view. For example, in a project about political polarization, one's political affiliation and beliefs could influence and affect data analysis. Or the sources where one typically gets their news could also have an impact. Additionally, geographical location could affect how one perceives data on specific topics. These personal lenses can create biases that can be difficult to identify. For example, my positionality as a cisgender, gay, White, middle-aged man living in a major city will affect how I analyze data and may inadvertently prevent me from including perspectives different from mine. I may naturally be drawn to stories reflecting my experiences and beliefs. Still, if I'm trying to include as many perspectives as possible, I need to be aware of my biases to check them throughout my process. For this reason, I encourage artist-researchers creating ethnodramas to include examples of their personal lenses when articulating their point of view.

The clearly articulated point of view also clarifies how the same dataset could yield different interpretations and ethnodramas. An artist-researcher uses the new knowledge gained from the literature review and their understanding of their point of view to craft a research question specific to their knowledge, interests, and experiences. They can also revisit the point of view as a touchstone on their perspective throughout all phases of the research process.

Articulating the Research Question

After completing the literature review and articulating their point of view, the artist-researcher begins drafting the **research question** that guides the creation of the ethnodrama. As ethnodramas rely on qualitative data from interviews and field notes, the research question signals that the ethnodrama will explore, describe, or explain a complex situation or phenomenon, rather than declare a concrete finding or work to prove or disprove a hypothesis. The research question should not lead to an answer of "yes" or "no," nor should it attempt to uncover positivist results.

In her book *A Director Prepares: Seven Essays on Art and Theatre*, American director and professor Anne Bogart (2001) writes, "Inside every good play lives a question. . . . We enact plays in order to remember relevant questions . . ." (p. 21). Bogart describes how she identifies that question as she prepares to direct a play and allows that question to infect the process and all those involved in the production. An ethnodrama's creative process *begins* with a question, and that's the research question. In the approach I outline throughout this book, an ethnodrama cannot exist without a question as the catalyst for creation. The research question is the central guiding principle for an ethnodrama and must be answerable through the creative processes in which the artist-researcher engages. As ethnodramas are a form of arts-based, qualitative research, their guiding research questions are generally inductive, which means they are *open-ended*. Research questions for an ethnodrama begin typically with *what* or *how* and often use words and phrases such as "explore," "describe," "illuminate," "unearth," "unpack," "generate," "build meaning," and "seek to understand" (Leavy, 2023).

An ethnodrama may have more than one research question, but I strongly recommend limiting your questions to no more than three. Effective research and compelling theatre are similar in that they both require focus. Limiting the number of research questions for consideration helps to maintain that focus. I have read several dissertations using qualitative research methods, including ethnodrama, which had a central research question and a long list of subquestions. I do not advise this as an approach when working with ethnodrama. I frequently work with only one research question. If I have two research questions, those questions serve different purposes. The first question often drives the creation of the ethnodrama itself, and the second question drives the audience's engagement with the material they experience through the performance of the ethnodrama. So the ethnodrama answers the first research question, and what the audience reports following their engagement with the ethnodrama answers the second question. More on this in Chapter 8!

The research question for an ethnodrama emerges from the knowledge gap that becomes clear through the literature review combined with the artist-researcher's point of

Participant population + Knowledge gap + Point of view → Research question

FIGURE 2.1 Equation leading to a research question.

view. The question should also consider the population of participants the artist-researcher will engage in the data collection process, the "who" they are interested in learning more about. Figure 2.1 expresses this combination as an equation leading to a research question.

For example, a group of graduate students in my course identified *making a living as an artist* as their topic of interest.[2] Next, each group member completed a mini literature review reflecting their interests in the topic and then articulated their point of view. Following those steps, the group came together, shared their findings and perspectives, and developed this research question: *How do self-identified artists navigate the relationship between their economic circumstances and artistic drive?*

The group wanted to speak with self-identified artists about this topic, so that became their participant population. Their collective literature review revealed several books, popular press articles, and online sources exploring the trials and tribulations of how artists make a living. Still, they found only passing references to how an artist's economic circumstances might affect their drive to create. The group did not uncover any ABR investigations around this topic other than a documentary film about working mothers as artists, which they identified as valuable to their research process but not a full exploration of their topic. They believed an ethnodrama could provide a new and innovative way of exploring what others had written about while highlighting the voices and stories of self-identified artists. Hence, these two areas became the knowledge gap they would work to fill. Based on their own experiences, the group also identified their curiosity about the necessity of "survival jobs" and how these additional jobs affected an artist's ability to create. This process revealed how their collective point of view contributed to creating their research question.

We can also review an example demonstrating a project with two research questions. In 2018, I created a project called *Of a Certain Age* that examined the experiences of performing arts professionals over the age of 65. For 2 years, I had been in conversations with Traci DiGesu, the Senior Activities and Volunteer Program Manager at the Waldman Living Room, a program of The Actors Fund, now known as The Entertainment Community Fund, about a potential collaboration between her organization and students in the Program in Educational Theatre at NYU's Steinhardt School of Culture, Education, and Human Development. Traci had identified that her older clients had invaluable insights about their vocational experiences in the performing arts professions and that students could benefit from hearing them. She also believed that students could provide a meaningful experience for these older professionals by listening to them, seeing them, and then performing their stories for them. Traci had seen other ethnodramas I had created, and she felt it was the suitable form for this project because her clients were less interested in performing their own stories and more intent on sharing their knowledge with others. We hoped the project would help us learn more about the effects and impacts of ageism on older people and society at large. We wanted to provide insights about ageism for social workers and clinicians who work with older populations and create allies for older people by disrupting ageist language and beliefs (Salvatore, 2020b).

Using her training as a social worker specializing in aging and gerontology, Traci provided me with some general literature on aging, and more specifically on aging as a performing arts professional, which allowed me to review pertinent literature on the topic. Traci and I also discussed our experiences working in the theatre, hers as a designer and mine as a director and playwright, and that we both wondered how our careers might shift and change as we grew older. We also were watching our parents reach the ages of many of the clients Traci worked with, and that witnessing created a unique perspective for both of us. For our project, we defined a "performing arts professional" as an individual who has worked or continues to work professionally in the entertainment industry in theatre, film, television, dance, and music. We knew we wanted to interview participants over age 65, which defined our participant population. We also knew from our knowledge of the literature that no ethnodrama existed about this group, and no study featuring the specific stories of these individuals had been widely shared. This became the knowledge gap that we wanted to fill. And finally, we knew that our own experiences in middle age and with our aging parents informed our point of view for this project. These points yielded the following research questions:

- *What are the experiences of becoming an older performing arts professional (over the age of 65)?*
- *How can gaining a clearer understanding of these experiences of older performing arts professionals help to combat ageism within the population at large?*

In this example, we answered the first question and disseminated our findings by creating the ethnodrama: interviewing participants, transcribing sections of the interviews, coding for recurring themes, arranging selections into a script, and rehearsing and performing the play for audiences. We answered the second research question by engaging our audiences in a postperformance activity. We invited them onstage to meet the actors and share what they learned from the ethnodrama through informal discussion. They also wrote their responses on small cards and deposited them into a box onstage. We then analyzed those written responses for recurring patterns to determine how the performance of the ethnodrama catalyzed a shift in audience perspective, which was the focus of the second research question.

When crafting the research question, it can also be helpful to consider the intended audience for the project. Sometimes, an ethnodrama can be created and presented to a community with a vested interest in the project's topic and the outcome of the investigation. In that case, the research question may use more specific language related to that audience's particular discipline of study, their shared experiences, and their relationships with one another. Other times, an ethnodrama may be created for a broader, more general audience. In that case, the artist-researcher should frame the research question in a way that does not assume inside knowledge of a particular subject area or experience. I typically create an ethnodrama that fulfills both of these possibilities, regardless of the project's origins. My theatre training has taught me to create productions that can be experienced and understood by a wide audience.

Sometimes, the possibility of ethnodrama as a mode of dissemination emerges later in the research process. A researcher might collect data and discover that an ethnodrama could be an appropriate way to disseminate their findings. Or an artist-researcher might create an ethnodrama from an existing dataset they did not collect. These cases create different circumstances to consider. Rather than the ethnodrama's research question driving the data collection process, the research question helps to define the artist-researcher's purpose for engaging with the preexisting data as an ethnodrama.

When Eric Marcus invited me to adapt his *Making Gay History* podcast into an ethnodrama, I had to adjust my usual approach to work from an already existing dataset. In our early conversations about the project, Eric expressed an interest in focusing on his interviews that recounted experiences before the 1969 Stonewall uprising, as he felt that this era of LGBTQIA+ history needed more attention. Eric's request overlapped with my own area of interest in early 20th-century LGBTQIA+ history, so this proved to be a great match. I also spent time in these initial conversations asking Eric about his data-collection process. In my role as the artist-researcher adapting this preexisting dataset, I wanted to understand as much as possible about how Eric recruited participants and conducted interviews, as that offered insight into how the dataset emerged and why certain patterns and themes existed. In the initial data review, I worked with Jamila Humphrie Silver, a member of the Making Gay History Board of Directors, as the research dramaturg for the project. We reviewed related literature to learn more about how historians and social scientists wrote about LGBTQIA+ history and social movements before Stonewall, and this process helped identify where this project could make a contribution. Jamila and I also discussed what we would be interested in exploring more as members of this particular community. We each also had past experiences creating ethnodramas about contemporary issues within the LGBTQIA+ community, which informed the project's point of view.

As I began to review Eric's transcripts of the interviews and to listen to the edited podcast episodes, it became clear that this creation process would be more complicated. Eric's request that the project focus on LGBTQIA+ history before Stonewall automatically eliminated several interviews from consideration, as they did not directly address this. Also, Eric's interviewing style was more open-ended and free-flowing than my interviewing approach for an ethnodrama. Sometimes, he used the same questions when interviewing, but the experiences of each individual mostly guided his interviews. Eric's interviewing approach stands to reason, as he trained as a journalist and did not set out to create an ethnodrama.

Following the literature review and conversations around a point of view for the project, we identified three research questions to guide our next steps:

- *What factors contributed to the emergence of the LGBTQIA+ community in the 20th century in the United States prior to June 1969?*
- *What are the key historical moments/movements for LGBTQIA+ people before the Stonewall uprising that people should know about as part of U.S. and global history?*
- *How can an understanding of LGBTQIA+ history before the Stonewall uprising help the LGBTQIA+ community to move forward into the future?*

Much has been written about the first two questions, so the project's main contribution to knowledge was using ethnodrama to activate the oral histories that Eric had gathered and to bring them to life on stage. The play would also achieve another of Eric's main intentions: to teach LGBTQIA+ history in high schools, colleges, and universities through student performances. The third question pointed to some audience activation following their experience with the performance. These research questions helped narrow Eric's extensive dataset to 20 interview participants who spoke explicitly about their experiences before 1969 and then guided the selection of which sections of the interviews to include in the scripting process. While arriving at the research questions occurred after the data had been collected and existed for many years, completing the literature review and articulating the point of view still played a significant role in the creative process. While the research question usually guides the interviewing process, in this case, the research questions allowed the team to make sense of an already existing dataset.

My most successful ethnodramatic scripts have emerged through answering well-defined research questions to which I genuinely did not know the answer. Of course, I entered with some prior knowledge or personal experiences with the topic at hand, and I might have even hypothesized about what I might discover. But invariably, what I found and learned through the ABR process was far more complex and nuanced than I anticipated. The research question is the touchstone for any ethnodramatic project and plays a central role in all subsequent steps of the specific process outlined in this book.

Generating Interview Prompts

After developing the research question, the artist-researcher can generate **interview prompts** to use in the data collection process with participants. I use "prompt" rather than "question" for a reason. Throughout many projects, I've learned that crafting an interview question that leaves space for a story to emerge can be challenging, but a statement as a command often does the trick. I use "command" in the grammatical sense, meaning an imperative sentence that gives a directive: "Turn to the next page in this book." I craft interview prompts that encourage participants to reflect on and discuss their experiences and beliefs related to the research question. However, it is important to clarify that the research question does not become an interview prompt in my data collection process; instead, it guides my overall inquiry, data collection, and analysis.

Interviews with participants should utilize open-ended prompts in the form of questions and commands. A participant should not be able to respond with a simple "yes" or "no." For example, when I worked on a project exploring how adults reflected on their childhood bullying experiences, I could have asked, "Were you bullied as a child?" and a participant could simply reply with "yes" or "no." End of response, because I didn't ask an open-ended question. The question also does not leave space for someone who bullied or witnessed bullying to respond. To counter these limitations of a **closed question**, I used a prompt phrased as a command and widened the scope of perspectives that could respond: "*Describe a moment from your childhood when you were part of an incident of bullying.*"

The prompt assumes that the participant agreed to an interview because they had something to say about bullying. Even if they hadn't been the object of bullying, they could still contribute to the discussion through their response. For example, a participant could respond by saying they had never experienced bullying as a child. Still, they could share a story about their niece or nephew's experience, providing valuable insights relevant to the overarching research question.

In a more recent VPL project, we interviewed participants from around the United States about their experiences with COVID-19. We began those interviews in March 2020 and continued gathering them through December 2021. When vaccines became available in December 2020, we adjusted our interview protocol to include a prompt about vaccination. Instead of using a closed question such as "Have you received the COVID-19 vaccine?" we used an open-ended question phrased as *"What is your experience with the COVID-19 vaccine and its rollout?"*

One could argue that this prompt assumes that a person received the vaccine, which is a fair argument. However, I would counter that a participant could respond and offer thoughts and opinions about their choice not to get vaccinated or their feelings about how officials rolled out the vaccine. The open-ended question allows multiple perspectives to emerge, all of which serve to answer the central research question.

The ability to transition a closed question to an open-ended prompt comes with time and experience, but here are some pointers to consider as you begin generating interview prompts:

- Can you answer the prompt with "yes" or "no"? If so, it's a closed question; you should rethink it.
- Begin revising by determining whether you want to shift to a command or a question.
- Draft a couple of different possibilities to see what could work. Imagine you were the person hearing the prompt during an interview. How would you answer it?
- Whichever draft prompt yields a more compelling answer is the one you should use.
- Practice over time and completing new projects will make generating open-ended prompts easier.

Some qualitative researchers conduct unstructured or semi-structured interviews using a large bank of prompts or themes, and they allow the interview participant to guide the flow of the conversation (Leavy, 2023). As the interview unfolds, the participant's responses dictate the interviewer's direction with their next question. The interviewer may also ask follow-up questions throughout the interview. While this common practice is widely accepted and often encouraged, I use a highly structured interviewing protocol that unfolds the same for each interview participant in the data collection process (Harrison, 2018; Leavy, 2023). Some researchers may view this structured approach as overly regimented or confining. However, the structure allows me to be more present as a listener and observer throughout an interview rather than becoming distracted by the need to assess where to guide the interview next. Anecdotal comments from interview participants have indicated that they appreciate the more structured approach, mainly because they feel seen and heard by me as the interviewer. I believe that's because they have my full attention. I offer the outline for my interview protocol in the next chapter, but I mention it here because the more structured approach affects how I generate interview prompts.

I conduct my interviews using 10 to 12 prompts, and each participant experiences the same set of prompts in the same order. I maintain this ordering from interview to interview, as it helps in the data analysis further along in the process. Sometimes, I may ask an interview participant to speak more about something they have said in response to a particular prompt, but I stay within the established structure. Asking too many follow-up questions can send an interview in all sorts of directions and down paths that are not help-ful to the overall inquiry. However, I finish every interview with the same two questions, intending to instigate another layer of conversation between myself and the participant. The next to last question is *"Is there anything else you would like to say about the topics we've been discussing?"*

This general question late in the protocol replaces the need for follow-up questions throughout, as it invites additional responses that earlier prompts in the protocol may have seeded. Participants sometimes circle back to an earlier part of their interview and build on it, or they offer something completely new. This question has also prompted par-ticipants to share a question they thought I would ask about "X," and since I didn't, they offered that question and answered it for me. Finally, this general follow-up question has often provided an invaluable response I transcribe and include in the ethnodrama. So you might wonder why I stick so rigidly to the established prompts and ordering and why I don't ask more follow-up questions along the way. The answer is about the interview par-ticipant's experience.

The interview process must focus on creating a positive experience for the inter-view participant, and to do that, the data collection process must be guided by an ethos centered on care. Yes, as the artist-researcher, I am working to collect data and answer a research question. However, if the power of working in this form comes from learning through another person's experience, the person sharing needs to receive my care. Listen-ing carefully, not interrupting a participant's flow, and creating space for them to share what they want to share in a given moment provide care. Not probing too deeply, even when I want to know more, provides care. Trusting that the prompts I've generated can catalyze an extended conversation and a deeper connection with a participant provides care.

Effective ordering of the prompts plays a vital role in reinforcing this ethos of care. When a participant finishes an interview with me, I want them to feel they've had a posi-tive experience and want to share the details of that experience with someone else. I want them to have discovered something about themselves that they didn't know before the interview started. Then, the interviewing process is not only about what I gather from it; the participant also receives something. I achieve this by providing structure and care, and thinking carefully about the narrative of the experience. Drawing on skills as a playwright and dramaturg, I order my interview prompts to create a logical, narrative-driven experience for the participant. I do not begin with the most challenging prompt. Sometimes, the first prompt may not seem to have an explicit relationship to the topic at hand, although there's always a connection in my mind. A participant's answers to the first prompt can provide me with helpful information about how they will respond to the overall interviewing experience. That initial assessment helps guide my delivery of the remaining prompts during the interview. I like to say that participating in an interview should not feel like cannonballing into a cold swimming pool on the first day the pool is open. Instead, participating in an interview should feel like sinking into a warm bath. An interviewing process can be pleasurable, even if it asks a participant to discuss difficult concepts, ideas, and experiences. To achieve that goal of pleasure, I have to create a posi-tive experience centered around care for the participant.

Hence the reason why I use this final interview prompt. I always ask a participant this last question: *"Do you have any questions for me?"* The simple offer to the participant to ask questions of me as the artist-researcher about anything—me, my life, the process, the subject matter of the interview, or anything else—deepens their trust in me and the project. If someone has spent 45 minutes to an hour sharing their experiences with me, they have every right to ask me any question they want. And participants frequently have questions. "Who are you again? How are you involved in this project? Why are you interested in this topic? What are you trying to say with this project? What's going to happen with this interview? Who else have you interviewed? How will this become a play?" And the list goes on. As you will learn in Chapter 3, many of these questions are addressed in the consenting process and discussed in the interview protocol before we begin with the interview prompts. Still, I answer a participant's questions as honestly and thoroughly as possible. We're at the beginning of the research process, and I want to convey that I mean no harm. I am not engaging in this process with any ill will or bad intentions. Ethnographic research in the social sciences, documentary theatre, and verbatim theatre has been criticized for decades for its potential to exploit participants. The purpose of the project and its interviewing process may be unclear. How the interviews will be used may be ambiguous. The interview unintentionally retraumatizes the participant. These are valid concerns, and because of them, I do my best to build trust with participants by letting them know as much as possible about the project's intentions throughout the research process. This final interview prompt is a fundamental part of trust-building, and I outline more about how I build trust in Chapter 3.

Let's consider the project about political polarization, called *Whatever You Are, Be a Good One*, to demonstrate how a group of interview prompts comes together. The Verbatim Performance Lab, my lab at NYU, created this ethnodrama to explore political polarization in the United States in advance of the 2022 midterm elections. In his book *Why We're Polarized*, Ezra Klein (2020) attempted to identify a framework for understanding the political problem of polarization, but he offered few answers or solutions. We wanted to use an ABR approach to uncover more information about polarization while also thinking about potential solutions. We identified our main research questions as follows: *What are the causes of the extreme political polarization that we currently experience in the United States? How can we overcome this polarization over the next 5 years?*

With those research questions in mind, my co-creator Keith R. Huff and I crafted a set of interview prompts to catalyze conversations with interview participants through which answers to our research questions could emerge. A trained team of interviewers conducted over 100 interviews from October 2021 through August 2022 with volunteers from across the country. Every interview used the same set of prompts asked in the same order.

Interview Prompts for **Whatever You Are, Be a Good One**

- How were you taught U.S. history, and how has that affected your political viewpoints?
- What are the core values of the United States, and where do you see them play out in your day-to-day life?
- How would you characterize the current political climate in the United States?
- Describe the last time you engaged in an in-person conversation with someone you disagree with politically.
- How has the ongoing conversation around inflation and the economy affected your day-to-day life?

- What issue do you think Americans could unite around, and what would it take to bring them together?
- Describe an experience when you felt that your rights were violated by a person, business, or government entity.
- What right is essential to the democracy of the United States, and what is the biggest threat to it?
- If you could ask a politician running for national office any single question, what would you ask them and why?

* * *

- Is there anything else you would like to say about the topics we've been discussing?
- Do you have any questions for me?

Notice that the prompts are a mixture of questions and commands. We arranged them to encourage a logical conversation, yielding valuable data to answer the research questions. Also, none of the prompts ask the participant to respond directly to either research question. If, as I've stated earlier, the research question functions as the overarching spine for an ethnodrama, the interview prompts should lead a participant to share something more specific. For example, I could ask a participant, "What do you think is causing all this political polarization?" but I'm not sure how interesting that will ultimately be to listen to in performance. That question also feels like it has the potential to elicit general responses that parrot back what the media might have to say on this topic. We wanted to uncover other perspectives on polarization, so our interview prompts required participants to engage with more specific thoughts and experiences. We cannot discover something universal without getting specific; specificity leads to universality, not the other way around.

The first question, "How were you taught U.S. history, and how has that affected your political viewpoints?" is similar to the ones initially used by Anna Deavere Smith as she developed her interviewing technique for her ongoing project *On the Road: The Search for American Character.* As she tells it in her book *Talk to Me: Travels in Media and Politics* (2000), Smith spoke with a linguist about particular questions that would cause a person's syntax to change, a moment that Smith described as "when language fails [us]" (p. 53). I interpret this description as asking a question that forces a person to construct meaning through spoken language in the moment rather than relying on some pat answer or understanding that they've already arrived at on a particular topic. The linguist recommended three questions: (1) Have you ever come close to death? (2) Do you know the circumstances of your birth? (3) Have you ever been accused of something you did not do? (p. 54). As written here, these are closed questions, but they can quickly become open-ended commands. Each of these questions prompts the participant to share a personal experience or a memory, which is an important way to begin. It personalizes the experience and primes the participant to share stories. Stories can be theatrically compelling, which then fuels an ethnodrama's theatricality. The source material must have theatricality to achieve a theatrical product.

Through my experiences with ethnodrama, I have learned to use two kinds of interview prompts with participants: story-generating prompts and philosophy-generating prompts. **Story-generating prompts** do what they say: They encourage participants to tell personal stories. **Philosophy-generating prompts** invite participants to philosophize and share their opinions on the topic. Rarely does a philosophizing prompt generate a story. It's possible, but the likelihood is low. Both kinds of prompts have value for the artist-researcher as they try to answer their research questions, but I recommend having more story-generating prompts than philosophy-generating prompts in a protocol. Listening to participants philosophize and share their opinions for long periods is not theatrically compelling and can be the death knell for many well-meaning ethnodramas. Stories tend to have more theatrical possibilities embedded from the start.

The bank of interview prompts for *Whatever You Are, Be a Good One* could have used more story-generating prompts, and I realized that in retrospect, once we had completed most of the data collection. As we reviewed the dataset to begin the scripting process, we had excellent responses that included a lot of opinions about what caused political polarization, how participants felt about the current political climate, and what they felt was important to consider for the country's future. The content of those particular responses seemed less theatrically compelling, but how the participants communicated their responses often made them more interesting. When there was a theatrically compelling story about a personal experience, those responses usually came from what I would categorize as the story-generating prompts:

- How were you taught U.S. history, and how has that affected your political viewpoints?
- Describe the last time you engaged in an in-person conversation with someone you disagree with politically.
- Describe an experience when you felt that your rights were violated by a person, business, or government entity.

These prompts catalyzed compelling content from the participants as they shared their personal experiences. I had learned this lesson before, but I needed the reminder. Story-generating prompts usually produce the most compelling material for an ethnodrama.

An examination of the interview prompts for *Of a Certain Age* illustrates a bank with more story-generating prompts:

- Describe the circumstances surrounding your birth.
- Describe your first professional job as a performing artist.
- Describe your most recent job as a performing artist.
- What is your favorite thing about working as a performing artist?
- Describe a moment in your life when you experienced or witnessed ageism.
- What is surprising to you about growing older as a performing arts professional?
- What advice would you give to someone at the beginning of their career as a performing artist?
- What, if anything, are you looking forward to in the next decade?

* * *

- Is there anything else you would like to say about the topics we've been discussing?
- Do you have any questions for me?

The four prompts that begin with the word "Describe" elicited stories from the interview participants about their experiences working in the performing arts, and those helped to answer our research question: What are the experiences of becoming an older performing arts professional (over the age of 65)? Some of the other prompts also generated stories, most notably "What is surprising to you about growing older as a performing arts professional?" but the likelihood was higher from the other prompts I highlighted.

So, it is essential to keep eyes and ears open for prompts that elicit stories, just as much as prompts that get at thoughts and opinions. But what's the best way to generate a list of prompts for consideration? Great question! To address this, let's consider a past project from my ethnodrama course that explored cancel culture following the uprising at the United States Capitol on January 6, 2021. This group of students was interested in how cancel culture manifested in the United States following January 6.[3] After completing their project need analyses and point-of-view statements, the group landed on two research questions: *What are the major consequences of cancel culture in contemporary American society? How does an individual's political and personal ideologies inform their point of view on cancel culture?*

Using these questions as a starting point, I asked each group member to brainstorm three to five interview prompts that could encourage a potential participant to share stories, thoughts, and opinions to answer their research questions. Following their individual brainstorming, the group submitted their prompts to me via email. I printed the individual prompts and cut them into paper strips, one prompt per strip. When the group members arrived at class, I handed them their envelope of prompts and three copies of their research questions printed in large font on pieces of paper. I instructed them to sort through the envelope of prompts and choose the ones they felt would elicit the most compelling and valuable responses from an interview participant. I told them to keep their research questions in plain sight (hence the printed copies) so that they could continually test each prompt's efficacy against the research questions' needs. Using prompts printed on slips of paper allows for easy moving around into categories such as "yes," "no," and "maybe." The artist-researcher can also place similarly worded prompts or similar intentions next to each other to see which one they prefer. This process can also unfold on a screen, using a Google document or other similar application, but I appreciate the ability to touch the prompts, pick them up, and move them around. Use a sorting method that works best for you.

After their first review of their prompts, this group came up with the following named categories with their prompts sorted under each one:

Personal Experience

- Describe a situation when you felt the need to censor yourself due to differing personal and/or political ideologies between you and another person.
- Describe a redemption story that you have been a part of or have witnessed.
- Describe a time in your life when you were accused of something that you didn't do.

- Describe a moment when you or someone you know has been canceled by others and what implications that had.
- Describe a moment in your life when someone challenged your political ideologies or personal beliefs.
- Describe a moment when you experienced or witnessed cancel culture?
- Describe a moment when you witnessed someone you've known getting canceled.
- Describe a moment where you found yourself canceling someone else.
- Describe an instance where you were the narrative authority on a situation.
- Describe a time when you were grateful for your right to have freedom of speech.
- Describe a time you supported a canceled individual? Why or why not?
- Describe a fear you have as a result of cancel culture.
- What is an instance where you offered a platform to a dissenting opinion?

Social Media

- How does cancel culture affect the way you use social media?
- How has social media impacted your political views or informed your moral beliefs?

Ideology

- What is the difference between hate speech and free speech?
- What does successful accountability look like to you?
- How do you define cancel culture?
- To what extent is cancel culture serving its purpose?

Not Sure?

- Do you believe there should be off-limits topics of discourse?
- Describe a moment in your life when you felt like your freedom of expression was hindered or censored.

Based on my suggestion of 10 to 12 prompts total, including the last two questions I always use, the group had some more decisions to make. They repeated the same review process but with greater attention to whether they wanted to include prompts from each identified category and how those prompts would generate the strongest possible dataset to answer their research questions. I also instructed them to consider how to order the prompts, thinking through how they would want to answer the prompts if they were a participant in the project. How could they create a positive experience for the participants as they discussed this difficult topic? The group came back with the following set of prompts:

- Describe a time in your life when you were accused of something you didn't do.
- How do you define cancel culture?
- Describe a moment when you experienced cancel culture or witnessed someone being canceled.

- Describe a situation where you felt the need to censor yourself due to differing personal and/or political beliefs between you and another person.
- Describe a time when you supported a canceled public figure.
- What about cancel culture scares you?
- What is the difference between hate speech and free speech?
- What do you think is the best way to hold someone accountable for their words and actions?

* * *

- Is there anything else you would like to say about the topics we've been discussing?
- Do you have any questions for me?

The group narrowed their list of 21 prompts to eight and added the final two. The bank of prompts included at least four story-generating prompts ("Describe . . ."), with the possibility that others might also elicit stories. The group also had a prompt asking participants to define "cancel culture." Given how much that term gets used in the media and passing conversations, asking participants to define it based on their own understanding created the possibility of demonstrating that it means different things to different people. The group's ordering of the prompts illustrated their understanding of how to create an experience for the interview participant. Starting with a personal memory, seemingly unrelated to cancel culture, then moving into a definition, followed by more personal memories and experiences, ending with more philosophy-generating prompts. Imagine yourself in the position of the interview participant and how your understanding of yourself in relation to this topic might shift, change, or solidify as a result of moving through this bank of prompts in this order.

Once the artist-researcher develops the bank of interview prompts, the urge to recruit participants kicks in, but they must complete other steps before speaking with anyone about the topic. Most importantly, the artist-researcher must address the ethics of the data collection process they are about to undertake. If operating independently, the artist-researcher needs to consider how to recruit participants ethically, obtain **consent**, and collect data. If the artist-researcher has an institutional affiliation, like a college or university, they may need to move through a review process with their institution's ethics committee.

The Ethics Committee Review Process

Given that creating an ethnodrama often relies on gathering interviews from participants, the artist-researcher must keep attention to ethics at the forefront of their process. As discussed earlier, ethnography has a long history of criticism for what it takes from those being "studied." For this reason, I refer to the people I interview as "participants" rather than "subjects," as, in my mind, this implies a different kind of relationship, more of a partnership in the data collection process. All researchers, artist-researchers included, are responsible for maintaining a strong moral compass as we work with other human beings. I call this practicing **good human beingness**, and I know it when I see it. Or rather, I know it is missing when I don't see it or experience it. Whether an artist-researcher works alone or as part of a team, independently or affiliated, they must practice good human being-ness, as it embodies the **relational ethics** necessary for working with other human beings.

When an artist-researcher works under the jurisdiction of a college or university, that institution's **ethics committee** governing research involving human subjects must vet the artist-researcher's proposed research process. These committees have different names from country to country. For example, in the United States, these committees are called institutional review boards (IRBs); in the United Kingdom, they are called research ethics committees (Delamont & Atkinson, 2018, p. 212). An ethics committee's vetting determines whether a project requires their oversight. If so, they will need the project to adhere to strict guidelines about the safety and welfare of the human participants in the research process. Ethics committee oversight emerged from the necessity to protect human beings participating in biomedical and social science research after decades of unregulated and harmful experiments on human subjects, most notably the Tuskegee Syphilis Study conducted by the U.S. Public Health Service from 1932 to 1972. An ethics committee review focuses on ensuring that the researcher has carefully considered the ethical implications of the research process for the participants and has obtained an individual's consent to participate. The ethics committee reviews each stage of the research process, from recruitment to consent to data collection to dissemination.

An ethnodrama engages human participants in a data collection process, so an institution's ethics committee may want to review and oversee the project. I have received mixed messages from my institution's IRB regarding my ethnodramas. At times, the IRB has reviewed a project, wanted oversight, and provided their approval of the procedures. Other times, the IRB has declared a project exempt from their oversight. Still other times, the same IRB has reviewed a project and determined that it does not meet the federal government's definition of research. These projects used the same research methodology and procedure in each instance but garnered different outcomes. These varied outcomes illustrate one of the challenges of engaging in ABR within academic institutions. Because I don't disseminate my research findings in a traditional academic format, such as a book or journal article, but rather as a play or theatrical performance, my institution's IRB often does not categorize my work as research. Additionally, because my ethnodramas typically showcase a variety of voices on a topic without declaring a specific finding or outcome, the IRB does not see me making any generalizable conclusions, a characteristic that contributes to the federal government's definition of research. Based on my experiences with my institution's IRB, I encourage any artist-researcher affiliated with an academic institution, whether a faculty member or student, to establish communication with their ethics committee early in the research design process. These initial communications can give an artist-researcher a sense of how their institution's committee thinks about ABR and can help inform their approach to the **procedural ethics** governed by the committee.

A typical ethics committee review application uses online submission software from a company specializing in research administration. The software breaks the application into various sections, and the artist-researcher answers questions about their project. Questions can be closed-ended, require a narrative explanation, or request uploaded documents. The sections of the application may take the following format:

• *Initial Screening Questions:* Information specific to the governing institution and questions that help to determine if the research project involves human participants.

- *Research Personnel:* Information about the artist-researcher, referred to as the Principal Investigator (PI), and any other research team members who will interact with human participants and/or have access to identifiable data. Students applying to an institution's ethics committee will need a faculty member named as the PI for their proposed project. For a doctoral candidate, this is typically the chair of their dissertation committee. In addition, institutions require proof that all research team members have completed training on interacting with human participants and handling sensitive data. Applications also require information about team members affiliated with other institutions.

- *Project Information:* Summary of the research project focusing on purposes, procedures, data types, and collection processes, basically what you're doing and how you're doing it. Because an ethics committee includes faculty and staff from various disciplines, the language should be accessible to a lay audience. This section could also contain questions about the project's funding and the proposed participants' geographical location. If a project requires international participants, there may be additional questions about how the data collection will protect participants in countries where surveillance is common.

- *Participants, Recruitment, Consent, and Privacy:* Who will participate, how will they be recruited and engaged in the research, and how will they grant their consent to participate? The artist-researcher needs to identify criteria for a participant to be included or excluded from a study and whether the study will involve participants from vulnerable populations, including children under the age of legal consent (e.g., 18 in the United States). Other vulnerable populations include incarcerated individuals, pregnant individuals, individuals with mental disabilities, or economically or educationally disadvantaged individuals. The artist-researcher will also provide copies of recruiting language and materials (flyers, posts, etc.), statements to participants, screeners that determine participant eligibility if needed, and consent forms.

- *Data Confidentiality and Risks and Benefits:* How are the collected data kept confidential and secure, and what risks or benefits might a participant encounter through the proposed research? The artist-researcher must explain how they will keep participants' identities confidential if necessary, and how they will store data (digital or analog), so that only members of the research team can access it.

- *Review Type:* What review type is requested? Based on completing the ethics committee review application, the artist-researcher can select a type of review for their project. The choices are typically Exempt, Expedited, or Full Board Review, and those designations are determined by the ethics committee and by a country's governing body. In the United States, the U.S. Department of Health and Human Services (2023) determined these designations (hhs.gov).

Once the committee receives the completed application, the review process begins. The committee will typically review and approve recruitment materials and consent or release forms that establish participant permission to use data collected through the interview process. It is common for the committee to ask for clarification or additional information about particular elements of the proposed research. I have had applications requiring multiple rounds of review before receiving final approval and clearance to proceed with the research. Artist-researchers should think carefully about their timeline for a project and plan accordingly by factoring in at least 1 to 2 months from the submission date to receive final ethics committee approval for a project. I also recommend developing a relationship with the administrative leaders of your institution's ethics committee and asking them for assistance when needed. I have had multiple conversations and discussions with administrators who have been incredibly helpful to me in navigating the IRB's questions about my work. Members of an ethics committee and the people who work to support them are not your enemies; they are doing an important job. Better to frame your relationship as collegial and collaborative, rather than adversarial and confrontational.

Achieving ethics committee approval for a research project feels like a milestone for any researcher, as the process can be challenging and time-consuming. That said, while the ethics committee process is often a necessary administrative step related to the procedural ethics of conducting research affiliated with an institution, we have a greater responsibility as researchers to be mindful of the relational ethics that unfold throughout our processes. Relational ethics connect more directly to the good human beingness I mentioned before. A member of the ethics committee does not follow you into a room for an interview with a participant, so it is up to you to keep the ethical considerations alive and at the forefront of your process. What matters most is what happens in the relationship between the researcher and the participant. I continue to revisit these ethical considerations throughout this book, demonstrating how to navigate them at each step of an ethnodrama's creation.

Moving Past the Gatekeepers

While ABR has gained popularity and credibility over the last 20 to 30 years, artist-researchers wishing to use ethnodrama as their research method may still encounter resistance from faculty members and colleagues who hold more traditional views. It may be difficult for someone who has published all their research in academic journals or books to understand the validity of an artistic process, a script, or a performance that creates and disseminates research findings. While this kind of traditional thinking and questioning can be frustrating and discouraging, I can offer some suggestions to counteract skepticism and resistance.

• *Know your form and why you want to use it.* If you want to use ethnodrama for your research project, know the form inside and out. While this book is a starting point and Chapter 1 has provided an overview, you have a responsibility to dig deeper. Your literature review should help to identify projects in adjacent topics that you can use to demonstrate that other scholars have used this form to great success before you. If you can situate your research among those previous projects, you may have an easier time convincing your colleagues and mentors about the efficacy of ethnodrama. Also, you must present a clear case about why you want to use ethnodrama rather than another qualitative research method. The "why" is very important. The argument for reaching a larger audience may be effective in this case. Depending on the size of the venue and the number of performances, an ethnodrama's production can reach many more "readers" than traditional forms of dissemination like journal articles and conference presentations.

• *Find your allies.* If you are a student conducting research for an advanced degree and you decide you want to use ethnodrama, then find a team of faculty mentors who are open to ABR. You may have to look beyond your academic department for faculty mentors who conduct ABR or who understand the breadth and scope of possibility within qualitative research. You should only undertake a research project with a supportive mentor or chair. For those junior faculty members considering tenure and promotion processes, it is essential to know the work of your direct colleagues at your home institution. By demonstrating interest and knowledge in what they do and how they do it, you may build a natural curiosity in them about your work. Understanding is a two-way street. Given that tenure and promotion require external review, you should also be ready with a list of arts-based researchers who are knowledgeable about ethnodrama and could evaluate your work. These connections become clear by attending academic conferences and serving as a peer reviewer for journals in your field.

• *Become comfortable with the languages of social science and theatre.* Not surprisingly, language has a lot of power because it provides legibility for what an arts-based researcher does and why they do it. Depending on your training, you may need to become more comfortable with the languages of social science or theatre. Early in my academic career, I learned that if I described my work in theatre using the language of social science, colleagues working outside of my discipline had an easier time understanding what I do. As a result, I grew more comfortable framing my creative work through a social science lens, specifically using the term "ethnodrama." This alternative framing has resulted in years of positive support from colleagues in sociology, political science, economics, applied psychology, curriculum and instruction, and international education. I have grown in my understanding of their disciplines, and they have become fans of ABR and ethnodrama. Conversely, if you are a social scientist, learning the language of the theatre will also help you to identify potential connections between your own processes and those practiced by artists and academic colleagues who make meaning through artistic creation and theatrical productions.

• *Prepare to explain yourself over and over again.* I would be lying if I wrote here that I no longer have to explain myself. Each time a new department chair or dean comes on board at my institution, I reintroduce my work in ethnodrama and why it is important and valid. Many faculty members have to go through this reintroduction process when leadership changes. However, it can be more challenging for an arts-based researcher because our methods are still frequently questioned. That said, I do have an advantage. Rather than asking someone to read my research publications, I can invite them to a performance. That invitation sparks curiosity, attendance, and, frequently, an easy conversion because of ethnodrama's innovative way of disseminating research findings. So while the repetition of explaining may be tiring, consider it an opportunity to expand the sphere of influence that ethnodrama and ABR can have.

Forging Ahead

While ethnodrama may seem unique and innovative for conducting and disseminating research, the methodology is still grounded in the basic tenets of sound qualitative research approaches. First, the artist-reseacher identifies a topic of interest, identifies gaps in knowledge, articulates their point of view, determines the population of participants they will speak to about the topic, and then identifies potential lines of inquiry. From there, the central research question emerges, guiding the creation of a bank of interview prompts used with the interview participants. The ethics of working with human participants remain in the artist-researcher's consciousness at each step. An ethics committee provides additional perspective and oversight for those affiliated with an institution. Moving into participant recruitment and data collection, these ethical considerations, which have mainly been theoretical and procedural up to this point, become practical, relational, and even more relevant.

ACTIVITIES

Research versus Art

Identify a traditional piece of qualitative research that impacted you. Spend 5 minutes freewriting about it. What about it impacted you and why? Take a short, 2-minute walk around your space. Now spend 5 minutes freewriting about a play or movie that impacted you. Again, what about it impacted you and why? Take another short, 2-minute walk. Review your free writing, noting the similarities and differences between the two experiences. What do you know now that you didn't know before the exercise? How might you bring this awareness about effective research and art making to your ethnodramatic creations?

Order the Prompts

Consider the list of prompts below for a project about the U.S. Presidency. They were crafted to catalyze answers to the following research question: *How do people living and working in the United States describe their thoughts and feelings about the U.S. Presidency during the 2024 election cycle?*

Currently, the prompts are listed randomly. Given the importance of ordering prompts to create an experience for an interview participant, how would you arrange them to achieve that goal?

- Tell me about a time when you felt directly affected by the actions of the President of the United States.
- Tell me about a memorable experience you've had voting in an election.
- Describe the circumstances surrounding your political upbringing.
- Describe a moment when you questioned the actions or decisions of the President of the United States.
- Do you have any questions for me?
- Describe your earliest memory of an election of any kind.
- Describe a recent conversation you've had about the past U.S. presidential election.
- Do you have anything else you'd like to say about the topics we've been discussing?
- If you look 3 years into the future, what do you hope the President of the United States will have accomplished?

- How did you learn about the U.S. Constitution?
- Tell me about a time when you felt inspired by a sitting U.S. president or a presidential candidate.
- What is the primary responsibility of the President of the United States?

Closed to Open

The initial brainstorming of interview prompts can often result in closed questions that result in "yes" or "no," one-word, or short-phrase answers. While closed questions might not be the best interview prompts, you can find ways to make them open-ended, as described on page 32 of this chapter. Look at the list of closed questions below and experiment with rewriting or rephrasing them to become open-ended prompts.

- Can you live without social media?
- Who should be responsible for educating young people about politics?
- When were you born?
- Has there ever been a time you changed your mind on a political issue?
- Did you choose the neighborhood that you live in?
- Do you trust a doctor to understand your medical needs?
- How comfortable do you feel discussing politics?

NOTES

1. *Making Gay History: Before Stonewall* can be licensed for production. For more information, please visit https://makinggayhistory.org/the-play.

2. The author is grateful to Candice Ding, Brittani Evans, Melissa Gabilanes, Jiawen Hu, Michael Kaplan, Carmen Meyers, and Samantha Weisberg for their work on this project.

3. The author is grateful to Lianne Davidoff, Ted Griffith, Ryan Howland, Rita Liu, Bridget O'Neill, Alex Oleksy, and Kat Todorova for their work on this project.

3   Data Collection

Data collection marks the moment in the creative process when the artist-researcher begins the relationship with their interview participants. Throughout this book, I frequently refer to the **dataset**, which is the interviews that emerge through data collection. "Dataset" sounds very clinical, but in the case of ethnodrama and other qualitative methodologies, the dataset contains numerous personal stories that living, breathing individuals have shared with another human being through a conversation that typically unfolds over a set period. After nearly 30 years of conducting interviews, I've learned that participants share surprisingly personal stories and honest thoughts and opinions with me, a stranger they've just met. I have experienced powerful emotions during these conversations, both as the interviewer and from the interviewee, and I have learned countless invaluable lessons about the topic at hand and the human experience more generally. I have been confronted by my own assumptions and biases, and I think some participants have been confronted by theirs. Nevertheless, the vulnerability that emerged in these exchanges has been striking and unforgettable.

Based on these experiences, I think of the interview as an intimate exchange between the interviewer and the interview participant. I use "intimate" here not in a physical sense but to emphasize the level of care and attention that the artist-researcher must bring to the data collection process. Care and attention must begin at the moment of first contact with a participant at recruitment, continue through the interviewing process and follow-up communication of thanks, and extend to the potential sharing of the participant's story in a script and performance. Because of the vulnerability and intimacy embedded in the data collection process, the artist-researcher must pay careful attention to the ethical considerations that ethnodrama can raise (Ackroyd & O'Toole, 2010; Leavy, 2023; Saldaña, 2011a; Salvatore, 2020b, 2025). A research process that involves interviewing participants and presenting the results in any format requires close attention to the legality and the ethics of the relationship between the artist-researcher, the interview participant, and the resulting data (Saldaña, 2011a).

In this chapter I discuss ways to recruit interview participants for a data collection process and suggest approaches to scheduling and confirming the interviews. I also address securing consent and offer sample language to include in a consent form. I share the outline for an interviewing protocol template I developed and refined over three decades to prioritize the interview participant's experience, ensuring that care and relational ethics guide the data collection process. The chapter also establishes best practices for recording interviews and collecting field notes.

Some Thoughts on the Process

Given that an interview participant for an ethnodrama has the potential to experience themselves as part of a script or performance and might encounter any number of discoveries and discomforts, the artist-researcher must keep this in mind when creating any new work. Having experienced a portrayal of myself on multiple occasions, I understand the feelings that emerge when I read my words in a script or witness an actor perform my words, gestures, and thoughts. I learned something through those experiences but wasn't always comfortable with what I learned. Sometimes, I felt embarrassed by how I spoke or moved my hands, or wondered why I related a particular idea in a certain way or shared a specific story. However, I had accepted an invitation or volunteered to participate in their process, knowing that what I had shared in the interview could be used in a script or performance. I also acknowledged that I contributed something during my interview that the artist-researcher chose to include in their ethnodrama. Because I have developed empathy for this experience, I engage interview participants carefully, ensuring they enter the data collection process of their own free will, with as much information about the project and the approach as possible.

My approach to ethnodrama implements a specific technique known as **verbatim performance**, which I define as "the precise portrayal of an actual person using their exact speech and gestural patterns as a data source for investigation, literally word for word and gesture for gesture" (Salvatore, 2023; Vachon & Salvatore, 2023). Verbatim performance amplifies the need for care in the portrayal of interview participants because of the strict adherence to their words and gestures as spoken during their interview. Seeing the specifics of how one presents material can highlight personal mannerisms and ways of speaking that the participant might not have ever noticed or acknowledged before seeing it performed back to them by someone else (Soloski, 2013; Vachon & Salvatore, 2023; Young, 2017). I continue to discuss why I use verbatim performance in ethnodrama in subsequent chapters of this book.

In my initial contact with any potential participant, I clearly state that verbatim performance will be a featured part of the project. I carefully describe the performance style to ensure that potential participants understand how an actor could portray them, and more recently, I even direct them to a recording of an actor delivering a verbatim performance. Participants may claim they know what "verbatim" means, but I want them to understand how the performance looks and sounds in this style. Still, until they experience a performance of themselves in the presence of an audience, it is difficult to fully grasp what will happen or how they will feel as it unfolds. My experiences with participants experiencing themselves in performance have been overwhelmingly positive. Many expressed gratitude for sharing their stories with a larger audience, and they appreciated the chance to see themselves in a new light. However, the numerous positive responses have been tempered by the few adverse reactions from participants who reported feeling misrepresented in performance. These complaints resulted from their experience of how they were performed, not from the content included in the script. So, even with the knowledge that I explained the process in advance and that we took the utmost care with sharing those stories and crafting the actors' portrayals, these moments remind me to maintain an empathic position for the participant's experience and to keep a mindset of care and the ethical considerations of this form always at the forefront of my mind (Salvatore, 2020b, 2025; Vachon & Salvatore, 2023).

I am vigilant about presenting my process honestly and openly to each interview participant, starting with a statement to participants at our initial point of contact and following with a statement of purpose in the written consent/release form. The interview protocol also includes multiple references to the verbatim nature of my work and how I will use the interview data. Participants can stop the interview at any time, refuse to respond to specific prompts, and request that sections of the interview not be considered for use in the ethnodrama. Participants always have the opportunity to choose their **identifier** (their actual name or a pseudonym) and to change the names of people or specific locations mentioned in the interview to offer and protect anonymity. All this information is shared at the beginning of the interview session and then repeated at the interview's conclusion. If a participant seems unsettled by their interview experience, I do not consider their interview in my analysis or dissemination. I do not want to offend, retraumatize, or endanger an individual participating in the research process.

Anna Deavere Smith, often cited as the creator of the verbatim performance style I use in the performance dissemination of my ethnodramas, describes that she only interviews people "who would scream it from the mountain top" (American Academy of Arts & Sciences, 2019). I have adopted Smith's ethos around participant recruitment because I believe participants should enter a research process willing, informed, and aware, beginning with the recruiting process.

Recruiting Participants

Artist-researchers can recruit interview participants in various ways, but their research question should drive their recruiting strategies. Remember from Chapter 2 that the research question for a project references the potential participant population. Since the criteria for interview participants played a role in crafting the research question, recruiting includes identifying participants that fit those criteria. Then, the artist-researcher must consider their geographical location, proximity to the potential **sample** or pool of participants, and the time allocated for the project to unfold. They must also consider their current relationship with the proposed participant pool. For example, is the artist-researcher a member of the community they propose to interview, or are they an outsider? Both insider and outsider statuses have implications for the ethics of the entire project, so the artist-researcher must be thoughtful about how they enter and engage with a particular community.

Suppose the artist-researcher has inside connections to a particular community. In that case, those connections facilitate awareness within the community about the project and create a willingness for volunteers to step forward more quickly. However, a preexisting relationship with participants might introduce bias, which could cloud the purposes of the research project. I encourage artist-researchers to be clear about their intentions and to separate their project as best they can from any other relationships they may have with participants within a community they already know. The artist-researcher might also propose interviewing participants in a community where they have no prior relationship. In that case, they must first consider ways to develop a relationship with that community to gain its members' trust and then engage in an interviewing process. I'm not suggesting that the artist-researcher has to embed themselves in a particular community before attempting to recruit participants. Still, it is essential to consider how to enter into a relationship with potential participants without a prior connection. In both cases, the issue of trust is at the heart of this. Participants must feel that they can trust the artist-researcher and their intentions. The trust-building process should begin at the moment of recruitment. A trusting relationship between the artist-researcher and the participant speaks to the broader importance of relational ethics, the "good human beingness" I mentioned in Chapter 2. While an artist-researcher may have received approval from an institution's ethics committee for their procedural ethics, they must maintain and monitor their relational ethics throughout the research process.

Depending on the project, the artist-researcher must also consider ways to cultivate a diverse pool of participants, and the project's needs dictate the scope of that diversity. For example, one project might require participants from across age ranges, while another might require participants in their 20s. Another project might require all participants to live in a particular state, and another might need participants from across the United States. In each of these instances, the artist-researcher should consider what techniques they can use to recruit as diverse a participant pool as possible.

One important rule I follow around recruiting and interviewing participants: I do not interview participants I know. I recommend that all artist-researchers working in ethnodrama do the same. Through past experiences, I have learned that when I interview someone I know, the interview tends to be less robust than when I interview a stranger or someone I've only interacted with on a cursory level. When I interviewed someone I know moderately well to very well, the interview participant seemed to leave out particular details in a story because we may have had a shared experience together, and they assumed I knew those details. Or we had a past discussion about a topic that is part of the ethnodrama project, so they skipped over some of those past thoughts. But in actuality, what they shared in that past conversation is why I thought they would be a good candidate for a project. If I am working on a project alone, I choose not to interview the person I know, even if they are a great candidate for an interview. If the project includes a team of people conducting interviews, I refer the person I know to another interviewer on the team. This choice reduces the possibility of a truncated response to a potential prompt. Experience tells me that participants are more honest and forthcoming with interviewers they do not know. The definition of what it means to know someone well is entirely up to the artist-researcher. In my case, I do not interview family members, friends, acquaintances I've interacted with more than once, or colleagues I work with closely.

To begin any recruiting process, consider the following questions:

- Who do I need to interview to answer my research question?
- What is my proximity to this community of potential participants? This might refer to geographical location, positionality, and relationality.
- Do I have connections to this community? If so, what are those connections, and how did I make them? Am I already a member of this community, or do I need to build connections?
- What are the best ways to inform potential participants about this project?

Recruiting participants for interviews for an ethnodrama typically relies on **purposeful sampling** and **convenience sampling**, which are also described as nonprobability sampling methods because they do not allow all members of society to participate (Leavy, 2023). Specific sampling techniques I use and recommend for ethnodrama include personal and professional connections, flyering, electronic posting, and **snowball sampling**.

If an artist-researcher has personal or professional connections, they can share information about the project with those connections and request that they participate in an interview. I sometimes seek out the voice of a scholar or expert on a particular topic because I want to include their perspective alongside those whose voices are less likely to be heard. My preliminary research and subsequent literature review often help identify people I would like to speak with and learn more from on a particular topic. If I have a personal relationship with a potential participant, I connect them with another member of the interviewing team, or ask them for recommendations of others to interview. While personal and professional connections can be a great way to start an interviewing process, I encourage artist-researchers to go beyond these proximal connections and think carefully about how their bias comes into play using only this kind of recruiting.

Flyering and electronic posting are similar in that both help to spread the word about a particular project. I think of flyering as using actual paper flyers posted in physical locations where potential participants might happen to be. In contrast, electronic posting uses a digital version of the information on a flyer posted to social media sites and email list services. In both cases, the recruiting materials should include the following:

- A brief description of the project, mentioning the topic or an overarching question as a hook
- A short description of potential participants
- A way to express interest in participating. This directs potential participants to contact the artist-researcher via a telephone number or email address, or refers them to a screening process to determine their eligibility for participation via a web address or quick-response (QR) code.
- If the project has received clearance and approval from an institution's ethics committee, a statement or stamp with an identification number indicates that approval. Materials also usually appear on the institution's letterhead and include their logo to identify the institutional affiliation to potential participants.

Sometimes, flyers or electronic posts also contain images or graphics to help spark interest; however, I caution against "busy" graphics or too much text. The recruiting materials should focus on the project's primary purpose and be presented clearly to the potential participant from the first moment of contact. During the recruiting process, it is essential to maintain accurate records for each interview participant, including the best way to contact them. You may need to contact a participant if a question emerges about their interview later in the research process. You will also want to keep participants informed about how the research process unfolds and let them know when they can see a performance of the ethnodrama.

For example, in 2009, I began recruiting participants for a project called *open heart* (2010), which explored the experiences of gay male couples living in open, nonmonogamous relationships. I wanted to learn more about how gay couples defined their open relationships and why they chose to live in them by speaking with couples who had been in their relationship for at least 1 year. I used paper flyers and electronic posts to recruit participants for the project, as represented in Figure 3.1. I posted recruitment flyers at local organizations frequented by gay men and sent an electronic version to academic departments at my home institution and other local colleges and universities for posting. I also adapted the language of the flyer for distribution over professional and nonprofessional list services and craigslist.org. Note that the flyer included my institutional affiliation, as required by the IRB.

I led the recruiting language with questions related to the project that could help to identify members of the potential participant pool. I briefly described that the process would involve two interviews, one with the couple and another with each partner, and I mentioned that the interview could become part of a theatrical performance. These two statements quickly identify my purpose and intent for the potential participant. In this case, I received a grant to support this project, so I could compensate participants for their time, which helped with recruitment. Finally, there was a telephone number to call if a participant was interested. Potential participants called that number, connected with a research assistant, and answered a series of screening questions to determine their eligibility for an interview (Table 3.1). Participants had to be 18 or older and have been in

FIGURE 3.1 Recruiting flyer for *open heart.*

TABLE 3.1. Screening Questions for Potential *open heart* Participants

- Do you live in the New York City area?
- Are you currently in a relationship with a man that has lasted for more than 1 year?
- How long have you been in this relationship?
- How old are you?
- How old is your partner?
- Are you and your partner in an open, non-monogamous relationship?
- Would you and your partner be willing to participate in two interviews about your relationship, one interview as a couple and one individual interview each?
- If you choose to participate in this study, you and your partner will be asked to visit a Manhattan office for two 60-minute sessions each. Would you and your partner be able to do this?

their relationship for more than 1 year to participate. Because I wanted to conduct the interviews in person, I also included a question about their geographical location. In one instance, I made an exception and conducted a set of interviews by telephone, but all other interviews occurred in person. If the participant made it to the end of the screening questions having answered "yes" to all, I received their contact information. Then, I contacted them via email or telephone to outline the next steps and schedule their interviews.

Once a participant identifies themselves as interested, and, as in the previous case, passes a screening process, they should receive a **Statement to Participants**. This statement provides the potential participant with more details about the project, so they have a better understanding and can make an informed decision about whether to continue with an interview. In addition, this moment provides the artist-researcher with the next opportunity to instill trust through honest and transparent communication about how the interviewing process unfolds. Here is the Statement to Participants for *open heart*:

Thank you for your interest in the open heart *project. The purpose of the project is to develop an interview theater piece [ethnodrama] that will explore the experiences of gay male couples living in non-monogamous, open relationships. The resulting theatrical performance will be presented at a venue to be determined.*

If you choose to participate, I will ask to interview you and your partner together, followed by an interview with each of you separately. Each interview will last approximately 30 to 60 minutes and take place in a [conference room at NYU] located at 726 Broadway in Manhattan. The interviews will focus on how you and your partner, together and separately, define your open relationship and your experiences in the open relationship. During both interviews, you will be asked to respond to a series of open-ended questions. Participation in this project is voluntary. You may refuse to participate or withdraw at any time during the interviews. With your permission, the interviews will be audio-recorded and transcribed. If you choose, your and your partner's anonymity can be protected by using a pseudonym identifier. For your participation, you and your partner will receive $40 for your joint interview and $40 for each of your individual interviews, for a total of $120 per couple.

This project could pose a risk for you and your partner because you will reveal intimate details about your lives. The project does give you and your partner the opportunity to speak together about your relationship, a benefit that may help increase your communication and could in turn strengthen your relationship as a result of participating in the process.

The outcome of these interviews will be a performance piece. Once the interviews for this project are complete, they will be transcribed, and selected pieces of interviews will be brought together to create a performance script. If your interviews are selected, you and your partner, as interview [participants] will be played by myself and/or another actor in the performance piece, using the words from your interviews verbatim.

If you and your partner choose to move forward with an interview, we can begin by scheduling your interview as a couple. We can schedule via email or telephone whenever you both are ready.

Based on this example, Table 3.2 outlines the content to include in a clear Statement to Participants. For the *open heart* project, if the participant provided an email address after the screener, they received this statement via email. If they provided a telephone number, I called them and read this statement. In both cases, if the participant and their partner chose to move forward, I scheduled the first interview with them as a couple. The participants received a hard copy of a consent form at the first interview and had time to review and sign it before the interview began.

In VPL's *Whatever You Are, Be a Good One* (Salvatore & Huff, 2022), the recruiting process followed a similar structure, but we utilized additional ways of recruiting and onboarding participants. We wanted to conduct interviews about political polarization leading into the 2022 midterm elections with participants from as many states and U.S. territories as possible, representing diverse lived experiences and political beliefs. We set an initial goal of 200 interviews, first thinking that we would work to collect two interviews from each of the 50 states. We later modified this goal to collect 200 interviews in proportion to the distribution of Congressional representatives for each state in the House of Representatives, adding the various U.S. territories as well. As a reminder from Chapter 2, the research questions guiding the project were as follows: *What are the causes of the extreme political polarization that we currently experience in the United States? How can we overcome this polarization over the next 5 years?*

The "we currently experience in the United States" implies that the participant pool would include people currently residing there. We did not limit our outreach to U.S. citizens, as we recognize that people live and work in the United States without holding citizenship and the right to vote, and we wanted to include their voices in this project as well. Given the scope of possibility for the participant pool, one might think recruiting participants would be easy. I certainly did. However, the commitment to interview participants from all 50 states and territories and across a spectrum of political viewpoints proved more challenging than I anticipated.

TABLE 3.2. Outline for a Statement to Participants
● Paragraph 1: State the overall purpose of the project. Include how the participant qualified to participate, if applicable.
● Paragraph 2: Detail the procedures for the interview. Include location, modality, proposed duration, and terms of participation.
● Paragraph 3: Review the potential risks and benefits of participation.
● Paragraph 4: Share how the artist-researcher could use the interviews. Note: It is important to be clear that by agreeing to participate, a participant also agrees to the potential for public performance of a section of their interview by an actor.
● Paragraph 5: Provide ways to schedule an interview.

We began our recruiting process by identifying connections that our interviewing team had to individuals and organizations around the country, where we could send an electronic flyer via email. We crafted a template for an outreach email and then used that to share the electronic flyer as widely as possible. We then created a series of social media posts on VPL's channels and encouraged the interviewing team to reshare those posts on their social networks (see Figure 3.2).

All electronic flyers and social media posts referred potential participants to an initial interest survey (Google form) that served as our screening tool to help track the diversity of our participant pool. The survey began with an initial statement to participants that introduced VPL, described the project, and included a link to the lab's website and an email address to ask questions. The survey asked participants for their email address, full name, city/town of residence, state/territory, and age range. Participants could select from a list of race and ethnicity descriptors based on those in the American National Election Survey (ANES) or choose to self-describe. We also asked an open-ended question about gender so that participants could identify in whatever way was most comfortable for them. We included a question about religion, again basing the choices on the ANES. We asked participants to choose whether they thought of themselves as a Democrat, a Republican, an independent, or something else. We also asked how the potential participants learned about the project. After about a month of recruiting and scheduling interviews, we added a final question asking potential participants to list three dates and times over the coming 2 weeks when they would be available to participate in an interview in a 60-minute block.

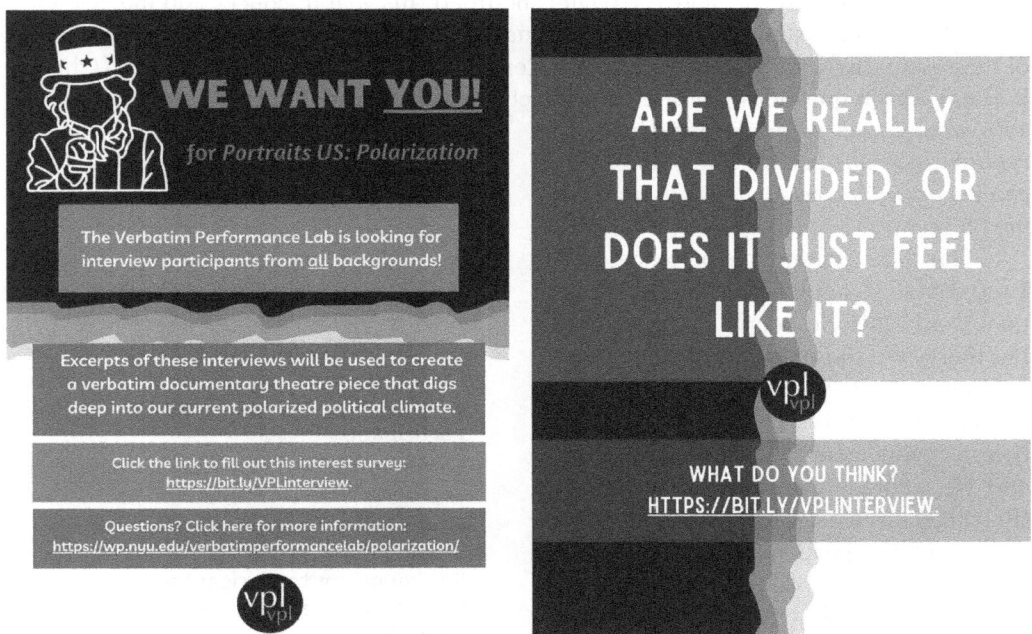

FIGURE 3.2 Examples of social media posts used to recruit participants for a project exploring the causes of political polarization in the United States.

We learned that including this as a survey question streamlined some of our email communication with the participants. As potential participants completed the initial survey, we emailed them a confirmation restating the project's parameters and followed that with an electronic release form using the online platform Docusign. After the participants had completed the release form, an interview team member contacted them to schedule an interview for one of their suggested dates and times.

Survey responses also helped us to track the demographics of the responding participants, as we could see where people were from and how they identified themselves by race, ethnicity, gender, age, and political affiliation. As more and more volunteers self-identified, we used the survey data to decide whom to interview and how to adjust and expand our recruiting. For example, many initial survey respondents identified as Democrats from the Northeast, which was unsurprising given our location in New York City and our affiliation with an institution perceived as very liberal. We used this information to develop more intentional recruiting processes to reach potential participants in other parts of the country and from different political affiliations. We learned that word-of-mouth recruitment via our interviewing team helped encourage more moderate and conservative participants to complete the survey and agree to an interview. We also created targeted social media posts specifically designed to appear in users' feeds in geographical areas needing more representation. Additionally, we targeted these identical posts to users of specific online groups on a particular platform. We paid a small fee for each of these targeted posts and found them helpful in spreading the word about the project.

We also used a modified version of snowball sampling, which relies on referrals and networking to locate potential participants for a project (Parker, Scott, & Geddes, 2019). In the case of this polarization project, after each interview, the interviewer asked the participant if they knew anyone they thought would be interested in participating. If so, they were encouraged to share the link for the initial participant survey with those possibilities. We believed that this approach could effectively engage more participants with conservative leanings. If the information about the project, along with a recommendation to participate, came from outside of our liberal institution, conservative individuals might be more inclined to take part. We learned that personal connections encouraged some participants to step forward and, in some instances, we needed to have preliminary conversations to explain the project in more detail.

Ultimately, we gathered 110 interviews from 37 states for what would become *Whatever You Are, Be a Good One*. We did not reach the goal of 200 interviews from all 50 states and territories, but we managed to interview participants from various lived experiences and political viewpoints. Our total sample could have been more diverse, but we honored the idea of interviewing participants who wanted to speak with us, those who were screaming from their mountaintops and in our direction. Our recruiting process demonstrated the pros and cons of working on a project about political polarization while being affiliated with an academic institution. In some cases, conservative-leaning potential participants did not trust that their anonymity would be protected and feared risking their jobs or social positions if their conservative viewpoints were somehow revealed and linked to them publicly. While we tried to be transparent about the process and reassuring about our intentions, I appreciated the reminder of how delicate recruiting, gaining trust, and interviewing can be. In a future iteration of the project, I would allow more time for the recruiting process and consider ways to build more meaningful connections in advance with organizations and individuals from across the political spectrum. That kind of deep relationship-building takes more time than I allowed for in this project, and I keep that in mind as I move into future projects.

Scheduling and Confirming

Once a participant agrees to an interview, the artist-researcher can schedule a meeting date, time, and location or modality. Your participant pool may determine the location and modality of the interview. If your pool is limited to nearby participants, you may conduct all of your interviews in person. If you plan to interview participants from a wider geographical area and will not travel to them, then your modality will be via online video conferencing (e.g., Zoom, Skype) or telephone. You may have established location or modality in your statement to participants, but I recommend restating it again at this scheduling moment.

Ideally, this process requires minimal back-and-forth by email or telephone and establishes respect for a participant's time, particularly since they are volunteering. I recommend the following points to consider:

- Offer the participant a range of time to choose from: "I'd like to schedule a time with you over the next 2 weeks."
- Offer your typical availability while also messaging flexibility. Also, consider when you tend to be the most attentive. For example, do not schedule an interview at 8:00 A.M. if you are not a morning person: "I tend to be available from 3:00 to 5:00 P.M. on Mondays, Wednesdays, and Thursdays, but I can also accommodate other times."
- Request three dates and times that can work for the participant: "Can you share three dates and times when you could potentially meet for an interview over the next 2 weeks?"
- Consider the time zone if interviewing by video conferencing or phone: "Can you confirm what time zone you're in so I can make sure I record the correct time on my calendar?"
- Consider a location if interviewing in person: "Can you suggest a convenient public location where I could meet you for this interview?"
- Do not meet participants who are strangers in their personal space. I always recommend public spaces or workspaces for interviews.
- You may also have space available through your institution or organization.

After a participant replies with their availability and I find a match to their schedule, I follow up as soon as possible, within 24 hours, with an email or telephone call that clearly states the date, time (with time zone), and location/modality for the interview. If the interview is taking place via video conferencing, I also offer a reminder about having access to a secure internet connection on the day of the interview. I have lost any number of interview participants at this stage in the process because I failed to reply promptly. Do not leave a participant waiting for you to respond. On the flip side, exercise patience as you wait for a participant to respond to you. I usually wait at least 48 hours before a follow-up requesting a response. I also send an email reminder or follow up by telephone the day before the interview. This reminder ensures that both parties are on the same page with the date, time, and location/modality, and no one is left alone and waiting.

Securing Consent

Once the artist-researcher has scheduled the interview with the participant, they should next secure the participant's formal consent to participate in the project. Securing a participant's consent is one of the most essential steps in any research process: It defines the agreement between the artist-researcher and the participant about what the participant is committing to do and how the artist-researcher will use the results of their participation. The integrity and ethical orientation of any data collection process are reinforced by how the artist-researcher manages the consent process. **Consent forms** for an ethnodrama should outline the project's purpose and include basic information about who will conduct the project and their affiliation. The form should also clearly articulate the project's dissemination plan. Since an ethnodrama's performance for an audience is a unique aspect of this particular research modality, the participant should understand that possibility up front. Hence, I advocate identifying ethnodrama as the research method from the start of the project. However, other researchers may wait until after completing the data collection process to make this decision. In these cases, the researcher uses ethnodrama only as the mode of dissemination. Suppose the researcher did not mention ethnodrama as a possibility during the initial consenting process. In that case, they have an ethical responsibility to return to their participants and ask for their additional consent for this performed dissemination. The consent form should also include information about the potential risks and benefits of participating in the interview process and a clause allowing participants to withdraw their permission to use their interview.

When I initially began working with ethnodrama and obtaining formal consent, I shared a paper copy of the consent form with the participant at their interview. In more recent years, I have shifted to digital ways of obtaining consent. Initially, I began by sharing a portable document format (PDF) version of the consent document via email and requested that the participant review it, sign off, and return it to me via email. I stored these digital copies on a secure, cloud-based server. Now, I almost exclusively use Docusign, an online platform that allows me to upload a PDF of the consent document, which becomes a template. I mark the parts of the document that require a participant's response, such as checking a box indicating they would like to be updated about the project's development or signing off with their agreement to participate. I can then enter the participant's name and email address, and the Docusign application sends the digital version to the participant for their review and signature. Once completed, Docusign returns an electronically signed PDF version of the document via email and stores it, so I can access it through the online application. This digital process is more efficient for obtaining consent, especially when working with a team of interviewers on a larger project.

What follows is a general template for a consent form for an ethnodrama, adapted from examples from two projects: VPL's *That's Not Supposed to Be Happening* (Huff & Salvatore, 2023) and Ryan Howland's (2022) *Yet through such connection . . . .* I list headings for each paragraph or section in this example to identify what content is covered. For an actual consent form, I do not include these headings. Additionally, I use "project/study" throughout, as I view them as interchangeable for ABR. The decision of which term to use is up to the artist-researcher.

[TITLE OF PROJECT]

INTERVIEW CONSENT FORM

What is this, who is doing it, and what is their affiliation?

You have been invited to participate in an ethnodrama project/study with the working title [Title]. This project/study aims to explore [the topic and/or a variation of the research question]. This project/study will be conducted by [artist-researcher's name and affiliation] as a part of their [dissertation study/faculty research/artistic creation].

What does the participant do, and what is the proposed outcome?

If you agree to be part of this project/study, you will be asked to take part in an open-ended interview concerning your own experiences related to the aforementioned project description and related topics. The outcome of these interviews will be a theatrical performance, and you, as an interview participant, may be portrayed by an actor in a live or recorded performance, using the words and actions from your interview.

How will the interview work? What happens after the interview?

Your interview will be recorded (audio/video) and then transcribed, and portions of your interview and the interviews of other participants will be arranged to create a script. That script will be rehearsed by actors working on the project, the lines will be memorized, and then the script will be used to create a live and/or recorded performance. Your characteristics, such as mannerisms, gestures, or appearance, may also influence the presentation of the script that results from your interview and the interviews of others. It is also possible that your interview may not be used in the project due to the limitations of time or duplicative material.

How does participation work and what are the risks and benefits?

Participation in the interview is voluntary. You may refuse to participate or withdraw at any time without penalty. During your interview, you have the right to skip or not respond to any prompts you prefer not to answer. You may also review your interview recordings and request that all or any portion of the recordings be destroyed. Participation in this project/study will involve [estimated number range] minutes of your time. No known risks are associated with your participation in this project/study beyond those of everyday life. Although you will receive no direct benefits, this project/study may help the artist-researcher understand more about the breadth and depth of experiences of people affected by the project's topics and themes.

How does confidentiality work?

Confidentiality of your interview records will be strictly maintained. While your real name will not be used if you choose to use a pseudonym instead, there is a limit placed on the confidentiality of this interview by the fact that actors and other members of the research and production team will have access to the audio/video recordings during the rehearsal and production process for the performance.

How can the artist-researcher be contacted with questions or problems?

If there is anything about the project/study or your participation that is unclear or that you do not understand, if you have questions or wish to report a problem, you may contact [artist-researcher's name, telephone number, email address, mailing address].

You will receive a copy of this document for your records.
Agreement to Participate

_____   _____

Participant's Printed Name   Participant's Signature and Date

Please note that this particular consent form does not give the artist-researcher permission to use the participant's voice or image in any way as part of the production process. Therefore, if an artist-researcher wants that option, they must state that clearly in the consent form.

This example should help you draft your own consent forms, but if you have an affiliation with an institution or organization with an ethics committee, please follow their protocol for consent forms. For example, some institutions offer an online application that helps to generate a consent form for a particular project. The artist-researcher plugs in details about their project, and the application renders the necessary language for the consent form.

After my institution's IRB determined that my arts-based projects were not research as defined by the federal government, I still wanted to have a model of consent that included a written document. I worked with an attorney to develop a **release form** to obtain consent from participants in my projects.[1] We based the language of my release form on a consent form but added more legalistic language to protect my creative process as the artist-researcher. *The main difference between a consent form and a release form is that, when a participant signs a release form, they relinquish any legal rights to their interview, including how the artist-researcher uses it.* The participant cannot exercise any control over artistic and aesthetic choices made in the production process. In theory, the release form eliminates the procedural ethical responsibility of the artist-researcher to engage in the process of **member checking**, which allows a participant to review their interview transcripts, request that sections not be considered, and make edits to what they said during the interview. Member checking has the goal of protecting participants and helping them maintain control over how the researcher uses their gathered testimony. Member checking also helps to disrupt the power differential between the researcher and the participant.

Even though I use a release form for consenting participants in my projects, I still value and uphold the importance of relational ethics over procedural ethics. As a result, I handle member checking differently and more immediately. I conduct a form of member checking at the conclusion of my interviewing protocol, which I introduce in the next section of this chapter, and I clarify how the participant can reach me if they want to review their transcripts in the future. When interview participants request to review their transcripts, I always honor their request.

Here is an example of an additional paragraph that might appear in a release form:

The transcript of your interview may be used by [artist-researcher's name], or they may authorize others to use the transcript of your interview in all manner, formats, and media, for performances and productions throughout the world. [Artist-researcher's name] shall own all right, title, and interest, including the copyright, in the transcripts, scripts, and performances that result from these interviews.

Notice that, just as before with the consent model, this paragraph specifically references the interview transcripts and does not include the use of the recorded interview. Even though I use a release form, I do not ask participants to sign away the right to their own recorded image or voice. If a particular process emerged in which I wanted to use a participant's image or voice in production, I would recontact them and introduce a secondary release form strictly for that purpose.

Additionally, there is a statement titled Agreement to Participate at the point in the release form where the participant signs. Here is an example:

AGREEMENT TO PARTICIPATE

I hereby acknowledge that I have read and understood the process as outlined above and that I voluntarily elect to participate in this interview without the promise of remuneration now or in the future. I hereby irrevocably grant to [artist-researcher's name], their successors and assigns, all rights to my interview, including my words, mannerisms, gestures, and appearance, for use in any and all media, whether now known or hereafter invented, throughout the world in perpetuity. I understand that while the purpose of this ethnodrama is to increase the understanding regarding the subject matter of the project, there is a possibility that the project may someday generate income for [artist-reseacher's name], their successors and assigns, to which I will have no claim.

The above language sounds intense, primarily because of the legalese that a release form necessitates. However, I again practice "good human beingness" regarding these processes. While the release form legally allows me to claim all rights and control over a participant's contribution to a project, I do not exercise that right. If a participant returned to me months after an interview and told me they didn't want me to include their interview in the ethnodrama or requested to see their transcripts and then asked me to change something, I would honor their request. And even in the most extreme case, in which an interview participant might contact me 2 days before an ethnodrama's performance and say that they have changed their mind and don't want their transcripts included, I'd ask them if we could have a conversation. In that conversation, I would listen to their concerns and provide additional context for how their transcripts contribute to the overall script and performance and how the project benefits from their contribution. I would also explain my position as the artist-researcher and the impact their choice could have on the overall script and performance. If they still wanted their contribution removed, I would honor their request and manage the consequences. If someone was screaming from the mountaintops at the moment of their interview and then decides later that they prefer to be whispering, that choice needs to rest with them. That's part of what I mean by "good human beingness"; I think it is the most important ethical decision an artist-researcher can make. The artist-researcher has the right and the responsibility to consider the aesthetic and artistic implications of these choices and to hold the position of the expert in those areas, but they cannot hold a participant's story hostage for the sake of art. Institutions and organizations will most likely require the artist-researcher to use a consent form, whereas a person working independently gains more protection by using a release form. Regardless of who has project jurisdiction, artist-researchers should always consult either their institution's ethics committee or legal counsel for advice and guidance regarding participant consent or release forms.

The artist-researcher should obtain written consent before the participant sits for an interview. Based on my experience, a participant may interview and provide excellent content, but I cannot include their responses in the ethnodrama without a completed consent form. In that case, I must reconnect with the participant to secure the signed consent form, which adds unnecessary time to the scripting process. Bottomline advice: Interview a participant only after receiving their signed consent or release form.

I encourage artist-researchers to interview at least twice the number of participants they expect to include in their ethnodrama. I follow this general guideline during my data collection process to ensure that I have ample responses representing multiple perspectives. However, I may also reach **saturation** with the emerging themes and ideas during the interviewing process, which means that data collection ceases to reveal new insights (Leavy, 2023). When I experience interview participants repeating the same ideas, even if their stories are unique, I take this as a sign that I am approaching saturation. Similarly, I carefully track the participants' demographics throughout the interviewing process, as I might also reach saturation of a particular lived experience or perspective.

From an ethical standpoint, the participant must understand from the top of their experience, beginning with consent, that I may or may not use their contributions in the script and performance because of time constraints or duplication of content. I include this in the language of the consent or release form and as part of the interview protocol, which I review in the next section of this chapter. There is a danger that a participant steps forward to share their stories and then feels upset, offended, diminished, or discouraged because I did not select a section of their interview for the script. That is not how I want participants to feel. Instead, I want participants to understand how the process works and why I might decide to include their contribution or not for this particular project iteration. Better to be transparent about this part of the process from the beginning.

The Interview Protocol

I use a highly structured **interview protocol** for my data collection process (Harrison, 2018; Leavy, 2023), which I have developed over 25 years and many projects. While its fundamental structure remains intact, I have continually updated its order, language, and terminology to incorporate my own learning and experiences, as well as developments and shifting norms in the broader field of qualitative ABR. The current protocol also reflects emerging technologies, such as online video-conferencing platforms. A structured approach to interviewing allows me to focus on listening, observing, and being a good host. As the interviewer, I am responsible for creating a welcoming atmosphere for the interview participants, so they feel safe and comfortable sharing their experiences openly and honestly. To create this type of environment for participants, an interview protocol should do the following:

- Use clear and accessible language to describe the process.
- Explain any terminology specific to the project that the participant needs to know.

- Restate important details covered in the consent process about data collection, analysis, representation, and dissemination.

- Determine how the participant would like to be identified in a scripting process.

- Order the interview prompts in a way that creates a scaffolded, positive experience for the participant.

- Provide multiple opportunities for the participant to retain control over what they share in the interview, including allowing them to make choices even after responding to the interview prompts.

I wrote about the importance of care in Chapter 2, but it bears repeating. The artist-researcher is responsible for creating an atmosphere of care during the interview process. This protocol ensures that the participant is informed about the interview, feels comfortable with how it unfolds, and maintains as much agency as possible.

The most current version of my interview protocol for data collection follows below. The protocol assumes that interviews will be recorded using audio and/or video. Because I disseminate using verbatim performance, the protocol includes details specific to that performance style. As other artist-researchers create their own interview protocols, if they are not using verbatim performance, this language should be modified or removed, as not all ethnodrama uses the conventions of verbatim performance in its data representation and dissemination. I present the text I speak in the interview protocol in italics; however, I do not read or recite it. I do my best to memorize those sections in a language that is comfortable and accessible for the participant. I encourage all artist-researchers conducting interviews to do the same. It allows for strong eye contact with the participant, reducing the process's formality and shifting the dynamic to more of an exchange between two people rather than feeling like one person is trying to get something from someone else. As long as the spoken version of the protocol covers the necessary information thoroughly, then the exact language can adjust to the individual conducting the interview. The language of the protocol can feel dense, so the more conversational the delivery, the more welcoming the process will become for the participant. The best way to achieve comfort with the protocol is to practice it many times before engaging with participants.

Interview Protocol

Before the interview begins, confirm that the participant has received a copy of the consent form, reviewed it, and signed it.

Let the participant know you will begin the process and start the recording device. Slate the interview with the following information:

- Your name
- Your location
- Date and time

Begin by thanking the participant for their participation and letting them know the approximate duration of the interview. Then, explain the process using the following language:

- *"I want to remind you that your participation in this interview process is voluntary. You can stop the interview at any time and/or refuse to respond to any particular prompt or question asked. Is that clear?"*

[The participant should answer with a verbal confirmation for the recording.]

- *"After our interview, I will review the recording and select and transcribe excerpts of the interview that may eventually be performed as part of [working project title]. An actor will use your words and gestures verbatim, based on the transcript, the recording, and my field notes, and then perform the section(s) of the interview in a live performance and/or for a video recording for release to a public audience. Additionally, as part of creating the script, other researchers, actors, and creative team members may hear/view parts of the recorded interview. I may also not use your interview in the project due to the limitations of time or duplicative material. Is that clear?"*

[The participant should answer with a verbal confirmation for the recording.]

- *"Please note that, in this style of verbatim performance, participants are often portrayed by actors of other races, ethnicities, genders, gender identities, ages, abilities, and orientations. We refer to this as* <u>portraying across identity</u>*, and its purpose is to heighten an audience's awareness and understanding of the content of a participant's response and to allow an actor to investigate and empathize with the lived experience of another. Do you understand this? Do you have any questions for me about this?* <u>On the final page of the release form, you could designate your preference related to this casting process, which will be noted and honored.</u>*"*

[The participant should answer with a verbal confirmation for the recording.]

- *"I will review all of this at the end of our interview, just in case something changes during our discussion. We're now ready for the interview. I will begin by asking you for some basic demographic information, and then I have a series of open-ended prompts that I'd like you to respond to. Are you ready to begin?"*

[The participant should answer with a verbal confirmation for the recording.]

- *"I'd like to ask how you would like to be identified for my scripting process. We can use your name or a pseudonym. Some examples are as follows: '27-year-old man,' 'Black business student,' 'White cis female, 20,' 'anonymous female architect,' and so forth. We can modify this after we finish, but can you say how you would like to be identified currently, so I have that recorded as part of our interview?"*

[The participant should clearly state their identifier for the recording.]

Note the participant's choice of identifier, as you will need to review it at the end of the interview.

Ask the participant to respond to the prompts regarding demographic information followed by the open-ended prompts:

Demographic Information
- *"What is your age or age range?"*
- *"What do you do for a living?"*
- *"Where are you from originally?"*

- *"Where are you now [at the moment of the interview]?"*
- *"How do you describe your identity?"*

*   *   *

Note: Depending on the topic of the proposed ethnodrama, you may want to ask additional demographic questions. For example, for *Whatever You Are, Be a Good One*, we asked, "What is your political affiliation?" The final demographic question is "How do you describe your identity?" I ask that question in this way for two reasons. First, not all participants think about identity in the way that I do or that many artist-researchers do because of our proximity to colleges and universities, where conversations around identity are commonplace. As a result, I've received fascinating and revealing answers to this question that completely upended my expectations and revealed my implicit and explicit biases. Second, this question allows the participant to express what parts of their identity might be the most salient for them. Knowing how they identify themselves is helpful rather than simply making assumptions based on how they present physically and aurally during the interview.

*   *   *

After gathering the participant's demographic information, proceed to the open-ended prompts.

- *"I have a series of open-ended prompts that I'd like for you to respond to. There is no right or wrong answer, and you should respond to them in whatever way seems appropriate."*

Interview Prompts

- Insert your project's prompts here and include the final two below.

*   *   *

- *"Is there anything else you would like to say about the topics we've been discussing?"*
- *"Do you have any questions for me?"*

A participant may sometimes ask for clarification about specific prompts. You may offer some clarifying details, but I encourage you to allow the participant to respond based on their initial understanding of the prompt. Sometimes, this process can reveal a profound or unexpected response, both for the interviewer and the participant.

After finishing the interview prompts, review the informational points from the top of the interview protocol while still recording to gather a second recorded verbal confirmation about the participant's details and preferences. Use the following language:

- *"Thank you for taking the time to speak with me for this project. I want to review some of the information we discussed at the top of the interview to ensure that everything is clear about how I will use this interview. After we finish, I will review the audio/video recording and transcribe sections of the interview. An actor may perform a section or sections of this interview in a live performance and/or for a video recording for release to a public audience. Any part of this interview could be used in the performance. We will use your words and gestures verbatim, based on the transcript, the audio/video recording, and my field notes. Other researchers and actors may also hear sections of the recorded interview as part of creating the script. It is also possible that we will not use your interview in the project due to the limitations of time or duplicative material. Is all of this clear?"*

[The participant should answer with a verbal confirmation for the recording.]

• *"At the top of the interview, I asked you how you would like to be identified in the scripting process, and you said _____. Is this still the case, or would you like to change your identifier?"*

[The participant should clearly state their agreement or a new identifier on the recording.]

• *"Are there any names of people, places, or things that should be changed in the transcribing process? If so, which ones?"*

[The participant should respond with the names that they want to be changed and could offer suggestions for pseudonyms if necessary.]

*   *   *

Note: If a participant requests changes, I encourage you to work to make the changes the same number of syllables as the original words whenever possible, as this helps to maintain the cadence and rhythm of the participant's speech. I share more about the relevance of this detail in Chapter 4.

• *"Are there any sections of the interview that you would prefer not to be used? If so, I will note that I should not include those sections in the transcribing process."*

[Participant should respond accordingly.]

Thank the participant for their time and participation, check that they have a copy of their consent/release form for their reference, and make sure they know how to contact you if any questions or changes arise after some time has passed.

Turn off the recording device.

I encourage artist-researchers to adapt this template to fit their project needs; however, I want to emphasize the importance of the review section following the interview prompts. By this point in the process, the participant has already heard this information in the protocol and read much of it during the consenting process. That said, this final review after they have experienced the interview is imperative. From an ethical standpoint, I want a participant to hear and read this information multiple times because different people process and understand information differently. When I complete the interview, I want to feel confident that I have given a participant every opportunity to change their mind, say "no," and have egress. I work in ethnodrama because I believe in the form's power to illuminate various perspectives. Still, I also know that ethnographic research can be deeply problematic if not handled with the utmost care. Ethnodrama elicits powerful responses through aesthetic choices made to represent data, but those choices must embrace a sound, ethically informed practice. Because I work at a university, I receive constant cues and reminders to consider the ethics of consent. However, regardless of the artist-researcher's connection to an institution, they must keep these ethical considerations at the forefront.

I begin the final section of the interview protocol by reminding the participant what I will do next in the process and how I might integrate portions of their interview into the ethnodrama and its performance. In my process, a reminder about verbatim performance is essential. Then, I ask them to verify their choice of identifier. Having experienced the interview, I want the participant to be able to adjust their identifier for scripting and performance if they so choose. Other researchers have wondered why I ask the identifier question at the beginning of the protocol and then again at the conclusion. This second ask cues the participant to reflect on what they shared in the interview and to consider whether they are comfortable linking that to their chosen identifier. This cue also instigates a form of member checking in that moment, as the participant reconsiders the content of the interview while it's still fresh in their mind. I have had participants shift their identifier to one that is more anonymous or one that includes their full name. I have learned that predicting a participant's choice is difficult, so this is another reason for the repeated question toward the end of the protocol.

I follow this question about their identifier with a question about the identities of any person, place, or thing, allowing the participant to request any name changes to protect someone else's anonymity. Again, asking this question after the interview prompts the participant to reflect on what they have shared. Many years ago, I was interviewed for someone else's project. I spoke about a couple that my partner and I knew, and I used their first names freely throughout. At the end of the interview, I remembered that neither of our friends was open about their sexuality with their families. I requested that their names be changed if the artist-researcher used that interview section in their play. The chances of my friends' families seeing this play were slim, but I still wanted to protect their privacy by changing their names.

The final question, perhaps the most important one, allows the participant to clearly state what parts of their interview are off-limits for consideration in scripting and performance. This moment is fundamental to building trust with the participant by demonstrating that they retain agency over what they have shared with me. Every participant should understand their option to identify sections of their interview that an artist-researcher should not consider. This option helps disrupt the power dynamic that can exist between an interviewer and a participant. Therefore, the artist-researcher must offer that space for reflection and choice.

I consider all three of these final questions a version of member checking immediately following the interview. The questions build trust and demonstrate care, and I want those feelings to carry over into how the participant feels after they leave the experience. I also make sure that the participant knows how to reach me in case, upon further reflection, they want to make changes to the boundaries they have laid through answering these last three questions. If a participant contacts me subsequently to review their interview, I share the sections that I have transcribed.

Conducting the Interview

With the interview protocol ready and with confidence gained from practicing it (see the activity at the end of this chapter), the artist-researcher can begin to conduct interviews.

I have found that interviewing gets easier with repetition and practice, but the first time out on a new project, armed with a new set of interview prompts, I always have some butterflies. Butterflies are a good sign. Their presence reminds me that I care about how the participant might experience the interview, which, as I keep emphasizing, is influenced by how the interviewer facilitates it. If the artist-researcher has prepared their protocol and feels comfortable and fluent with its language, then the participant should also sense this comfort as the interview unfolds.

Generally, I do not share interview prompts with a participant before the interview. Because I work with verbatim performance in disseminating the data, I am interested in how participants respond to each prompt when they hear it for the first time during the interview. If I share the prompts in advance, participants tend to prepare their responses, which affects their authenticity. I have developed a sensitivity around prepared responses, so when I listen to the recording of an interview I have not conducted, I can usually sense when a participant received the prompts in advance. The responses have few, if any, pauses for thought or reflection and sound quite polished. These are not automatic indicators that prompts have been shared in advance, as some participants may be skilled and confident with responding in the moment. Still, they do cause me to listen more carefully to the interview to see if I can determine what happened. When a participant asks to see the prompts in advance, I explain that I am most interested in experiencing their candid responses in the moment. I also remind the participant that they can pass on any prompt I ask, so they are free of pressure or obligation to answer anything they do not want to answer. Suppose the participant continues to request the prompts before the interview. In that case, I engage them in a conversation to see if they genuinely want to participate. A need to see the prompts in advance may indicate that the participant has some reticence about sitting for an interview. They may not be a good fit for this particular project, which is fine. Not every participant needs to participate in every project.

I have made exceptions to this general rule related to accessibility for participants who have offered why having the prompts in advance could help them. For example, when we interviewed participants about their experiences with the COVID-19 pandemic, one participant dealing with long-term COVID expressed that they would benefit from seeing the prompts in advance. They reassured the interviewer that they did not want to prepare answers beforehand, but the effects of long COVID made it difficult for them to process information quickly in the moment. Having the prompts ahead of time would allow them to understand the flow of the interview and feel more comfortable leading up to the interview. We gladly made this modification for the participant. We had yet to interview anyone with long-term COVID, and we wanted this point of view included in our dataset. As the saying goes, there are exceptions to every rule, and this exception certainly was warranted. The artist-researcher should make their own decisions about handling this part of their interviewing process. One could argue that sharing the prompts in advance has more advantages than disadvantages for a particular project or when working with a specific community of participants. Regardless of the artist-researcher's decision, they should work for as much consistency as possible across their process and be clear about the circumstances when they make any exceptions.

How the interviewer conducts themselves during the interview can also impact the participant's experience. To foster a positive experience for the participant, artist-researchers should consider the following recommendations:

1. **Be alert.** To the extent possible, work with the interview participant to schedule the interview at a time convenient for them, but also when you're the most alert. Do your utmost to be at your best when you're collecting data.

2. **Dress appropriately.** What we wear sends messages to the participants with whom we interact. If you dress like you care about the exchange that's about to take place, the participant will take the interview seriously. Now, I'm not suggesting you bust out your pantsuit, jacket, or tie. Instead, consider the time and location of your interview. If you're meeting someone for an afternoon coffee, then dress for an afternoon coffee. If you're meeting someone at their place of employment and they work in a corporate office, consider how you might enter that environment with respect. If you're meeting online, think through your presentation online.

3. **Enter with curiosity.**[2] If a participant has stepped forward for your project, that's a strong indicator they feel they have something valuable to contribute. However, not every interview will yield material for the ethnodrama. A participant may have an off day, or you may have an off day as the interviewer. These moments happen, and they are just additional dynamics within the process. Give everyone the benefit of the doubt, but don't assume anything as you enter the experience.

4. **Keep the focus of the interview on the participant.** The interview is not about the interviewer. The interviewer should not become the center of attention or the primary speaker; instead, they should take on the role of active listener and avoid interrupting and interjecting as much as possible. Part of the reason I created such a structured interview protocol is to keep myself in check as the interviewer. Anybody who has spent a significant amount of time with me knows that I'm a talker. When interviewing someone else, I must avoid shifting into a two-way conversation or dialogue. I focus on active listening and staying fully present for the participant, and I am not responding to the prompts. I offer the prompt and then listen. If the participant wants to hear my thoughts on something, I defer to the final prompt of the interview when I ask the participant, "Do you have any questions for me?" Then, I'm happy to answer whatever questions they have.

5. **Do not ask follow-up questions.** Some of you are aghast at this statement. "What? No follow-up questions? What do you mean, no follow-up questions?" I mean precisely that. If you care about prioritizing a participant's experience, you'll follow this advice. No follow-up questions. If a participant responds to a prompt, and you are more curious about something they said, simply say, "Can you talk more about that?" If the participant wants to, they will. If they don't, then move on. From my perspective, an interviewer should not probe and pry. Other qualitative researchers may disagree, but I strongly feel that an interview should not feel like an extraction. The participant should control the sharing process as much as possible. "But what about my project? My dataset? My research question?" Remember, it's not about you. It's about the participant and their experience in the interview. "But I know this person has more to say on this prompt, this topic!" Do not assume the participant wants to share what *you* think they have to say or what *you* think they know. Accept what the participant has shared and move on. Your next to last prompt is, "Is there anything else you would like to say about the topics we've been discussing?." If the participant has additional things they want to say, that is their moment.

6. Stay quiet. Again, this is hard for me, and I will clarify what I mean. Staying quiet is closely linked to recommendation #4. By quiet, I don't mean silent, stoic, and without emotion. I mean, listen actively and offer very few verbal affirmations. I do a lot of nodding, smiling, "hmm"ing, and "uh huh"ing, meaning that I offer affirmations that are more about messaging "Keep going, I'm with you" rather than agreeing, disagreeing, or adding in my two cents. I also frequently say, "Thank you for that response," before I move on to the next prompt.

7. Do not take notes during the interview. Don't do it. I know you want to, and I'm telling you not to do it. Instead, keep your full attention on the participant as they're responding to you. Do not pause in between their responses to write things down. Stay with them the entire time. Your focused yet soft eye contact with the participant should invite them to keep talking and sharing with you. If you are back and forth between writing things down on a legal pad and listening to them, you are splitting your focus and sending an unconscious and unintentional message that you're not so interested. Content is important, but not more important than the person in front of you doing the sharing.

8. Mind your body language. Your nonverbal communication can significantly impact how a participant responds to your prompts. Make sure you sit comfortably, preferably with your feet flat on the floor and your arms in a neutral position, like with your hands in your lap. Crossed arms and legs are both defensive body language positions and can subliminally and unintentionally message that you're uninterested or upset by something someone is saying. Also, be aware of nervous fidgeting and try calming it as best you can. You want to message to the participant that you are confident and comfortable with the process.

9. Check your recording device. Whatever you do, don't forget to do this. As you might imagine, getting through an interview and learning it didn't record can upset you and the participant. Check your recording device in the presence of the participant. Have a brief conversation about the weather and play it back to ensure your device works properly. If you're using a recording application on your smartphone, switch the smartphone to airplane mode so you don't get a call or a text message that might turn off the recording application. If you're interviewing in a public place with a lot of noise, check the sound level of the recording to make sure you can make out what the participant is saying.

10. Keep going. Don't stop the interview unless the participant asks you to stop or you encounter some kind of emergency. Go to the bathroom before you begin. If you feel like the interview is not going well, keep going. The participant has set aside their time for you, and you must honor that. Stay open. I have had plenty of interviews start slowly. Then, suddenly, something shifts, and the participant shares something extraordinary that answers my research question and finds its way into the ethnodrama. Do not give up on the interview participant. Be patient and remain curious.

An interviewing process should never focus on exploiting a participant's vulnerability. However, specific prompts may cause discomfort because of what they ask a participant to consider and reflect upon. That act of sharing may leave the participant vulnerable because of what they choose to share. We must also trust an interview participant's ability to say "yes" to participate and make informed choices about what to share. As outlined before, the participant has agency and choice in the written consent process, and at the beginning and end of the interview protocol. Similarly, suppose a participant struggles with their emotions or seems uncomfortable during the interview. In that case, I follow up after the prompts to determine if the participant wants to eliminate the entire interview or particular sections from consideration for the ethnodrama. Even if the participant continues to say "yes," I pay close attention to how I use the interview in the ethnodrama, if at all. If the participant expressed discomfort during data collection, they might also feel uncomfortable with an actor's portrayal of their material on stage. Sometimes, I have had a participant arrive for an interview stating that they hoped their participation would be therapeutic in some way. I quickly reminded them that I am not a therapist and that this is not a therapeutic process. There could be therapeutic by-products from participating in a discussion of a particular topic, but the primary purpose of the interview is for research and artistic creation, not for therapy.

I had an experience on a project about bullying where I doubted the participant's "yes" for inclusion. Late in the staging and rehearsal process, I realized that the script included a longer excerpt from a participant about her experiences with online bullying as a teenager. She shared openly and with emotion how negative and impactful the experience had been for her but had given permission to use all parts of the interview. As I watched the production come together in rehearsals, I realized that the audience would have one experience with this participant. I also wondered how the participant would respond to seeing this story replayed onstage. The assistant director and I reviewed the entire interview to see if we could incorporate other sections. We even considered cutting the piece altogether for fear of retraumatizing the participant if she attended the performance. After much deliberation, I reminded myself and everyone else that the participant had said "yes" and that we should trust her and trust the interviewer's original instincts to transcribe this section for consideration. When the participant came to see the performance, we all felt nervous about how she might respond. Following the performance, the participant approached the interviewer, who also portrayed her in the performance. She shared how powerful it had been for her to hear her own story shared onstage in front of an audience and that it had helped her to find some peace with that moment in her past. She also hoped that she would someday be able to share the performance with her young daughter to demonstrate that she had survived a challenging experience and had moved forward with her life. I share this anecdote as a complication around our roles as artist-researchers. We have ethical responsibilities to protect and care for our participants, but there is a difference between caring and infantilizing. That difference is grey at best and, more often than not, complicated and murky. I encourage all artist-researchers working in ethnodrama to act with great care and listen and trust when a participant says, "Yes, please share my story." If you have been clear, they should be able to trust you, and you should trust them. Their "yes" to you should matter.

This does not mean that I have not encountered complications with participants. As I approach the premiere performance of any new project, I always notify all participants about the status of their interview on a project. Each participant receives an update about whether their interview became part of the script, and all participants receive an invitation and complimentary tickets to attend a performance. In one recent instance, I notified a participant about the upcoming performance and that their interview would not be part of the ethnodrama this time. I explained that we had interviewed over 100 participants and that this performance run would use excerpts from 50 participants. I then invited the participant to attend the performance as my guest. The participant then wrote back demanding compensation, stating that $200 was appropriate for their time being interviewed. They also accused me of purposefully leaving their voice out of the production because of their identity. A member of our interviewing team conducted this interview, so I could go back into the records for this particular participant and ascertain that they had completed and signed the release form for the project. The form clearly outlined that there would be no compensation for participating and that we would not use all interviews in the resulting performance. I replied to the participant with their signed copy of the release form, pointing them to the paragraphs of note, and thanked them again for their participation. This example demonstrates precisely why I restate important information about the process in the written consent and during the interview protocol, and why maintaining clear and consistent records is so important.

Recording the Interview

When I first started collecting interviews in the mid-1990s, I used a handheld cassette tape recorder or a mini-cassette recorder and conducted all of my interviews in person. I modeled my process from what I had read about Anna Deavere Smith's process, so much of my protocol and practices evolved from that specific way of collecting data. Now that we're in the 21st century, technology has expanded and allows easier access to digital audio and video recording. VPL shifted its work to an online environment during the COVID-19 pandemic and created several successful pieces during lockdown. Those projects required us to interview using online video-conferencing platforms like Zoom, and we learned to leverage this transition to our advantage. We also discovered that we could create interview-based projects that recruited participants from beyond our local community without traveling and embedding ourselves in those areas.

Essentially, there are three ways to conduct interviews:

- In-person interviews with audio or video recordings
- Video-conferencing interviews
- Telephone interviews

Even with the additional technology and capabilities available to us as researchers, I still prefer the in-person interview. Many artist-researchers now use video recorders to collect their interview data, but I like audio recording only, as it is less intrusive than a video recorder. Even though video equipment can be as simple and portable as a smartphone and a mini-tripod, the presence of a camera can make a participant feel more "on the spot." That feeling can affect how they share their experiences. The presence of a video recorder also affects me as the interviewer, allowing me to get a bit lazy. Without video as a crutch, I stay more connected during the interview, paying close attention to the participant's gestural responses, facial expressions, physical attributes, clothing choices, and the interview setting. These physical elements are just as important to me as the content of what the participant is sharing.

In-person interviewing does limit the artist-researcher's ability to recruit participants for a project, depending on their ability to travel. If recruiting for a project draws from the local population, in-person interviewing becomes more likely. If a project demands a more comprehensive geographical span, in-person interviewing may be limiting and unrealistic. Additional factors such as travel budget, time to gather interviews, and specificity of the participant pool could limit the possibility of in-person interviews. If a project requires an ethics committee's approval, the artist-researcher should include in-person and other forms of interviewing in their application to allow for greater flexibility. Articulating that possibility in advance prevents the need to go back and request a modification, which can take valuable time away from the data collection process.

As I described, video-conferencing applications like Zoom or Skype have changed the data collection process forever, and I continue to experiment with these platforms in my work. Video conferencing has many advantages, including affordability, convenience, and in-application recording and transcribing functions. Most institutions provide their employees and students with access to these video-conferencing applications free of charge, allowing for audio and video recording of the interview. Because they now offer live transcribing for subtitles as an accessibility feature, the application also produces a rough transcript of the recording. This transcript can provide an initial starting point for later transcribing and scripting. Video conferencing also allows the interviewer and the participant to speak from a location of their choosing. Home, office, car ride, outside: wherever the twain shall meet. Both parties can be comfortable, and there's no need to find a common meeting place.

The video-conferencing applications also allow the potential participant pool to widen if the research project does not include geography as a delimitation. For example, Daniel Kenner created an ethnodrama investigating how music therapy helps patients with dementia. Daniel wanted to speak to clinicians working with this particular population, and his potential participant pool widened because he used video conferencing. His dataset included interviews with clinicians from across the country and worldwide, ultimately allowing for richer findings and a more dynamic ethnodrama. During the COVID-19 pandemic lockdown, Ashley Hamilton and her team of artist-researchers with the University of Denver Prison Arts Initiative interviewed participants inside and outside Sterling Correctional Facility in Sterling, Colorado. The team of incarcerated men working on the project conducted interviews via video conferencing from inside the prison. Neither of these projects would have come to fruition without this new technology.

For all of their great benefits, these video-conferencing applications require much thought and care for practical use, starting with a strong internet connection. The artist-researcher must consider their connection and ask the participant to check theirs in advance. When using these applications, I suggest including something about this in your statement to participants to ensure they have an internet connection to handle the application. The need for a stable connection raises important ethical questions about accessibility, as participants in a project that collects data using these applications must have the financial means to afford all necessary access. As anyone who has used these applications knows, they can freeze or lag at any point, even with a strong and reliable internet connection, disrupting a participant's response. I have experienced multiple moments of frustration over a momentary freeze in a recording that makes an otherwise strong response from a participant unusable because I can't make out the missing part of what they said.

When using video-conferencing applications, the artist-researcher should carefully consider how participants frame themselves in the camera accessed by the application. This camera could be built-in on a desktop or laptop computer, a moveable add-on webcam, or a camera in a smartphone or tablet. These devices provide numerous opportunities for camera angles and framing, many of which can be quite challenging. Ideally, the participant should frame themselves in their camera so that they can be seen from midchest up. To use video-conferencing applications effectively, I suggest the following check-through before starting to record an interview:

- Encourage the participant to keep their camera device stationary and still, if possible. Staying seated or standing in one place rather than moving around is best. Also, they should position their device so they look forward and into the camera, not down at the camera.
- Provide minimal direction to help the participant, but don't overdirect, as this can cause nervousness. Use your "good human beingness" to guide you on this.
- Headphones or earbuds can help with sound quality and audio recording.
- The participant should not sit in front of a window with the sun streaming behind them. That could also affect the visual quality of the recording. In general, avoid any intense light coming from behind a participant.

During the interview, the artist-researcher should also consider that these video-conferencing applications default to switching the view back and forth to whomever is speaking at the time or making a louder noise. An accidental cough or a louder "uh huh" from the interviewer can shift the application's camera focus away from the participant during their response, which then causes a lost moment of what happened with their physicality. If that physical data is important, the interviewer can mute their microphone after they share each prompt so their microphone will not pick up any stray noise from their end. Some applications also offer the option to pin the speaker, which should also help. The applications also provide the ability to record just the person speaking or the gallery of participants on the call. The second option would include both the participant and the interviewer. The benefits of these video-conferencing applications far outweigh the deficits, but artist-researchers should use them carefully to achieve the best quality recording of an interview.

Telephone interviews are the least optimal of the three options, but they are possible. I have conducted telephone interviews in the past, and those interviews have found their way into my dataset and then into an ethnodrama on multiple occasions. The artist-researcher cannot see the participant's appearance, physical gestures, or surroundings through their observations. Still, some of this information can come from the participant. For example, I have asked a participant to describe their location at the time of the interview, including details about their room, where and how they're sitting, what they can see, what the weather is like outside, and so forth. I also explained to them that if they were to become a part of the script, our costume designer would like to know what they were wearing at the time of the interview, so I asked them to describe their physical appearance to me, including what they were wearing. This question could be a bit awkward, so I frontload the question with the reason for why I am about to ask it. This information eliminates discomfort on both sides, and participants share whatever they feel necessary and comfortable sharing.

Interviewers can also record telephone calls on a smartphone using any number of third-party applications. These applications record a telephone conversation as it unfolds without any additional recording device. I record telephone interviews using a speaker phone and a recording device. I make sure that I test the sound levels at the top to make sure that the recording device is close enough to the speaker. The main factor to consider here is the confidentiality of the interview given the use of a speaker phone. Make sure you are in a secure location in which sound does not bleed into a public area where other people could overhear your conversation. Given that the protocol asks the interviewer to slate at the top, this allows the participant to know the interviewer's location and that it is secure and private. Again, if using a smartphone as the recording device, make sure it is switched to airplane mode to prevent any incoming calls during the interview.

Regardless of how the artist-researcher conducts and records their interviews, they should maintain the confidentiality of the recording. I also recommend downloading interviews from smartphone devices and third-party applications as soon as possible after the interview to ensure that an accidental loss of a recording device or an application crash does not cause the loss of an entire dataset.

Gathering Field Notes

Beyond using the interview protocol to gather data, the artist-researcher should also record **field notes** that document their observations during the interview. These field notes can include the participant's appearance, physical behaviors, and surroundings. If the artist-researcher used an audio recorder to document the interview, these field notes become particularly useful for the production process when an ethnodrama becomes a piece of ethnotheatre. Actors find the notes useful as they work to create their performances because they provide details about how a participant appears and behaves. Designers can use them to develop a production's physical and visual world. Field notes can also assist with the initial sorting and coding processes, as they include demographic information that could come into play when considering which participants to include in an ethnodrama. While some may think video recording eliminates the need for field notes, I disagree. Gathering detailed field notes remains an essential part of data collection, as the process requires the artist-researcher to focus on the interview participant and the circumstances of the interview as they unfold in real time, which raises the stakes for paying close and careful attention.

Field notes emerge from the interviewer's perception of what unfolds during the participant's interview, and perception is informed by all five of the interviewer's senses: sight, sound, smell, taste, and touch (Harrison, 2018; Small & Calarco, 2022). Traditional ethnographic field observation, in which an ethnographer embeds themselves in a community for some time, engages multiple senses. The typical interview for an ethnodrama relies more on what the interviewer hears and sees. An artist-researcher's positionality influences their perceived observations, which is why the reflection that unfolds when articulating the point of view is essential (remember Chapter 2!). The artist-researcher should work to reduce subjective judgment, opinion, and interpretive analysis in their field notes whenever possible, while simultaneously recognizing the impossibility of complete elimination. Let's consider the following example. If I conduct an interview and observe that a participant is wearing a green sweater and has shoulder-length brown hair, I would write:

The participant is wearing a green sweater and has shoulder-length brown hair.

This sentence states my observation based on what I perceived using my sense of sight. We might quibble about different shades of green or brown, but I'm not sure how useful that would be for this process.

Another version of the same note might be:

The participant is wearing a beautiful green sweater and has short brown hair.

By assigning the adjective *beautiful* to this observation, I've introduced my opinion, making the observation more subjective. And describing the participant's hair as "short" is relative. Depending on the observer's opinion, a participant's shoulder-length hair could be long or short.

Let's look at another example that considers tone of voice. Suppose I interview a participant about housing in New York City and ask them to describe a negative experience with a landlord. In that case, I may encounter a response that includes some loud talking. To record my perception of the moment in a field note, I might say:

When asked about a negative experience with a landlord, the participant spoke louder than during the other parts of the interview.

This note indicates my perception of what I heard as the participant spoke at this particular moment in the interview. Another version of the same note might be:

The participant got really angry when I asked them about a negative experience with a landlord.

This version introduces my opinion and some analysis of the same moment. I have interpreted the raised volume of the participant's voice as anger and included that judgment in my field notes. This version of the note may misrepresent the participant's experience or even assign intention to the increased volume in their voice. These examples demonstrate once again the importance of self-awareness on the part of the artist-researcher. As the saying goes, "Our perceptions are our reality," but that does not mean that our reality matches the reality of our participants. The artist-researcher must consider how their lived experience affects their observations at each step in the data collection process and do their best to acknowledge that position and control the urge to assign opinions and interpretations in their field notes.

To assist with organizing my thoughts as I collect field notes, I have created a document called the **Participant Characteristics and Physical Surroundings Survey**. I arranged the information as a two-page document with two prompts on each page. I complete the survey for each interview that I conduct. In the unusual situation in which I interview two participants at the same time or a participant more than once, as in the *open heart* project referenced earlier, I collect field notes for each interview. So, in the case of *open heart*, each couple I interviewed had three surveys: one for the couple's interview that included observations about both participants, then one survey for each participant's interview.

I do not take any notes during the interview, but rather stay fully engaged and work to build trust with the interview participant. Harrison (2018) refers to this process as "postinterview note-taking" (p. 73) and advocates for it because "experiencing something with an eye toward documenting it—the constant urge to jot something down and/or snap a photograph—can produce a qualitatively different experience from being fully present in the moment" (p. 77). My instinct has always been that it would be distracting if I wrote field notes in front of an interview participant while they were speaking to me. I want to avoid this kind of distraction for a participant when I interview them for a project.

The artist-researcher should focus on the interview protocol and prompts during the interview, noting observations about the participant's appearance and behaviors. Once the interview is complete, they can thank the participant, part ways, and immediately record all of the details they can remember from the interview on the Participant Characteristics and Physical Surroundings Survey. Very little time should pass between the interview's end and the survey's completion, as reflecting and articulating what just transpired "enhances one's understanding and recollection of the experience" (Harrison, 2018, p. 74). Emerging interviewers panic whenever I lay out this procedure and the expectation of no note taking during an interview. They don't trust themselves enough to remember important details. Based on my experience, if you pay close attention, you will recall the gestures and movements that capture a participant's essence and are most important for the process. This level of detailed observation takes practice, but the artist-researcher can develop the skill over time. I have been conducting interviews for nearly 30 years, and I can still remember certain participants' specific physical gestures linked to something they said in their interviews, mainly because the moments were unforgettable. Enter the interview experience with curiosity, as mentioned before, with a genuine interest in the participant, what they will say, and how they will say it. Trust yourself to remember, and you will, if the detail is essential to a participant's essence.

Here are the prompts for the Participant Characteristics and Physical Surroundings Survey:

Interviewer Name:
Participant Identifier (name or pseudonym):
Date and Time of the Interview:

Provide a brief, detailed description of the participant and their surroundings based on your observations and experiences during the interview. Focus on observations you can make using your five senses.

- **Physical Description:** *Approximate height, weight, hair color, eye color, hairstyle, clothing, shoes, glasses or no glasses, jewelry, or any other defining elements. Please also include information here about how the participant described their identity at the top of the interview.*

  Note: This last sentence, which asks how the participant described their identity at the top of the interview, is essential to include here, as an interviewer's perceived observations cannot record all identities, especially those that may be invisible to the five senses.

- **Physical Behavior:** *Gestures, movements, position(s) while sitting or standing, changes in position, focus or lack of focus, repeated small gestures, activities while speaking with you, and any other defining gestures.*

- **Specific Location:** *Describe the physical surroundings where the interview took place. What kind of space were you in? Colors? Knick knacks? Furniture? Formal or informal? Memorable objects or elements of the space? Who else was around? Private or public?*

- **Geographical Location:** *Where did the interview take place for the participant? For you? Do(es) the neighborhood(s) have name(s)?*

These four basic prompts provide guidelines for recording objective observations about the participant and their surroundings during the interview. Below is an example of how I answered these four prompts when I conducted an interview for *Whatever You Are, Be a Good One.*

- **Physical Description:** *Approximate height, weight, hair color, eye color, hairstyle, clothing, shoes, glasses or no glasses, jewelry, or any other defining elements. Please also include information here about how the participant described their identity at the top of the interview.*

The participant described herself as a "religious old lady from Utah" but hesitated when describing her identity. The participant presented as a White woman and told me she is 77 years old. She has chin-length, blondish-brown hair, with a part on the right side. She has blue eyes and smooth skin. She wore a burgundy red top with an open neckline and a blueish-green pin or bow at the center. There is no other jewelry of note that I can remember. I think she is of average height and weight, as I saw her walk into the frame. I'm going to guess 5′ 6″ and 140 lb. The participant did not wear glasses.

- **Physical Behavior:** *Gestures, movements, position(s) while sitting or standing, changes in position, focus or lack of focus, repeated small gestures, activities while speaking with you, and any other defining gestures.*

The participant looked into her camera for most of the interview. She occasionally looked off to her left. She also sometimes leaned back away from the camera, mostly when laughing about something from the interview. She also occasionally looked down momentarily before answering a question or prompt. There were also moments in the interview when she threw her hands up in the air (mostly toward the end). There was also a moment where it sounded like she was tapping on a surface. Toward the end of the interview, the participant read something to me from social media, and when she read, her eyeline shifted to the left. The participant did not make any additional defining gestures beyond the ones noted earlier.

- **Specific Location:** *Describe the physical surroundings where the interview took place. What kind of space were you in? Colors? Knick knacks? Furniture? Formal or informal? Memorable objects or elements of the space? Who else was around? Private or public?*

I conducted the interview using Zoom. I was in my office at NYU. The participant was in her apartment. I could see a light-colored couch behind her and a painting on the wall behind her, mostly shades of green with some yellow. There were bookshelves on either side of the couch. There was also a way out of the room on the right side. Two frames were hanging on the left wall. The frames seemed to contain certificates.

● **Geographical Location:** *Where did the interview take place for the participant? For you? Do(es) the neighborhood(s) have name(s)?*

The participant was in her apartment in downtown Salt Lake City, Utah. She told me she could look out her window and see the capital building just a few blocks away. I was in my office at NYU on the east side of Washington Square Park in Greenwich Village, NYC.

The Physical Surroundings and Participant Characteristics Survey structures the interviewer's field notes for use by an actor, the director, and the designers. Notice that an actor performing a section of this participant's interview has information about how she engaged with me as the interviewer via Zoom, by looking directly into her camera most of the time, except when she looked down momentarily after a prompt. I also noted that she threw her hands into the air at later moments in the interview, so depending on the selection from the interview used in a script, an actor might incorporate that gesture as well. These notes also help a director as they coach an actor's performance and think about how to stage the interview in production. A costume designer has a description of the participant's clothing, hairstyle, and accessories, all of which could help to select costume pieces for the actor. If a scenic designer wanted to create a physical space that resembled the actor's home, they have details to work from in my description of the room where the interview took place. All parties can access that recording since the interview took place on Zoom. That said, I recorded these observations without looking back at the recording, and I think they represent specific and memorable elements of the essence of this particular participant. Had I conducted the interview and only recorded the audio, the notes on the participant's movements would become even more critical. Why did she look down after the prompts? Why did she look to the left when she read something from social media? What does throwing her hands in the air represent? These are compelling questions that an actor can imagine answers for while still honoring the original movements of the participant. By allowing an actor to interpret the physicality of some of these moments, they can humanize the interview participant in performance and move away from simple imitation, caricature, or mimicry.

Some Closing Thoughts

As emphasized throughout this chapter, the artist-researcher must prioritize care for each participant they engage with through their data collection process. Each interview represents a moment when the participant constructs meaning about their personal experiences and how those answer the broader question guiding a particular project. Participants speak their understanding into existence by saying it aloud to someone else, frequently a complete stranger, and often for the first time. As a result, the interview may be a transformative experience for some and an emotional experience for others, filled with feelings that run the gamut. Regardless of that spectrum of experience, the interview participant should feel happy they chose to speak. The facilitation of that experience lies in the hands of the artist-researcher, and they need to hold space, extend care, and bear witness as the interview participant constructs meaning in their presence.

ACTIVITIES

Practicing the Protocol

Spend some time rehearsing the interview protocol on pages 62–65 of this chapter. Once you can deliver it comfortably without referring to notes, record yourself delivering it. Listen to or watch the recording and consider what energy you are conveying. How might that energy affect an interview participant's willingness to share stories about their experiences with you?

Self-Interviewing

Choose a set of interview prompts shared in Chapter 2 and write each prompt on an index card. Sit down in a quiet place with the stack of cards in the order outlined in the chapter. One at a time, answer each prompt based on your own experiences. Record the interview as you move through the prompts. Once completed, take some time to reflect. How did you feel as you responded to each prompt? How did you feel once you completed the interview? Did the experience leave you feeling positive? Negative? Indifferent?

You can repeat this same exercise with interview prompts for your project. The process remains the same, as do the questions at the end. But add this question: How does your experience with your project prompts inform any edits or changes you might make to the prompts or their order?

Observation Exercise

Observe someone in a public setting using the Participant Characteristics and Physical Surroundings Survey on pages 76–77. For example, a cafeteria or coffee shop is a great place to observe someone eating, drinking, and/or conversing. Using the various prompts in the survey, practice making observations about the person you selected using your five senses. On another day, repeat the exercise, but do not take notes while observing. Observe for 15 minutes, then leave the location. Wait 15 minutes and attempt to complete the survey. This exercise will help you to practice remembering observations without writing them down as they occur.

NOTES

1. Thanks to Alix Claps for her guidance and expertise.

2. Thanks to Jonathan Angelilli for this lesson.

4   Data Analysis
and Interpretation

Once a **dataset** exists, the artist-researcher moves forward in the creative process by analyzing and interpreting the data. As discussed in Chapter 2, an artist-researcher can create an ethnodrama using data they collected themselves or work with data from someone else. Regardless of the origins of the dataset, the artist-researcher should use their overarching research question to guide their analysis and interpretation of the data. Their purpose should be to find and highlight moments in the dataset that provide insights and answers to the research question.

The artist-researcher must remember that they cannot force the dataset to say something it doesn't, as this can lead to a myopic view of the topic they are exploring. The researcher may have a hypothesis about what they might discover. Still, they must remain open to what the dataset reveals and the possibility that their belief is incorrect. I have worked on projects in which I thought my interviews would surface a particular set of experiences confirming an idea I had formulated about how the data might answer my research question. During the data collection process, I even convinced myself I had heard those experiences many times. Then, when I got to the analysis and interpretation of the data and paid closer attention to what was there, I realized that I had made an assumption about what I might discover—a step away from the data for a period of time provided some distance. When I relistened to the interviews, transcribed the sections that resonated with me, and analyzed them for recurring themes, a surprisingly different answer emerged.

Similarly, the artist-researcher cannot change the demographics of the participants in the dataset after completing the data collection process. If a project requires a diverse population of participants, then the artist-researcher must recruit intentionally and track those demographics throughout the interviewing process. Discovering that particular perspectives or viewpoints dominate a dataset can be challenging at the point of analysis and interpretation. Even with intentional recruitment and demographic tracking as described in Chapter 3 for *Whatever You Are, Be a Good One* (Salvatore & Huff, 2022), a project may still conclude with a dominant point of view or experience represented. If that's the case, the artist-researcher can find a way to account for that in the scripting process, which I discuss more in Chapters 5 and 6. Transparency around the composition of the dataset can be helpful and essential. In a more traditional qualitative study, a statement describing the composition of a dataset might appear as a limitation of the particular project. With ethnodrama, the artist-researcher must consider whether to present or acknowledge that limitation in scripting and performance. As a reminder from Chapter 3, the artist-researcher should not coerce or force participation; participants should be "screaming from the mountaintops."

Because I began my work in ethnodrama thinking like a playwright, I did not apply the language of qualitative research to my approaches until later in my career. I developed my approach to sifting through interviews to find the "golden moments," participants' responses I knew an audience needed to hear. My artistic sensibilities guided my process, and I trusted my instincts. Artist and scholar Andrew Freiband (2023) refers to these sensibilities as **artists' literacies**, characterizing them as "a framework for considering art-making as a form of deeply-insightful social research, and then applying the knowledge acquired to creating systemic change" (para. 3). I agree that artists have unique ways of thinking about data, and our unique "literacies" have validity when used to analyze data, solve problems, and create change. Golden moments from interviews also emerged through searching for answers to my research question. I use the plural "answers" because I am not on a positivist journey but rather a meditative journey that allows multiple answers to the question to emerge via the various perspectives that work their way into the ethnodrama through the analysis process.

Moving forward, I begin with suggestions about organizing a dataset. I then share a process for analyzing interviews to identify moments that address the ethnodrama's primary research question. This analysis process moves through three rounds: an initial round, a transcribing round, and a binning round. First, I review the initial process of choosing what to transcribe. Then, I describe how to present interview data as transcripts, followed by how to code those transcripts for recurring themes that answer a project's central research question. I also explain how to identify emergent themes through individual and collaborative coding techniques.

Organizing the Dataset

Depending on the scope of a given project and the number of participants interviewed, an artist-researcher might find themselves swimming in a lot of data. Based on what I've described so far, up through the initial data collection process, each participant interviewed will already have the following pieces of data:

- A signed consent form
- A recording of the interview
- Field notes from the interview via the Participant Characteristics and Physical Surroundings Survey

⬩ Any additional notes or correspondence from the process thus far that should be reviewed during the transcribing and subsequent analysis process, including requests made by the participant regarding their interview and its use (e.g., sections that should not be considered for the project)

When I first started making plays from interviews, I labeled a manila folder with the participant's identifier. That folder held their signed consent form and my field notes from the interview. Next, I marked each cassette tape of the recorded interview with the participant's chosen identifier and the interview date. I stored these folders and cassettes in a filing cabinet and then added interview transcripts to each folder as I moved through the analysis process. Now that I work with digital copies of data, I have moved to a cloud storage system. The cloud storage is password-protected to maintain the confidentiality and security of each participant's data. An external hard drive for digital storage can provide an additional layer of confidentiality and security if preferred. Storing data digitally also saves space and allows easy file backup to prevent loss or accidental erasure. I use the same basic organizing principle of a digital folder for each participant and name it using their chosen identifier. The initial digital folder uses their actual name because the participant returns the digital consent form before their interview. Once they have selected their identifier during the interview, I change the name of their digital folder to match their selected identifier. This change process demonstrates the need for a critical element of data organizing: a spreadsheet tracking interview participants through the data collection process.

An organizing spreadsheet is necessary for any ethnodrama creation process, as it can provide the artist-researcher with an at-a-glance reference for how their data collection, analysis, and interpretation processes unfold. Suppose the artist-researcher uses an online surveying tool, like a Google Form, to recruit participants. In that case, the tool generates a spreadsheet in Google Sheets that collects each participant's responses to the recruiting survey. The resulting spreadsheet can then be adapted with additional columns to track each participant. If the project uses a team of interviewers to collect data, each team member should have access to the spreadsheet to update the essential information as the process unfolds. Here are some examples of categories that can be helpful columns on a data-tracking spreadsheet:

⬩ Participant's full name
⬩ Contact information (email address or telephone number)
⬩ Demographic information necessary for the project
  ○ Examples could include age or age range, gender identity, race/ethnicity, religious affiliation, political affiliation, geographical location, and so forth. Whatever information is necessary to help ensure that the dataset includes a variety of identities and experiences. Each of these examples could become a column on the spreadsheet.
⬩ Statement to participant shared (date)
⬩ Interviewer's name (if there is a team of interviewers)
⬩ Date and time of scheduled interview (include time zone if needed)

- Modality of interview (if using multiple modalities—in person, online, telephone)
- Consent form sent (date)
- Consent form received (checkbox)
- Recording of the interview uploaded to the participant's folder (checkbox)
- Interview transcribed and uploaded to the participant's folder (checkbox)

Each artist-researcher can find their unique way of using this spreadsheet system, but I highly recommend creating some form of centralized tracking. I work with Google Suites, so I can even hyperlink directly to a participant's digital folder from a Google Sheet if necessary.

A participant's digital folder contains all of the materials gathered through the interviewing process in their digital form:

- A signed consent form
- A recording of the interview in its entirety (audio, video, or both)
- A copy of field notes from the interview via the Participant Characteristics and Physical Surroundings Survey
- Digital copies of typed transcripts of the interview (more on this shortly)
- Any additional notes or correspondence from the process thus far that should be reviewed during the transcribing and subsequent analysis process, including requests made by the participant regarding their interview and its use (e.g., sections that should not be considered for the project)

I recommend including the participant's identifier in the file name for each of these pieces of digitized data to help locate misplaced or misfiled pieces in the event of any errors in organizing.

Given that these participant folders contain so much information about each participant, the integrity of the storage needs careful consideration. The artist-researcher and other interviewing team members must not share access with anyone not cleared to work with the dataset. Additionally, when I work with a team of interviewers, I ask them to work with the folders for the participants they interview and to stay out of the folders of other participants. Again, this is to maintain confidentiality for the interview participants to the best of my ability. As a reminder, the participant was notified on the consent form and during the interview that other team members might access their interview data as part of the creative process. Still, I want to limit the traffic through the folders as much as possible. This limitation also prevents accidental erasure or misplacement of data. If the interviewing team becomes part of the analysis and interpretation process, I grant access to the necessary segments of the dataset for them to review. After I complete a project, I remove access to the dataset and download the complete dataset from the cloud application to a hard drive to prevent further access in the case of a data breach or hack.

Even with this digitization of the dataset, I still use hard copies of certain pieces in my analysis and interpretation process, namely the interview transcripts. So, let's move to that part of the process.

Initial Round: What to Transcribe

An artist-researcher analyzes a dataset to identify its recurring patterns. These patterns represent the findings inherent in the dataset and offer initial answers to the research question. These recurring patterns may also provide a way of organizing the findings for dissemination in an ethnodrama and subsequent performance. Ethnodrama, like most methods of qualitative ABR, relies on a process called **coding** to identify the emerging meanings in a dataset. When an artist-researcher codes data, they isolate moments within the dataset that somehow begin to answer the research question. Leavy (2023) describes the coding process as a way to "reduce and clarify the data generated" (p. 165). Using the idea of the "golden moment" of an interview as a metaphor, we can think of coding like sifting sand and looking for pieces of gold. The excess information falls away, and the moments of meaning begin to shine through. Saldaña (2021) describes a **code** as "a short word or phrase that symbolically assigns a summative, salient, essence-capturing, and/ or evocative attribute" (p. 5) to a section of a piece of data, so the entire **transcript** of an interview may contain several shorter moments categorized with different codes.

When the artist-researcher faces a dataset of recorded interviews, the first step of the analysis process requires a major decision: Will every interview be transcribed in its entirety? Some qualitative researchers elect to transcribe each full interview. This approach has the benefit of documenting the entire interview in text format, allowing the full transcript to run through coding software such as ATLAS.ti or NVivo. Using particular codes identified by the researcher, these software programs determine where those codes appear in the transcript, pointing the researcher to recurring patterns among the transcripts in the larger dataset. The software can identify those patterns across all of the interviews, thus providing the researcher with identifiable chunks of the interviews for further analysis. The researcher may also manually code these full transcripts, reading each transcript carefully and identifying where each participant has spoken about one of the specified codes. Whether using a manual approach or software to assist with coding, transcribing the entire interview takes additional time and energy, creating excessive text that doesn't get used in an ethnodrama's scripting process.

In my initial approach to coding, what Saldaña (2021) refers to as first-cycle coding, I relisten or rewatch each interview in its entirety, noting sections of the interview that meet the following criteria:

- The section is continuous and 2 to 3 minutes long.
- The section somehow answers or addresses the project's overarching research question.
- The section is theatrically compelling.

I limit my excerpts to 2 to 3 minutes because a monologue spoken by a single character in a traditional play script is typically 2 to 3 minutes long. This length generally reflects how long an audience will maintain attention with one person speaking in a performance. Suppose I encounter a longer section of an interview that meets the additional two criteria of answering the research question and being theatrically compelling. In that case, I note it for consideration, but I try to stay with the 2- to 3-minute parameter. I also choose continuous sections of the interview. I do not splice 1 minute from one section and 2 minutes from another to create a 3-minute section. Other artist-researchers allow for this editing and splicing together, making it appear that sections from two separate moments occurred together in the same thought process. I choose not to do this splicing in my work because I use verbatim performance for dissemination, which embraces that how someone says something is just as important as the content of what they say. I also question whether this kind of splicing and editing interferes with the authenticity of the participant's testimony and raises questions about the ethics and integrity of representation. The participant delivered their response a certain way for a reason, so we should maintain the integrity of the response. Cutting the participant's spoken journey from one moment and attaching it to another potentially dilutes or misrepresents the participant's experience. In theatrical terms, an actor's performance of a participant's response should have **unity of time**, meaning that their performance unfolds across the same amount of time it took for the participant to say it in the original interview.

I select sections based on their relationship to my central research question. To help make this distinction, as I listen, I consider the most important ideas this participant shared that address the project's *research question*. Notice that I focus not on how the participant answered the interview prompts but on how their responses to the prompts answered the project's research question. This distinction is essential, so I keep the research question in plain sight throughout the analysis. I also stay mindful of my positionality and biases as I review the data and its relationship to the research question. Hence, reviewing my written point of view (Chapter 2), which includes an awareness of potential biases, is crucial to this process.

I also consider sections that I interpret as theatrically compelling, which we can call **theatrically compelling coding**. So what exactly does that mean? For me, it means two things:

1. What parts of this interview could be dramatically interesting in performance?
2. What parts of this interview must an audience hear?

Please note that "dramatically interesting" does not automatically mean that the participant is sad or angry. A participant could be relaying an experience with humor, or one that is humorous. Drama tends to exist when conflict is present, but conflict does not necessarily mean something negative is unfolding. As artist-researchers consider what is dramatically interesting, I encourage them to broaden their definitions of what that could mean. Artist-researchers should listen for "complete stories, unique explanations, surprising declarations, and struggles for meaning," as these ways of sharing information would appeal to an audience in performance (Salvatore, 2025). Suppose the research topic lends itself to serious responses. In that case, it can also be helpful to consider sections that answer the research question and bring lightness or levity to the dissemination. Levity allows the audience space to breathe before moving on to another piece containing relevant and potentially more serious information. An audience responds to how a performance changes in tone; an ethnodrama, like any strong script, should reflect a variety of tones to help maintain the audience's engagement. The artist-researcher can look for these possibilities during this initial round of coding and analysis.

A theatrically compelling section must also answer the overarching research question, but the response might also include other characteristics. It is important to consider sections of an interview that may be compelling because of *how* the participant shared their thoughts and ideas. For example, how a participant responds in a particular moment could make that moment dramatically interesting in performance. Consider these questions:

- Does the participant begin to answer a prompt confidently and then suddenly realize halfway through that they want to say something else?
- Does a participant express an emotion in their response that somehow contradicts the content of what they're saying?
- Was there something about the location of the interview that caused the participant to respond in a particular way?
- Does the participant describe a location or an experience so vividly that I can see it in my mind's eye?

I select certain sections of an interview to transcribe during the initial analysis process because I can answer "yes" to one of these questions. These considerations illustrate where artistic sensibility comes into play, and an artist-researcher working in ethnodrama is responsible for thinking about this. Always consider: What opportunities does a particular section of an interview provide for a theatrical exploration? This approach privileges the art making in the ABR process. These reasons are also why I choose to relisten or rewatch before transcribing, as a typical transcript of an interview may not reflect how someone speaks. But more on this in the transcribing section of this chapter.

I sometimes select a section from an interview that straddles two interview prompts, meaning that part of an answer near the end of the response to one prompt may connect to the beginning of the following prompt. This is a valid section for consideration, and there are ways of indicating the presence of the interviewer's spoken prompt, both in scripting and performance. I love to include these moments in a script, as they remind the audience that I've created the play from interviews conducted with actual participants. These kinds of reminders are essential for an audience, so they remember the source of the play: the actual words spoken by real people.

Once I have reviewed the entire interview, I create a table listing the sections I identified as meeting the previous criteria. Table 4.1 reflects a fictional participant I might have interviewed for *Whatever You Are, Be a Good One*. After rewatching this fictional interview, the result for the participant might look like that in the table.

TABLE 4.1. Participant Identifier: 47-Year-Old Woman	
3:50–6:15	Disagreement with brother during 2016 election
10:23–12:50	Taking a social media break
15:47–18:30	Effects of grocery prices on voting
25:28–27:45	Questioning politicians about their voting records
37:18–40:10	Hope for the future of civics education

The top row of the table includes the fictional participant's chosen identifier. Then, I've listed five interview excerpts that meet my criteria for being the appropriate length, answering the research question, and offering opportunities for theatricality. The left column includes the timestamp for the section in the overall recording, and the right column contains a short phrase that summarizes the section's main idea. This short phrase is an example of a code. I store this table in the participant's main data folder.

I have also used this initial coding technique with an ensemble in a creative process in which multiple team members conduct interviews. Each interviewer can undertake this initial coding process with their interviews. The other team members can also review the interviews as a form of investigator triangulation to determine if the selections align with their perceptions of the research question and the theatricality of the selections (Leavy, 2023). When I work with one or two longtime collaborators, some of our processes around triangulation are more automatic and occur through conversation, so we may not require this table. However, when working with a larger team or a new collaborator, I implement this table step to document the initial coding process.

Now that I have this list of possibilities from the participant's interview, I chose up to three sections to transcribe. Again, I do not transcribe all the sections I have identified, but rather the three sections that best meet the criteria for inclusion in the dataset moving forward. I believe it is vital to cull the dataset at each step of the analysis process. The table provides a record of the sections that I thought were the best possibilities, but by limiting myself to three, I am making choices about what I think will make for the best possible ethnodrama at each step of the process. This method may raise questions about "missing something," but if it concerns the artist-researcher, they can revisit the other interview sections if needed. The transcribing process provides yet another opportunity for coding that examines the content of a participant's response and how they delivered it.

Transcribing Round: How to Transcribe

Once the artist-researcher has determined whether they are transcribing the entire interview or selecting sections through an initial coding process, they can transcribe the dataset. The act of transcribing used to mean listening to recordings and typing along. For the average typist, this process can be annoying and frustrating: the stopping and starting of the recording, the frantic attempts to keep up with a particularly fast talker, and the distracting background noise of the interview location. These elements can contribute to many frustrated feelings, even for the best typist. Some artist-researchers hire transcribing services like Rev.com to prepare transcripts; however, they must state that up front in an application to their institution's ethics committee. In recent years, with the advent of machine-generated transcription, uploading an interview recording to an interface like Otter.ai has significantly reduced my transcribing time. Otter.ai creates a machine-generated transcript of the recording that I then download and use to begin the process. Of course, the machine-generated version contains errors, but it provides a starting point for the ultimate transcript that I include in my larger dataset.

Before we dive into how to transcribe, let's set some context. As I describe this process, I use definitions and examples from VPL, developed in collaboration with my colleague, associate director, Keith R. Huff. In VPL, we think of scoring a transcript as another way of analyzing and coding qualitative data. We describe the process as **coding**

for speech because we analyze a speaker's specific speech pattern and cadence to notate those patterns through transcribing. Interpreting these patterns helps us make sense of a participant's interview responses. Now let's review some basic terminology associated with documenting spoken text on the page.

- A **transcript** is the written record of the audio of a conversation, interview, or media artifact that reflects as accurately as possible what was conveyed. When an artist-researcher listens to an interview, they transcribe what they hear to the page.
- To **transcribe** is to document the words spoken in a conversation, interview, or media artifact. As the artist-researcher transcribes, they create transcription on the page.
- **Transcription** is the written notation of language that results from transcribing.

So, a transcript contains transcription generated by transcribing. Another way to think about this: Transcription is the words on the pages, and the transcript is the document comprising those pages.

Traditional qualitative research tends to present transcription on the page the way we're used to reading prose (Madison, 2018). I present most of this book in prose blocks following conventional grammar, spelling, and punctuation rules. I refer to the transcription of spoken text presented as prose as a **flat transcript**. I use "flat" to describe a transcript presented this way because it provides no additional information to the reader other than the content of what someone said (Salvatore, 2020b). Flat transcripts also tend to contain **buffed transcription**, meaning edited and polished. When I say that transcription has been buffed, I mean that most, if not all, of the pauses in speech, filler words, disfluencies, and repeated words or phrases of the speaker have been removed or corrected in the transcribing process. These corrections are common in qualitative research and popular journalism. For example, look at any transcript of a political debate published by a media outlet and compare it to a recording of that debate. You most likely find the published version has been buffed and, therefore, is an inaccurate representation of what was actually said.

I frequently find myself in discussions with colleagues working in the social sciences about this choice "to buff or not to buff." Some colleagues recommend removing disfluencies in a participant's speech when transcribing to present a participant's response more clearly to an audience. In one instance, at a suggestion during an academic presentation, I chuckled at such a recommendation. When my colleague asked me why I was laughing, I replied that what they recommended removing and editing was the most revealing part of the participant's response. If an artist-researcher wants to use flat, buffed transcripts, that is an acceptable choice, but there is a responsibility that goes along with that choice. A flat, buffed transcript is an edited transcript. There is an ethical responsibility to notate it as such when used in any data presentation, regardless of the venue or outlet. There is another way to transcribe, which provides more insight into *how* someone spoke. This approach demonstrates an additional layer of ethical sensitivity, which demands closer and deeper listening to a participant's response. I now present it for your consideration.

As I first became acquainted with interview theatre through Anna Deavere Smith's plays *Fires in the Mirror* (1993) and *Twilight: Los Angeles, 1992* (1994), my process of transcribing interviews is informed by the published versions of these early works. More recent publications of Smith's plays, like *Let Me Down Easy* (2018) and *Notes from the*

Field (2019), are presented as prose. Using Smith's early published work as inspiration, I transcribe what a participant says verbatim, including all filler words such as "ums" and "aahs," verbal stumbles, and the disfluencies. What emerges from this process is **raw transcription**, as opposed to buffed transcription. I also arrange the transcription on the page so that it notates the rhythmic pauses and tempo of a participant's speech pattern, also known as their **cadence**. As I transcribe an audio recording, each time the speaker pauses while speaking, I begin a new line of text by pressing "return" on the keyboard. Also, if a participant speaks for a long time without a break or pause and that speech doesn't fit on one typed line, the text continues to a second line, and I reverse indent to notate that the speaker's cadence continued unbroken. A reverse indent is also known as a "hanging indent." The resulting transcription looks more like verse on the page, so much so that Smith has referred to her work as "organic poetry" (Dominus, 2009; Saldaña, 2011a). Other qualitative researchers may refer to this style of text presentation as "poetic transcription" (Madison, 2018, pp. 133–134) or use the tools and techniques of discourse analysis to generate transcription (Gee, 2014). Since the resulting transcript reveals a participant's rhythmic way of speaking, it has similarities to a musical score, so I refer to it as a **scored transcript** (Salvatore, 2020b). A scored, raw transcript is a more specific and nuanced way of presenting qualitative data. It considers the speaker's speech patterns, reveals what someone said verbatim, and illustrates visual information about how someone spoke. The raw transcription must reflect a speaker's disfluency to notate how they spoke. Table 4.2 outlines examples of common disfluencies adapted from those identified by the American Speech–Language–Hearing Association that an artist-researcher could encounter in transcribing.

The artist-researcher can also decide how to transcribe words that a speaker may contract but in which no contractions exist in formal writing or moments when the speaker drops the ending sound of a word. For example, a speaker may say:

- *gonna* instead of *going to*
- *wanna* instead of *want to*
- *gotta* instead of *have to*
- *tryin'* instead of *trying*

Some researchers may question the need for this choice or wonder if notating these specific ways of speaking somehow demean or poke fun at a participant. If the attitude is that only participants who speak a certain kind of way have valuable insights to contribute, then that may be the case. If the researcher or the audience for the research holds that bias, then this choice could cause a reason for pause. However, I challenge that assumption and question what that says about the limitations of written language to express something about an individual and their experiences.

TABLE 4.2. Examples of Common Disfluencies
• Whole word and phrase repetitions
○ "Well, well, I don't agree with you."
○ "And also like in that- like in that magazine, there are print ads."
• Sound and one-syllable word repetitions
○ "I w-w-w-wish you wouldn't say that."
○ "There- there- there was a man in front of me."
• Interjections
○ "I, um, have to make a phone call."
• Revisions
○ "I had- I found my keys."
Note. Based on material from American Speech–Language–Hearing Association (www.asha.org/public/speech/disorders/stuttering).

The artist-researcher must then notate where the speaker pauses in their speech pattern to take the raw transcription and create the scored transcript. When we teach transcribing in VPL, we identify three reasons that pauses in speech tend to occur: syntax breaks, emphasis, and breath. Figure 4.1 offers examples of how these speech breaks might present as transcription. In each example, the end of the line of text indicates where the speaker paused. In the example for breath, the speaker spoke through to the end of the third line without taking a breath, which is indicated by the reverse indent.

Artist-researchers new to this scoring process frequently ask how to judge whether a pause is long enough to warrant starting a new line of text. In reality, there is no practical way to time a pause to make this decision. Each of us may hear a pause differently, so scoring is also impacted by the person doing it. However, I have developed a process that allows a group of transcribers to come together around what constitutes a pause by working through a series of excerpts from different speakers' audio recordings. The group members transcribe each excerpt independently and then compare their transcripts to scored transcripts we created in the lab. We have discovered that taking a group through three or four rounds of this process moves them closer together in how they hear pauses. We use this process to develop a form of inter-transcriber reliability around hearing and notating speech patterns and cadence.

Ultimately, the scored transcript serves two purposes. First, it provides the artist-researcher with additional information about how someone speaks. Second, it offers an actor performing the transcript some guidance about how to speak the text, while also increasing the potential for discoveries about why someone speaks the way they do. A scored transcript can provide powerful insights into the mindset of the interview participant at a given moment (Salvatore, 2020b). For this reason, I recommend that artist-researchers analyze and present interview data using this scored format.

In her book *Talk to Me: Travels in Media and Politics*, Anna Deavere Smith (2000) writes:

> I think we can learn a lot about a person in the very moment that language fails them. In the very moment that they have to be more creative than they would have imagined in order to communicate. . . . It's in language that I think we can find the other. . . . I am able to study a person's language and breaths very carefully because I can record it, and listen to it over and over again. I think it's about finding that moment when syntax changes, when grammar breaks down. Those are the moments I should study, if I want to know who a person is. (p. 53)

Smith's observations raise essential questions about more traditional approaches to presenting qualitative interview data. When we present spoken text in a flat transcript as

- Syntax breaks
  Well, in all due respect to my-
  to Tom, I'll pass.

- Emphasis
  What we need to thi- rethink
  is the
  entire
  war
  on
  terror.

- Breath
  Uh, what I would do, and I've made that
  very clear that I would bring our
  troops home by the end of my
  term.
  That's my plan.

FIGURE 4.1 Presenting speech breaks as transcription.

prose and delete all filler sounds, pauses, stumbles, and disfluencies, we offer a sanitized portrait of a participant, implying they made no mistakes and had no struggle with making meaning of their experience. A flat transcript focuses solely on the content of what the speaker had to say but ignores the possibilities that lie in what Smith describes in the earlier passage as moments "when grammar breaks down." Many well-meaning qualitative researchers argue that "cleaning up" a transcript presents a participant in a better and more positive light. I argue that this cleaning process is a form of erasure, and I question the ethics of the choice. Ignoring how a person speaks may be well-intentioned, but it removes and silences a dimension of the participant's experience during their interview.

Even with the additional information the scoring provides, a scored transcript cannot capture everything about how someone spoke on its own, hence the importance of using the recording of an interview as a reference as well. I have had multiple examples from my own work in which a transcript's content implied a particular emotion or feeling for a speaker's delivery. However, when I reviewed the interview's audio recording, I was surprised by how the speaker shared the content. I remember one particularly striking example from an interview conducted by a student with a participant who described her experience at the Westgate Mall in Nairobi, Kenya, during the terror attack there on September 23, 2013. When I first read the transcript and experienced the participant's description of a grenade rolling past her and her younger brother in the mall as they sought cover during the attack, I imagined she would sound distraught as she told the story. However, when I listened to the audio of her interview, I heard something very different. The participant told her story with control and a sense of calm, as if she recounted what she had for breakfast that morning. I had made assumptions about how the speaker would sound based solely on my reading of the content, and my assumptions were incorrect. My positionality and personal experiences affected my interpretation of the data on the page. Artist-researchers should be mindful of the interplay of these variables throughout their analysis process.

Let's review an interview excerpt that ultimately became part of *Whatever You Are, Be a Good One*. The interview participant chose the identifier "Zach, 24-year-old man." Below is an example of the excerpt presented as a flat, buffed transcript, which is the typical way to present qualitative interview data.

I think we're at a deeply unsustainable place where people believe on a fundamental level that those with different political beliefs than them aren't their community members, aren't just rivals in that sense, but are like deeply evil people who should be exterminated. And that's tough as a nation to come back from. Just looking through the lens of world history, when you reach a place where rival factions decide that anyone who disagrees with them is the enemy, it's very difficult to rebuild those bridges. And so I think that the majority of that is driven by specific bad faith actors who have a desire to create instability because our system of government doesn't work for their desire to wield as much power as possible in any way that is possible. And I have my political beliefs. I believe that the majority of that is driven by bad faith actors who are for the most part nationalist conservatives, but who are much more nationalist than they are conservative. And I don't think that the tone of their political beliefs, or the nature of their political beliefs, matter so much as the tenor of them. I think there are a lot of people in this country who want a stable, functioning democracy, who want to help others. But having people in positions of power with large bullhorns who can and will wield that power to destabilize our system just inherently fractures our ability to function in this democracy.

This flat presentation of Zach's spoken words as prose provides information about what he said during the interview. Based on how this transcript notates what Zach said, we might assume that Zach feels quite confident in what he says. Now let's look at the same section presented as a scored, raw transcript.

I think we're at a deeply unsustainable place
where
people believe on a fundamental level
that
those
uh
with different political beliefs than them
uh
aren't just-
aren't-
certainly aren't their community members
uh
cert-
aren't just
you know
rivals in that sense
but are
like
deeply
evil people
who
uh should be exterminated.
And um that's tough
as a nation
to come back from
just
looking
through the lens of world history
when you-
when you reach a place
where rival factions
decide that-
that anyone who disagrees with them
uh
is the enemy.
Um
it-

it's very difficult
to-
to
rebuild those bridges.
Um
and so
I think that
the majority of that is driven by
specific bad faith actors
who have a desire to-
to
uh create instability
because our system of government doesn't work for their desire
to wield as much power as possible
in any way that is possible.
Um
and I
you know
um
I have my political beliefs.
I believe that the majority of that is driven by-
by
uh
bad faith actors
who are for the most part nationalist conservatives
uh but who are much more nationalist than they are conservative.
Um
and
I don't think that
the
uh the tone of their political beliefs
or the nature of their political beliefs
matter so much as the tenor of them.
Um
and that
um
I-
e-
I think there are
a lot-
a lot- a lot
of people in this country who want a stable functioning democracy
who want to help others.
Uh but
having people in positions of power with large bullhorns
who can
and will wield that power

to-
to destabilize our system
is
um
it just inherently uh fractures-
fractures
our ability to function in this democracy.

The scored transcript conveys the same content but provides more information about how Zach delivered it. Some key points to consider:

- The scored transcript shows Zach's speech pattern, which is not nearly as smooth as the presentation in the flat transcript. In fact, Zach spoke in fragments, sometimes single words.
- Zach used many filler words like "uh" and "um." These words and the more fragmented cadence may indicate a different level of confidence than the flat transcript.

Now, if you go back and review the flat transcript and compare it to the scored transcript, you will notice that the flat transcript removes the filler words and any repetition. These edits in the flat transcript flatten Zach's presentation and present a one-dimensional understanding of his response, whereas the scored transcript adds another dimension and allows for more complexity as we analyze and consider how Zach responded to the prompt and how he created meaning for himself during the interview. We can see this simply by looking at the presentation of the first sentence:

FLAT, BUFFED PRESENTATION:

I think we're at a deeply unsustainable place where people believe on a fundamental level that those with different political beliefs than them aren't their community members, aren't just rivals in that sense, but are like deeply evil people who should be exterminated.

SCORED, RAW PRESENTATION:

I think we're at a deeply unsustainable place
where
people believe on a fundamental level
that
those
uh
with different political beliefs than them
uh
aren't just-
aren't-
certainly aren't their community members
uh
cert-

aren't just
you know
rivals in that sense
but are
like
deeply
evil people
who
uh should be exterminated.

In the simplest of terms, the flat, buffed transcript makes it appear that Zach delivered more of a prepared answer, whereas the scored, raw transcript illustrates that Zach constructed meaning in the moment. His breaks in cadence, filler words, and repeated phrases illustrate a more complicated response to the interview prompt. The scored transcript provides more information to inform an artist-researcher's analysis, interpretation, and dissemination. Zach's moments of disfluency reveal his meaning making process. As Anna Deavere Smith (2000) said, "Those are the moments I should study, if I want to know who a person is" (p. 53). If we're caring artist-researchers, we should work to understand a participant more holistically by also investigating how they speak, rather than simply taking the content of their speech and using it for our own purposes.

An artist-researcher can decide how to present their textual data, but they should acknowledge how they present the written transcription when disseminating their findings. That acknowledgment helps prepare the audience to receive it as intended and explains why the artist-researcher made their particular choice. From my perspective, which you can probably already glean from what I've written so far, *the scored, raw transcript represents the most accurate, honest, and ethical way of presenting spoken interview data for consideration by an audience.* This method of analysis, like any method, requires practice and experimentation. Still, the benefits of investing time and energy in this kind of data presentation far outweigh the deficits of extra time needed. The increased attention and time required to create a scored, raw transcript automatically causes the artist-researcher to engage in **deep listening**, a term that my colleague and frequent collaborator Sarah Bellantoni uses to describe what it takes to create a scored, raw transcript and then, ultimately, also to perform it. Deep listening requires concentration, focus, patience, and an openness to discovering something new and unexpected.

Each of us has a unique way of speaking and sharing stories. The artist-researcher needs to be sensitive to that individuality throughout this transcribing stage of the analysis process. Deep listening helps to open up the possibilities of hearing uniqueness. Interview participants respond to interview prompts in different ways. If we listen closely enough, we can begin to hear and notate those differences in the transcription and thus provide actors and audiences with powerful insights into the mindset of the interview participant at that particular moment. Through deep listening, I can identify the difference between a participant saying something for the first time in an interview, something they've never said before, versus repeating a story they have told multiple times. Using the scored transcribing methods I've described, I can notate the transcription to see that difference visually on the page. By being aware of the difference between something said for the first time and something said many times before, the artist-researcher can use those different deliveries to help create theatrically compelling moments in an ethnodrama and the subsequent performance of the data. How a participant has delivered their content also plays a crucial role in developing dramatic moments in a script—more on this in Chapters 5 and 6.

Formatting and Organizing Transcripts

As outlined earlier in this chapter, the artist-researcher needs to organize their dataset to locate and track the various pieces of information for each participant while maintaining the integrity and confidentiality of the data. Transcripts from each interview are stored in the participant's folder. Throughout the years, I have developed a system of organizing and tracking important information for each transcript from an interview. This system has expanded through the larger projects we have engaged in for VPL. Beyond the transcription of the spoken text, we include the same information at the top of each transcript, allowing easy sorting and tracking. The template for the top of each interview transcript contains the following information presented as single-spaced text:

Title of the Excerpt:
- A line or phrase from the actual transcription in quotation marks that summarizes the main point of the excerpt

Project:
- Name/working title of the project

Interviewer:
- Name of the interviewer

Date of the Interview:
- Date interview was conducted

Transcribed:
- Name of the transcriber and date transcribed; often the same as the interviewer, but not always

Timestamp:
- Section of recording that matches the transcribed excerpt

Transcript Location: (optional)
- If using a cloud server (e.g., Google Drive or Dropbox) to store data, include a hyperlink to the participant's folder in the cloud

PARTICIPANT IDENTIFIER (in capital letters, like the name of a character in a script):
- Text of the interview here (single-spaced)

Here is an example of the top of Zach's transcript from the excerpt just offered:

Title: "Bad faith actors"
Project: Portraits US: Polarization / *Whatever You Are, Be a Good One*

Interviewer: Cassidy Kaye
Interview Date: 4/11/2022
Transcribed: Cassidy Kaye, 4/11/2022
Timestamp: 14:32-16:52

ZACH, 24-YEAR-OLD MAN
I think we're at a deeply unsustainable place
where
people believe on a fundamental level . . .

Most of this information is self-explanatory, but the first piece of information, the title, requires additional explanation. I title each interview excerpt with a line or phrase from the transcription to help me remember why I selected the excerpt in the first place. The title functions similarly to a newspaper headline, as it crystallizes the content of the particular excerpt. Because the title serves as a quick summary, it also helps in later steps of the coding process. We can also think of the title as an example of ***in vivo* coding** (Leavy, 2023; Saldaña, 2021), which uses the actual words of interview participants to develop codes. Saldaña refers to *in vivo* coding, also known as verbatim coding, as his "first 'go to' method with interview transcript data" (2021, p. 138). The artist-researcher takes another step forward in the analysis process by titling the transcript.

The timestamp when the interview excerpt starts and ends in the recording becomes particularly important when the artist-researcher wants to review that section while scripting and when an actor wants to review it as they prepare for a performance. Similarly, if the artist-researcher uses a cloud server like Google Drive to store their data, a hyperlink to the participant's folder can foster efficiency in locating needed data pieces in a scripting or rehearsal process. The PARTICIPANT IDENTIFIER indicates the speaker of this particular excerpt. I capitalize it as I would capitalize the name of a fictional character who is about to speak in a traditional script. The transcription of the section begins immediately on the following line.

I suggest using Google Docs for all transcript excerpts, as this platform allows for easy recording and tracking of any changes and updates to the transcripts. This tracking ability becomes especially useful when working with scored, raw transcripts in a rehearsal process. I always say that a scored transcript is a living document that needs to serve the actor working with it in performance. Given that the transcript should reflect how the actor hears the pause from their review of the recording, Google Docs allows the actor to make adjustments, which are then easily accessible by other creative team members on a given project. As the artist-researcher selects excerpts to transcribe, I recommend creating an individual document for each excerpt and using the excerpt's title as the document's electronic file name. The file name facilitates easy discovery and access when searching for data in the scripting process. Page numbers on each document are helpful as well.

Finally, choose a font type and size, and stick with it through the transcribing process. This detail may sound nitpicky, but when you begin the scripting, you'll thank me, as it maintains consistency and allows for easy integration of individual transcripts into a full script. Cutting and pasting text from an excerpt into a working script becomes easier if all excerpts are in the same font. Additionally, if you choose to score your transcripts, consistent font type and size will maintain your scoring as you move the excerpt into the script. The more variation in your transcribing font selection and size, the more likely you will need to go back and rescore many pieces to get a consistent and properly formatted script. You should apply the same principle to line spacing as well. I recommend single spacing for transcripts, but you should adhere to your preferences. Consistent formatting and presentation of the transcripts allows the artist-researcher to move into the next coding phase with confidence.

Binning Round:
Coding Data into Bins

Following the transcribing round, which includes the coding of speech, the analysis process moves to another round of coding, which involves identifying recurring themes, patterns, and intersection points within the larger dataset that emerged through the interviewing process. Each artist-researcher should construct their ethnodrama in a way unique to their project, research question, dataset, point of view, and personal aesthetic. The artist-researcher must continue to be aware of their point of view and monitor how it affects their coding of data in this next round (Ackroyd & O'Toole, 2010; Salvatore, 2025).

For this coding round, the artist-researcher reads the transcripts to determine their effectiveness and connectedness, and places similar sections into **thematic bins** (Anzul, Downing, Ely, & Vinz, 1997). These thematic bins represent codes that emerge based on how the data present to the artist-researcher as they read. Sometimes, the interview prompts lend themselves to assisting with this coding round, meaning they might provide some organizing principles. That said, I do not recommend purposefully trying to code based on answers to the interview prompts. Remember that you crafted the interview prompts to catalyze responses that would answer your overarching research question. So often, sections from entirely different parts of interviews come together to discuss the same theme in unified or contradictory ways. The artist-researcher should remain open to the possibilities that present themselves during this round of coding. Prepare for surprises to emerge.

If an artist-researcher works alone, they can begin by independently reading through their dataset and noting patterns. As mentioned earlier, they may also upload their interview transcripts to coding software. Reading the dataset and hearing it in one's head represents a traditional approach to this coding process. However, suppose an artist-researcher has the ability and the resources, namely other human beings, to hear their data out loud. In that case, I recommend listening to the data read aloud whenever possible. Remember, an ethnodrama is ultimately a play, and playwrights write plays to be heard and seen, not read in isolation like a novel or a traditional journal article. Therefore, if you're using ethnodrama as your research modality, hearing your data aloud is an integral part of this round of the coding process. Yes, you listened to the excerpts spoken by the participant during their interview, but at this point, I find it helpful to hear the data spoken in other voices. The lone artist-researcher can code a dataset on the project, but this can easily lead to myopic data analysis. Triangulation with trusted colleagues around a dataset can provide a more holistic analysis, particularly if those colleagues have different points of view, other ways of moving through the world, and different positionalities.

In **collaborative coding**, an ensemble of artist-researchers may review the transcripts in a dataset by reading them aloud, identifying each transcript's main idea or theme, and noting this on the excerpt and on a spreadsheet that tracks the reviewing process. During this out-loud data sharing, the ensemble can listen for emergent recurring patterns and identify and track them into the previously discussed thematic bins. Collaborative coding could also unfold with a lead ethnodramatist and a trusted colleague. The duo can code as described for the ensemble but with more individual silent reading and notating followed by sharing and cross-referencing.

At this coding stage, I prefer to introduce a collaborator called a **dramaturg** to my process. A dramaturg in a traditional theatrical process can play many production-related roles, from providing historical research for a team of artists producing a play to creating program notes and audience engagement activities to accompany a production. In a new play development process, like scripting an ethnodrama, a dramaturg helps to "create an environment where a new piece of theatre can be conceived, developed, and grown, and a playwright can be nurtured" (Trencsényi, 2015, p. 102). In the case of an ABR process, substitute the word "playwright" with "researcher" or "artist-researcher." Regardless of the word you use for the creator, the dramaturg's role is the same. They help to facilitate the creation of a new play by supporting the primary creator. Some might also describe this role as akin to a thought partner or critical friend (Costa & Kallick, 1993), as they provide another perspective during this round of coding. The dramaturg's presence contributes again to a triangulation around data analysis and interpretation. They help to keep the artist-researcher's point of view from being the only one in the coding process. I've worked with dramaturg Sarah Bellantoni for over a decade. Our collaborations have yielded several original plays, many mentioned and cited throughout this book. For those using ethnodrama for a dissertation project or promotion review, clearly outline the dramaturg's role in advance, so your committee members and evaluators understand the nature of this person's involvement in your project. Then, describe this person's role and acknowledge their contributions accordingly in the methodology section of your dissertation or review materials.

If I have an ideal set of working conditions, I do a two-step coding process in this third stage that uses collaborative coding in the first step and a dramaturg in the second step. To illustrate, I describe this two-step process as it unfolded for *Of a Certain Age* (Salvatore, 2018). Each of the eight researcher-actors[1] on that project conducted interviews and then followed the transcribing process described earlier. Before engaging in any interviews, the researcher-actors interviewed one another, transcribed a section of the interview, and then performed their fellow ensemble member back for the group. I always engage an ensemble in this process, so that they understand what it feels like to be performed back by someone else. It is a form of empathy building and ensemble building, and a clear example of how to navigate the ethics of this work (Salvatore, 2020b, 2025).

Once the researcher-actors completed their interviews, coded for specific sections, and transcribed them, they uploaded the necessary materials to each participant's folder. I then printed hard copies of each transcript for each participant, placed those transcripts into a physical folder with the participant's name, and assembled those folders in a group. We gathered as a team, and each researcher-actor received the assembled folders for the participants they had interviewed. I posted the research questions around the room, so they were in plain sight and could serve as a constant reference point for our next step as

a group. I instructed everyone to take a few minutes to review the contents of their folders and to pull transcripts from each person whom they felt directly addressed the posted
research questions. I also asked them to consider sections they felt an audience must hear.
As a reminder, I use these guiding parameters in the initial coding round, and I return to
them in this binning round. Once each researcher-actor pulled their sections, we began
to read them aloud. One person started, and we listened to that transcript. Then I asked if
anyone else had a transcript related to what we had just heard, either agreeing with it or
contradicting it. If the presented excerpt did not produce a connection to someone else, we
moved on to another excerpt that answered the research questions and needed to be heard
by an audience. As we moved through this read-aloud process over 2 hours, we heard
multiple sections from multiple participants and collectively noted recurring patterns. For
example, hearing the data helped identify the recurring experience of many participants
feeling invisible as they grew older. This pattern became an essential thematic bin in the
second part of the coding process. This collaborative coding also identified participants
whose interviews did not yield data that answered our research questions. We noted these
observations for consideration in the next stage of the coding process. This 2-hour session
was not a full review of the dataset, but hearing excerpts of it aloud gave us a greater sense
of its possibilities. Again, the multiple positionalities of the interviewing team provided
various perspectives on the same interview excerpt and allowed for dialogue about the
participants and their shared thoughts to emerge across the ensemble that would eventually perform these stories. I collected the folders at the end of the session, as any notes the
ensemble had made on the transcripts would be helpful in the next phase of our review
(Salvatore, 2020b).

Using the information gathered from this group share, I moved into the second step
of the coding process: reviewing the full dataset with the dramaturg Sarah Bellantoni. We
met in person over 3 days for this second step and also consulted with assistant director
Andy Wagner, who was reading the material separately offsite. Sarah and I worked in
a large space with room to spread out the data to facilitate our coding. We used single-
sided hard copies of the transcripts for this process, but other artist-researchers might feel
comfortable working digitally at this stage. The choice is yours. As shown in Figure 4.2,
spreading the data on a table or the floor helps to organize and facilitate emerging connections and possibilities.

Sarah and I split the stack of 37 participant folders between us, and we reviewed each
transcribed section individually, noting in pencil the main idea or theme of the section in
the upper corner of each transcript. In addition to reading independently, we also read
sections aloud, listening for patterns, repetitions, connections, and contradictions. Using
our working notes and Andy's additional observations, Sarah and I created piles of related
excerpts by theme, which became our thematic bins. After this second step, we had the
following thematic bins:

- Making a living
- Collaboration
- Memories
- Auditioning
- Casting

FIGURE 4.2 Dramaturg Sarah Bellantoni seated with the data spread out on tables during the binning round of coding for *Of a Certain Age*. Photo courtesy of the author.

- Lying about age
- Effects of aging
- Ageism
- Invisibility
- Longevity
- Advice to younger professionals

These thematic bins provided the beginning of a structure that we would ultimately consider when we began scripting the ethnodrama (Salvatore, 2020b).

Sarah and I then reviewed the transcripts in each thematic bin to identify which participants found their way into them and how many interview excerpts each bin had overall. We tracked this on a large piece of newsprint, listing each participant's name and a tick mark for each interview excerpt that made it into the thematic bins. A digital spreadsheet could track this counting as well. This deeper review of the data helps the artist-researcher determine which interview participants to include in the ethnodrama. As described in Chapter 3, I interview at least twice as many participants as I think will be included in the ethnodrama, with the understanding that not all of those participants will become part of the script. This review of the thematic bins' contents also helps identify participants with more than one interview excerpt that could become part of the script. Once I get to the scripting process, I like the option for participants' voices to appear more than once in the ethnodrama.

Relative to *Of a Certain Age*, Sarah and I began our analysis and coding with data collected from the 37 unique participants. This round of analysis reduced the number of potential participants for inclusion in the script to 21. To achieve this culling process, we considered the following questions:

- What recurring subthemes or patterns are present in this bin?
- What contradictory ideas are present?
  - Contradictory ideas from two or more participants presented in conversation with one another can create dramatic tension.
- What unique perspectives are present?
  - Unique perspectives contribute to the originality of any research.
- Is more than one participant articulating the same idea, and if so, who is presenting the idea in the most compelling way?

To the last point, we identified transcripts in which participants shared the same idea, then determined which participants had stated that idea in the most original or dynamic way. So when more than one participant offered a similar response to answer the research questions, we used the theatrically compelling code to decide which piece to include and, by extension, which participant to include in the play. For example, one participant described how they had been impacted by ageism in the entertainment industry in a philosophical way, whereas another participant shared a specific story about her friend's experience with voiceover casting. The friend was cast for a voiceover role, and when she arrived at the studio to do the recording, the director expressed shock at her age. While both participants shared important information about ageism, we decided that the story about the actor's experience recording the voiceover provided a more impactful example of how ageism manifests itself in this vocation. The story was more theatrically compelling and provided opportunities for staging. The theatrically compelling code often serves as the "tiebreaker" when two interview excerpts cover similar ideas.

We also considered how a participant's positionality could expand the representation of voices that would find their way into the ethnodrama. We thought about the overall demographics of the dataset and identified that the project could reach a wider audience if we included voices from as many different lived experiences as possible. Therefore, we considered race and ethnicity, gender, gender identity, age, and vocational role within the performing arts professions. We had interviewed many actors for this project, but we also wanted to represent the experiences of other vocations within the performing arts. We identified interview excerpts from a theatre director and a makeup artist, as these two perspectives provided additional insights into how aging plays out in vocational roles beyond acting.

As we moved through this process of identifying redundancy, some participants came to have only one interview transcript for consideration in the ethnodrama. In these cases, when a participant's folder contained only one selected interview excerpt, and we felt strongly about including that excerpt in the eventual scripting process, we returned to that participant's interview recording and listened for additional moments that might allow us to expand that participant's presence in the script. In at least three cases, relistening to the interview revealed additional data that

TABLE 4.3. Prescripting Classification and Selection of Participants for *Of a Certain Age*

Sorting into thematic bins	Reviewing thematic bins	Conclusion of analysis
37 participants	21 participants	16 participants

helped make the case to include that participant in the scripting process.

When we arrived at the end of this step of the analysis, Sarah and I reduced the number of potential participants to consider in the scripting process to 16 (see Table 4.3). The data for these 16 participants moved forward into the scripting process for *Of a Certain Age*.

Sometimes, the coding steps just described can switch in order depending on the project's parameters, the origin of the dataset, or the moment when ethnodrama emerges as a possibility. Eric Marcus's interviews for *Making Gay History* (2002) serve as an excellent example. As discussed in Chapter 2, through completing our literature review, reviewing 108 interview transcripts, and listening to the podcasts in the series, research dramaturg Jamila Humphrie Silver and I identified three research questions. We also narrowed Marcus's large dataset of interviews to a subset of 26 interviews that featured participants speaking about their experiences before the Stonewall uprising in 1969. Another round of reviewing the transcripts and the podcast recordings reduced the number to 17 interviews, featuring 20 potential interview participants (see Table 4.4). Eric occasionally interviewed two participants simultaneously if they were in a partnership or living together. During this round of review, we tried to be very conscious of the demographics of the participants we considered for inclusion in the script. We wanted to ensure that as the ethnodrama developed, we focused on considering as many different lived experiences as possible. We did not want to perpetuate the erasure of the lived experiences of trans people of color, especially given that the ultimate purpose of the project was educating young audiences about LGBTQIA+ history, and the voices of trans people and people of color played significant roles in that history.

Once we had identified the smaller group of interviews for consideration, we then coded the transcripts of the podcasts for sections that addressed our three research questions. Production dramaturg Sarah Bellantoni and assistant director Mackie Saylor joined Jamila and me for this collaborative coding process. Together, the four of us coded and scored the selected excerpts from each interview podcast for speech pattern and added timestamps for where the excerpts appeared in each podcast episode. We then coded

TABLE 4.4. Classification and Selection of Interviews from *Making Gay History*

Interviews under consideration from Eric Marcus's entire dataset	Selected interviews that deal with pre-Stonewall uprising experiences	Interviews that are coded and scored for speech pattern
108 interviews	26 interviews/ 30 participants	17 interviews/ 20 participants

the interview excerpts from these 20 participants and developed four thematic bins that related to our research questions:

- Historical context
- Catalysts for change
- Movements for change
- Change/evolution

We placed the interview excerpts into these bins, identified who was speaking in each bin, and examined how different points of view and experiences were represented and referenced. At this point, we made some adjustments to which participants' material we included, based primarily on redundancy and representation, and we still landed with 18 participants. These four bins and their contents became the basis for scripting the ethnodrama. While the organizing process and the multiple rounds of coding remained the same as they did in the *Of a Certain Age* process, some of the major decision points occurred at different moments, primarily because of the availability of full transcripts already and the size of the original dataset.

The coding process with *Whatever You Are, Be a Good One* relied on similar coding steps but across a larger group of collaborators. A team of trained interviewers[2] conducted interviews with over 100 participants across 9 months. Each interviewer picked sections from their interviews to transcribe, they created scored transcripts, and then we arranged the participants' data into groups based on geographical location. Given that this project investigated political polarization across the United States, we split the country into five geographical areas (National Geographic Society, 2009): Northeast, Southeast, Midwest, Southwest, and West.

We then sorted the interview excerpts into those five geographic bins based on the location of each participant at the time of their interview. We wanted the final ethnodrama to include the voices of 50 interview participants, so we had to reduce the dataset by more than half. To make these decisions, we gathered a collaborative coding team of six members,[3] some of whom had conducted interviews and had some familiarity with the contents of the dataset, and others who had not engaged with the dataset. Each team member reviewed the interview selections from particular geographical areas. For example, I reviewed the interview excerpts from all participants living in Southeast states. As a team, we arrived at 10 interview excerpts from each region, 50 excerpts total, reflecting a broad diversity of states, political viewpoints, gender and gender identities, and races and ethnicities. In our first rehearsal, the 10-member acting company[4] read the excerpts from each region aloud, and after hearing all 50 pieces in a day, we made some final substitutions to the selections (see Table 4.5).

These 50 excerpts became the selections used throughout the performance run of *Whatever You Are, Be a Good One*. I discuss how this project's performance worked in Chapters 7 and 8. Again, in this third example, the coding process followed the same basic principles of three rounds of analysis, but we modified the parameters of each round slightly to fit the overall goals of this specific ethnodrama's needs.

After completing the binning round of analysis, the artist-researcher better understands what the dataset has revealed about their research questions and how many interview participants might become part of the ethnodrama. As stated at the beginning of this chapter, it's important to remember that we cannot make a dataset say something that it

TABLE 4.5. Sorting and Coding Excerpts for *Whatever You Are, Be a Good One*		
Interviews conducted; excerpts selected, transcribed, and scored by the interviewing team	Excerpts sorted by geographical region and reviewed by a six-member team through a collaborative coding process	Excerpts read aloud by the 10-member acting ensemble; final selections made
104 interviews	Northeast, Southeast, Midwest, Southwest, West	50 excerpts representing 50 individual participants; 10 participants from each the five geographical regions of the United States

doesn't reveal, nor can we change the demographics of the dataset we collected. The dataset is the dataset; we work with what we've collected. We cannot force data to say what we want them to say or what we think they should say. We can only present what the data reveal through our analysis.

Wrapping Up

As this chapter on data analysis comes to a close, let's review the three rounds of analysis proposed throughout:

1. Initial round: Select two to three excerpts from a participant's interview that are 2 or 3 minutes in length, answer the research question, and are theatrically compelling.
2. Transcribing round: Code for speech patterns to create scored transcripts.
3. Binning round: Code for recurring themes, patterns, and interconnections among the various interview excerpts and participants.

While I've broken the analysis process into three rounds, these rounds are interconnected and influenced by the research question and the artist-researcher's point of view. In cases where a team of interviewers collects data and/or a team works through a collaborative coding process during the binning round, the points of view of all team members begin to affect the data analysis process. Hence, the importance of the research question as the overarching guide. Additionally, my training and experiences as a playwright, director, and dramaturg all impact my analysis process because I am thinking about how these various pieces might come together in a script and, subsequently, in a performance. As I move through the analysis process, I am thinking about the dramaturgy, or the structure, of the script. I emphasize the importance of theatrical training when using ethnodrama, as the artistic and aesthetic lenses are present throughout this analysis process. It's why I identified the theatrically compelling code and now name it as essential for analysis in ethnodrama.

As we move into the following chapters about dissemination, the importance of artistry becomes even more apparent. The selections that emerged in the analysis now have to come together as a script and then a performance.

ACTIVITIES

How Do You Like to Organize?

Open up your computer's drive and look at how you manage your files. What are the characteristics of your organization, and why do you choose to do it that way? Have a similar look at your desk, bookshelves, and/or filing cabinets. How are those areas organized, and why? Are there patterns in how you organize? If so, what are they, and how can you use those patterns to create your own organization system for a large dataset that emerges from conducting data collection for an ethnodrama?

Flat Transcript versus Scored Transcript

Choose a short excerpt of a media artifact (90 seconds to 2 minutes) from a famous speech by a politician or cultural leader. Make sure that the speech is available as an audio or video recording. As you listen to the speech, create a *flat transcript* of the excerpt. Take a short break and then return to the artifact and your flat transcript. Now, relisten to the artifact and create a *scored transcript,* noting the speaker's cadence by taking a hard return whenever the speaker pauses. You may have to listen to the artifact several times to accomplish this scoring. Review the section on transcribing for additional guidance. Once you've completed the scored transcript, examine the two versions (flat and scored) side by side. What does the scored transcript reveal about the excerpt that is different from the flat transcript? How might this information be useful in a data analysis process? In a dissemination process?

How Do You Speak?

Find a quiet space where you can record. Turn on your recording device and respond to this prompt: "Describe a memorable moment from your first day of school." Your story should be no longer than 2 minutes. Try to ensure that your story has a clear beginning and ending. Do not write out your story and read it. Respond in your own voice, as if you were answering a question someone asked you on the spot. Your response should be conversational, not practiced and rehearsed. Set aside the recording for some time (a full day is best), then come back to it. Now, using your recording as a reference, transcribe and score your story about your first day of school. Beyond notating the pauses in your speech pattern, make sure to include all verbal disfluencies (stutters and stumbles) and filler words ("like," "um," "uh," etc.). Once you have completed the scored transcript of your story, consider the following questions:

1. What did you learn about your way of speaking through the transcribing and scoring process?
2. What did you learn about how you tell a story through the transcribing and scoring process?

NOTES

1. The researcher-actors for *Of a Certain Age* included Amalia Adiv, Rai Arsa Artha, Josh Batty, Megan Conway, Sherill-Marie Henriquez, Suzy Jane Hunt, Keith Morris, and Hayley Sherwood.

2. The interviewing team for *Whatever You Are, Be a Good One* included Zeina Abdeldayem, sebastian alberdi, Jae Eun An, Taylor Beckman, Melany Bermejo, Adriana Bustamante, Averil Carr, Robyn Chao Phan, Theodora Dirrim, Davor Golub, Lauren Gorelov, Ryan Howland, Keith R. Huff, Cassidy Kaye, Daniel Kenner, Pallovi Komma, Alyssa Korman, Lindsay Kujawa Barr, Margot Levinson, Ariana Luque, Maya Masa'deh, Camila Matamoros, Lucy Medeiros, Elle Mera, Francisco Morandi Zerpa, Alexia Navarro, Martina Novakova, Michael Roberts, Carly Rubin, Joe Salvatore, Nava May Saylany, Sammie Taxman, Renee Troxler, Smrithi Prema Venkatraman, Nicole Villagomez, Yaoyi Zhang, and Zimeng Zhao

3. The collaborative coding team for *Whatever You Are, Be a Good One* included Sarah Bellantoni, Lauren Gorelov, Ryan Howland, Keith R. Huff, Joe Salvatore, and Tammie L. Swopes.

4. The acting company for *Whatever You Are, Be a Good One* included Averil Carr, Jessamyn Fitzpatrick, Topaz Gao, Noah Jackson, Devin Joyner, Kayla Matters, Michael Roberts, Daniel Teutul, Ari Weiss, and Ran Zhu.

5 Scripting

Getting Started
and Basic Scripting Conventions

Once the artist-researcher completes their data analysis and separates the larger dataset into thematic bins, they can consider how their selections might come together in an ethnodrama. This transition from dataset to script also represents a critical moment for the artist-researcher. Until this point, the steps in the research process may resemble those in more traditional qualitative research. However, as the scripting process begins, the artistic and aesthetic sensibilities of the artist-researcher must come to the forefront of their work and guide the creation of the dissemination document, the script. In Chapter 1, I wrote about the importance of theatre training for the artist-researcher, and this scripting step is where the need becomes most evident. The artist-researcher must begin to think like a playwright and director to create the most effective ethnodrama possible, conveying the research findings while simultaneously functioning as a compelling script that can lead to a dynamic ethnotheatrical performance. For these reasons, starting with this chapter, I now refer to the artist-researcher as the **ethnodramatist**. A dramatist writes plays, so the term "ethnodramatist" acknowledges the primary role that the artist-researcher takes at this point in the process: a playwright creating a script.

As the ethnodramatist enters the scripting process, they should ask themselves, "What plays have been memorable for me and why?" "What published research studies have been memorable for me and why?" Usually, when I pose these questions to students in my class, they discuss their ideas in small groups and then arrive at similar conclusions for both: The stories are clear. If the story is unclear in either case, the audience cannot follow the play's message or the research findings and thereby cannot learn from either.

This chapter outlines ways to think through the initial stages of the scripting process, starting with facing a stack of data and deciding how to begin the script. I introduce two basic scripting conventions, the monologue and the duet, which I have found helpful in arranging material to create meaning for performers and audiences. I offer examples of each of these conventions from various plays. After gaining an understanding of these conventions, the ethnodramatist can move on to Chapter 6, where I introduce more complicated scripting conventions that expand the possibilities for ethnodramatic creation.

Entering the Scripting Process

As the artist-researcher transitions to ethnodramatist, moving from the data analysis process into the scripting process, it is not uncommon to feel anxious and overwhelmed. While they may have arranged hard copies or digital "stacks" of transcripts into thematic bins, the ethnodramatist now faces the proverbial "empty page" that any playwright confronts as they begin a new project. I have faced this empty page multiple times, and the initial feeling of dread is always the same. Again, I return to the writing of American director Anne Bogart (2001) in these moments. She states:

> Every time I begin work on a new production I feel as though I am out of my league; that I know nothing and have no notion how to begin and I'm sure someone else should be doing my job, someone assured, who knows what to do, someone who is really professional. I feel unbalanced, uncomfortable and out of place. I feel like a sham. In short, I am terrified. (p. 84)

Yes, Anne, exactly. I feel terrified as I write this book, wondering if I have anything helpful to say to anyone about ethnodrama. We have to acknowledge these feelings, particularly as we begin. Bogart is a director but has spent her career creating original works in collaboration with playwrights and actors. She understands the creative process intimately and the fear that comes with the act of creation. Again, Bogart says, "We all tremble in terror before the impossibility of beginning. It is important to remember that a director's work, as with any artist, is intuitive" (p. 85). Now, read this again: "It is important to remember that any *artist's* work is intuitive." And, all together, one more time: "It is important to remember that any *ethnodramatist's* work is intuitive." Do you see what I did there? I'm using slight variations on Bogart's words to demonstrate that the ethnodramatist needs to embrace their intuition. Now, you might ask, "What will my dissertation committee or tenure review committee say when I tell them that I'll rely on my intuition as I disseminate my research findings?" Remember, in Chapter 2, I advised you to find mentors and colleagues who would understand or be open to an arts-based approach to research. However, you also have a responsibility to articulate how and why you're making choices as you move your data from thematic bins into a script, and this articulation places your training as an artist and researcher on full display. As the ethnodramatist, you must understand the implications of your choices and be able to define how the logic of those choices informs your scripting process. With these thoughts in mind, embrace the terror of beginning and make some choices. To help get over that initial fear you might feel, keep these points in mind:

• **Your ethnodramatist intuition comes from your knowledge of your process up to this point and of the dataset.** You know the steps you've taken to get here. Feel confident in that. You are also the expert on this dataset, so embrace your expertise and don't shy away from it. Trust that your knowledge and intuition will guide you.

• **The beginning is the beginning of Draft 1. There will be more drafts.** None of the choices you make in this first draft are final. Nothing is set in stone. Actors usually perform Draft 9 or 10 of a script I create. Plays don't just pop out of a playwright's head onto the page in a finished form. If only it were that easy. Scripting is an iterative process over many drafts, just like any other genre of writing.

• **You will make new discoveries by working with the data in the scripting process.** Be ready to have your mind changed. It happens. Stay open, and your research findings will become stronger and more precise as a result.

• **Don't be afraid to return to the dataset.** You may need to relisten to an interview or several interviews because a new connection or insight arrives. Don't panic. Go back in, listen with fresh ears, and see what emerges.

• **Be in conversation and in collaboration with others as you script.** As mentioned in Chapter 4, a dramaturg, thought partner, or critical friend can be invaluable as you think through how to piece your discoveries together for an audience. Find someone you trust and share ideas with them. It also helps if they're open to ethnodrama or other ABR and understand how to read a play. You may be surprised how difficult reading a play can be for some people.

• **Keep this all in perspective.** In the very first interview-based play I ever made and performed with my performance partner Kate Nugent, I had a lot of anxiety. I worried about the script, as it was my first public-facing project, and it had been a few years since I performed. We were premiering the work in front of many friends and colleagues, and while, on the one hand, that was comforting, on the other hand, it raised the stakes. During our rehearsal process, I was struggling with a lot of self-doubt, and our stage manager, Kaz Reed, turned and looked at me and said, "Joey, it's just a skit in a skithouse." I remember we spent quite a few minutes laughing at the term "skithouse"; the laughter, coupled with the reality of what Kaz was saying, calmed me down. Kaz has since passed away, but she's never far from my mind when I'm making a new work. I've used the turn of phrase "skit in a skithouse" so many times at some of the most high-pressured moments in my career as an artist and academic. It lowers the temperature every time and reminds me that no matter how "important" I think what I'm doing is, I'm not curing cancer or solving a major world conflict. I'm making a play. And while that play may be important and potentially impactful, it's still just a skit in a skithouse. Perspective. Thank you, Kaz.

In addition to keeping those calming points in mind, answering some basic questions as you enter a scripting process can help you move beyond your initial fear and resistance. Answering these questions can lay a solid foundation for the process that's about to begin.

Questions to consider when entering an ethnodrama scripting process:

• What answers do you have for your research question as a result of the coding and analysis process?

• How do those answers represent multiple perspectives from your dataset?

• How many participants' voices do your thematic bins contain?

• Do you want to make a definitive statement that answers your research question?

• Do you want to offer multiple perspectives on your research question?

- How will these participants' voices and their multiple perspectives come together to offer answers to your research question?
- How are you thinking about the structure of your play?
  - Will it have multiple scenes?
  - Will the play be arranged chronologically or thematically?
- Will the play be performed by one actor or multiple actors?
- Will each actor perform one character or multiple characters, which means that each actor performs various roles?
- Will you include the interviewer's presence through an actor embodying them on stage or through some other mechanism by which the audience hears/sees the interview prompts? Is the interviewer's presence necessary, or are the interview prompts even essential for the audience to hear/see?

Your scripting process will ultimately yield the answers to these questions, but they are essential to consider as you begin.

Also note that, as I enter the scripting process, I intentionally shift my language to refer to any participant who becomes part of an ethnodramatic script as a *character* in that script. While "character" might imply a fictional representation, these testimonies are not fictional. Rather, actors perform them in a fictional construct. Hence, the shift to the term "character." This shift does not change how I practice care in re-presenting these testimonies, but it acknowledges that the process has now expanded more deeply into a creative, arts-based exploration and dissemination of the data.

It may seem early in the process to consider how many characters' voices to include in the script and how many actors will perform those characters, but I recommend making preliminary decisions and then remaining open to changes as the scripting process unfolds. These initial choices help create guidelines for working with your dataset. Otherwise, it can feel overwhelming. It may also seem odd or out of order to think about casting actors before finishing a script; however, the number of characters' voices included in the ethnodrama and how many actors will perform those voices can significantly impact a script's structure. For example, when Anna Deavere Smith performs one of her solo works, she portrays one person at a time in a series of monologues. She moves fluidly from one person to the next and rarely, if ever, portrays two people simultaneously, as if they were conversing with one another. Even for an actress as virtuosic with this form as Smith, switching back and forth between people in dialogue is very difficult to achieve, not to mention challenging for an audience to follow.

In developing a script for an ethnodrama performed by an ensemble of actors, as with *Of a Certain Age* (Salvatore, 2018), I can decide that I want eight actors to portray two characters each, for a total of 16 voices in the play. In this case, I want the audience to experience the versatility and virtuosity of the actors as they each play multiple characters. Actors playing multiple characters also affect how the audience experiences data dissemination. When actors play more than one character in a performance, a director can make this choice evident to an audience through costuming and how the actors perform. These choices can help maintain an audience's critical engagement with the material rather than having only an emotional response, a vital goal of 20th-century German playwright and director Bertolt Brecht (Brecht, as translated by Willett, 1992), and one that informs all of my work in ethnodrama. I discuss the performance theory supporting these choices when I share more about ethnotheatrical production in Chapter 7. Most importantly, during the scripting process, these choices dictate elements of the script's structure and offer more options to arrange the various selections. I can have multiple actors on stage, each playing a different character, which allows me to construct and arrange "conversations" between characters about particular topics even though I interviewed each of them separately.

The ethnodramatist should also consider whether to use **composite characters** in their scripting process. When choosing participants to include in an ethnodrama, some ethnodramatists may find it necessary to create composite characters by combining related excerpts of interviews conducted with separate individuals to form one fictional character. Drama therapist Darci Burch (2019) created an original ethnodrama called *The Space Between Us All: Playing with Dissociation* that examined the experience of dissociation among drama therapists in their work. She conducted 20 interviews with clinical colleagues, primarily from in and around New York City. During her scripting process, Burch realized that even using pseudonyms as identifiers would not entirely protect the identities of the interview participants who wished to remain anonymous. To address this challenge, she reexamined her coding process, looking for sections of interview transcripts from her participants that made similar points about a particular topic. She then combined sections from various participants to create a single voice on a topic, and that composite voice became a character in her script. Sometimes, an individual participant's responses might become part of more than one composite character. Burch's choices to create composite characters in these ways added the additional necessary layer of anonymity for her interview participants, and "in this way, one character was not identifiable as a single interviewee and one individual was not necessarily connected to one particular character" (p. 33). Given that the audience for Burch's piece was primarily local drama therapists and that the field is relatively small, she made a solid ethical choice that protected the privacy of her participants and informed the structure and dramaturgy of her ethnodrama (Salvatore, 2025).

Similarly, Ryan Howland (2022) used composite characters in his video project *Yet through such connection . . .* , an ethnodrama examining how theatre educators in rural Vermont might become more intentional with anti-racist and inclusive practices in their drama classrooms. Following his data collection process, Howland recognized an ethical obligation to protect the participants' identities in his dataset, given their existing personal and professional overlaps. Using Burch's work as inspiration, Howland created four fictional composite characters: The Teacher, The Artist, The Student in the Locker Room, and The Unfortunately Cast Student (p. 88). He asked each actor to create "an easily identifiable but unique character profile" (Burch, 2019, p. 33) for the composite character they were performing. Howland provided the actors with the field notes he had gathered during each interview and "encouraged them to [identify] gestures, costume possibilities, and ideas for vocal qualities to bring into the performance" (p. 89). He then used those choices to coach each actor into a performance of the composite character. These choices, combined with the compositing during the scripting process, allowed for additional layers of ethical care for the participants.

While composite characters offer excellent options for helping to protect participants' anonymity, I encourage ethnodramatists to proceed with caution when using this technique. Given the ongoing discussion of the importance of ethics and care woven throughout this book, it is essential to note how Burch and Howland demonstrated strong ethical care with their choices to create composite characters, both for participants and audiences. They thought carefully about their options and emphasized the need for compositing based on the size and familiarity of the communities they worked with on their respective projects. They also ensured that their audiences understood that the characters portrayed in the performance were fictional composites of the participants they had interviewed. An audience should have an awareness and understanding of what they are experiencing in the performance of an ethnodrama, and using composite characters amplifies that need. As Saldaña (2011a) indicates, a composite character is a work of fiction, compared to an ethnodramatist presenting a participant's response as delivered during the moment of the interview.

I also recommend alerting interview participants that their shared responses could be combined with other participants' responses to create a fictional composite character. Sometimes, that possibility is difficult to anticipate, so there are two options. The first option is to outline the possibility of composite characters during the consenting process and within the interview protocol. Then, the participant is aware of the potential for that choice from the start of the process and can decide whether to continue their participation. The second option utilizes a member-checking process in which the artist-researcher reconnects with the interview participant, alerts them that they selected sections of their interview for inclusion in the play, explains the composite character creation process, and asks the participant for permission to use their interview this way. Again, this offers the participant the option to agree to the composite character choice or to request that their interview excerpts not be used this way.

As a reminder from Chapter 3, I conduct a form of member checking as the interview protocol concludes. Some qualitative researchers engage in member checking throughout the scripting process to ensure that interview participants feel comfortable with the selections chosen for inclusion in the dissemination process. Because I code, analyze, script, and disseminate using verbatim performance, I commit to preserving the authenticity and integrity of the verbatim delivery of participants at the moment of their interviews. Allowing for changes after the fact dilutes that authenticity and integrity. When gaining consent of participants for a project, I alert them that an actor will perform them verbatim and offer a link to a video example of what a verbatim performance looks and sounds like. After providing all that information, I leave it to the participant's discretion to decide whether to proceed. This approach is my protocol for member checking in ethnodrama; others will have alternative approaches. I encourage artist-researchers to use member checking however they see fit and at various points in a process if they choose.

Finally, as the scripting process begins, it is important to think about a target running time. Based on my experiences as an audience member and creator, an ethnodrama should be between 45 and 90 minutes long and performed without an intermission. This self-imposed time limit affects the number of interview selections and characters I can include in the script. I also usually prefer that each character appear in the script more than once, so I typically limit myself to 12 to 18 characters in an ethnodrama (Salvatore, 2020b, 2025). Hearing from a character more than once helps to create a more complex portrait of the character rather than simply having a smattering of singular moments from many different voices. That said, I have also had the experience in which a participant made one crucial point that bears no connection to anything else that anyone has said, but they made it in such a unique or impactful way that I chose to include their voice as a character only once. The range of 12 to 18 characters, each appearing more than once with two 2- to 3-minute excerpts, has tended to produce an ethnodrama that runs approximately 90 minutes without an intermission. Ethnodramas that run longer tend to lose their effectiveness and impact. Remember that the ethnodrama in performance must reveal the research findings while maintaining the audience's attention. If you lose the audience, they lose your findings.

Productions of plays often unfold in two halves and include an intermission. The audience and the performers take a short break after the first half of a play, usually as the storyline arrives at a critical moment for one or more characters. After the short break, the audience returns to learn how the play ends. This more traditional way of thinking about narrative and plot structure focused on a protagonist and their journey through a set of experiences sets up a more passive way for the audience to consume the story and messages of a play. I avoid having an intermission in an ethnodrama because the form benefits from a tight presentation that unfolds in one sitting and keeps the audience focused on constructing their meaning via the presentation of data.

Students often ask me how to establish a narrative in ethnodrama when it features multiple voices and perspectives. How can an audience understand the play if it does not follow a typical narrative structure? In performance, the ethnodrama must convey research findings to an audience in an aesthetically pleasing way (Ackroyd & O'Toole, 2010; Saldaña, 2011a), but a traditional narrative structure is not the only way to accomplish this. Rather than having the audience follow the journey of one protagonist, I want the audience to actively follow their own journey with the data. I advocate for a thematic organization and progression of ideas, as that has the potential to create both an analytic and aesthetic experience for the audience. I structure an ethnodrama as a series of scenes, each addressing one of the central findings that emerged in the data analysis process. The thematic bins provide the structure for those scenes. Then, I order the scenes so the audience can experience the data and draw their own conclusions.

I think of the script's performance as a meditation on a set of perspectives, themes, and ideas that emerged through the data collection and analysis process. Those various perspectives float in and out of the audience's consciousness as the ethnodrama unfolds in performance. Based on their own perspectives and experiences, each audience member acknowledges and notices different moments as they float in and out. So rather than construct a fictional character with experiences that lead them to some self-revelation that the audience witnesses on stage, I arrange a set of characters' perspectives and experiences into a collage of ideas. The audience's experience is active rather than passive because they are responsible for making meaning. Yes, I have made choices about what to include and arranged those choices into an experience. However, just as a visual collage often asks the viewer to make meaning of its layers, ethnodrama can instigate the same process. It can offer findings to an audience while simultaneously asking them to deepen and personalize the findings based on their point of view and analysis of what the ethnodrama presents to them. If the ethnodrama tells the audience what to think, the experience becomes more pedestrian and ultimately a boring time in the theatre. The learning from the ethnodrama lives at the intersection of the characters' experiences with the audience's experiences as they analyze and interpret via the presentation of the data.

Beginning the Script

With the interview selections sorted into thematic bins, preliminary decisions made about the number of characters to include and actors to perform, and a goal set for running time, the ethnodramatist can begin to arrange interview selections into a script. The beginning of an ethnodrama serves the dual purpose of engaging an audience in its subject matter and helping them understand that they are experiencing a play based on collected and analyzed data. As the ethnodramatist prepares to script the opening of an ethnodrama, they can consider the following questions:

- Will the topic of the ethnodrama be defined in some way?
- Will the overarching research question be referenced in some way?
- How will the beginning of this play help the audience understand what they are about to experience? What are the rules of engagement?

Since an ethnodrama typically follows a unique structure compared to a traditional play, I establish **rules of engagement** early on in the script to prepare audiences to engage with the research findings as critical thinkers rather than cathartic responders. These rules of engagement can indicate how I created the play. *Of a Certain Age* opened with a soundscape featuring the voices of the team of researcher-actors who had conducted the interviews, speaking parts of the interview protocol. Sound designer Darren Whorton used the audio recordings of the interviews to pull snippets of the protocol from each interviewer and then wove them together to demonstrate how a participant would have experienced the beginning of the interviewing process. We did not include the voices of the interview participants, as that request had not been part of the consenting process. This opening prerecorded soundscape provided the audience with information about how we conducted the interviews and reminded them that the play was created from the words of real people.

Some might argue that details about the creative process belong in a program note rather than in the performance itself. While I also include a program note whenever possible, there is an ethical responsibility to incorporate this information into the performance. Only some people read a program note carefully, if at all; therefore, I recommend finding creative ways to build the rules of engagement into the play itself. In a more traditional, narrative-driven play, we might refer to these details as **exposition**, information about events that happened before the action of a play's story begins, that helps the audience to better understand the characters' current state of affairs in a play. In the case of an ethnodrama, the rules of engagement serve a similar purpose as exposition.

Depending on the topic, research question, and intended audience, sharing more about the topic and the research question as an ethnodrama begins can help bring an audience together "on the same page" as the performance unfolds. In the same way that a dissertation might include a section in its introduction that defines terms that will appear throughout the document, the opening of an ethnodrama can provide a similar overview of terminology. In the first section of *Towards the Fear* (Salvatore, 2014), an ethnodrama examining the experiences of adults with bullying, social combat, and aggression, I used a series of participants' responses to a prompt asking them to define "social combat" as a way to introduce that term. That collection of voices wrestling to define the term led to two sociologists offering their academic definitions. Those scripting choices allowed for an explicit introduction of the topic, while also nodding toward an overarching research process. The use of multiple voices also demonstrated that different participants can define a term in various ways, including the academics who use it in their research.

I also use a scripting convention that helps an audience know who speaks at any given time, mainly since actors typically play multiple characters in my ethnodramas. The first time a character appears in the play, the actor playing the character begins their particular section and then pauses, usually about 5 to 10 lines into their speech, and another actor onstage announces the identifier for the character that the participant selected for themselves during the interview process. I usually identify the moments for these announcements in the speeches during the scripting process, but they often adjust slightly through the rehearsal process. This announcement happens each time a new character appears for the first time. If that character returns later in the script, they are not reintroduced: I rely on the actor's ability to accurately portray the character and the audience's ability to invest in that portrayal to know who is speaking. Other conventions include projections or voiceovers to identify and announce the presented character. Any of these choices can be effective, but the ethnodramatist should make a specific choice, introduce it as a convention from the beginning, and use it consistently throughout the script and performance (Salvatore, 2020b).

I also recommend finding ways to acknowledge the interview process throughout the script, so that the audience understands from listening to the spoken text that the characters are responding to prompts introduced by an interviewer. As early as possible in an ethnodrama, I include a section of an interview in which a character references something about the interview process, be it about an interview prompt or the interviewer's presence. Again, using an example from *Towards the Fear*, the spoken text of the play begins with a character identified as Bartlett, a 46-year-old man, saying:

BARTLETT
Huh
(deep breath)
How does aggression manifest itself in my day-to-day life? That's a- wow, that's a- you're
    asking some very good questions. You guys have done a good job with this *(laughs)*.

Bartlett restates the interview prompt "How does aggression manifest itself in your day-to-day life?" which illustrates details about the data collection process. He also acknowledges the presence of the interviewer when he says, " . . . you're asking some very good questions." By opening the ethnodrama with this portion of Bartlett's response, I provide the audience with insight into the research process and remind them that this play is not about fictional characters. This excerpt also establishes that the actors will perform the interview excerpts verbatim throughout the performance. Bartlett interrupts, repeats himself, and appears tongue-tied in trying to formulate an answer to the question, later saying he "wasn't quite prepared for these [questions]." I include moments like this at the beginning of the script and then incorporate them in later moments as a subtle reminder for audiences that they are experiencing the spoken words of real people responding to interview prompts. In the same way that Shakespeare generally repeats any detail important to the action of a play at least three times, I repeat this convention of reminding the audience that they are experiencing research dissemination in the form of a play (Salvatore, 2025).

Another way to demonstrate the interviewing process is to share the interview prompts in the script to trigger the characters' responses. I use this convention less often in ethnodrama, as I do not code an interview for responses to specific prompts, nor do I tend to use the prompts to organize the script. Instead, responses from various prompts could work their way into a thematic bin, so I find the prompts less useful as an organizing principle. However, in *Making Gay History: Before Stonewall* (Salvatore, 2020a), I did include Eric Marcus's voice as the interviewer throughout, mainly because he asked follow-up questions, so it became difficult to remove his comments while still maintaining the rhythm and cadence of the original conversation. Each ensemble member embodied and vocalized Marcus's questions or interjections throughout the performance. Below is an example from the ethnodrama featuring Marcus's interview with the pseudonymous "Paul Phillips," an attorney hired to work in the Colorado state attorney general's office in the 1960s. I assigned Marcus's comments to Actor #10.

PAUL PHILLIPS
I thought one time I just didn't want to go through life this way and uh
I didn't know any other way to keep from it.
And I was just completely
uh
down and out so to speak.
I gave up
practically.
Finally my dad come to me one day and told me what uh
he had heard.
Whether he heard it or how he found it out but somebody musta told him.

ACTOR #10
What did your dad hear?

PAUL PHILLIPS
He didn't tell me.
He
told me things-
he told me that he had heard
that I was not natural
sexually.
He said, "We'll go up to uh-
to Mayo Clinic
get your examinations and see if we can find out
what causes it
what to do about it."
So he puts M- Mother and I in the car and we go up to uhm
Minnesota.
That was back in the days

when you couldn't get a place to stay
couldn't get a place to eat.

ACTOR #10
Because you're Black.

PAUL PHILLIPS
Cause you're Blacks.

ACTOR #10
What did you do?

PAUL PHILLIPS
Buy crackers and bologna i-
in the store and take 'em out and eat 'em.
Stuff like that.

ACTOR #10
Where did you sleep?

PAUL PHILLIPS
Got a tent.
We got one of these uh
10 by 12
tents
and we stayed in the tent at night.
Take all of that and put it together
it's awfully hard on anybody.
I don't care if he's white or black or green or yellow.

ACTOR #10
Right.

PAUL PHILLIPS
That kind of pressure is terrific.

ACTOR #10
How old were you then?

PAUL PHILLIPS
I was still quite young.

ACTOR #10
Were you still in high school?

PAUL PHILLIPS
Yes, I think I was still in high school.

ACTOR #10
You must have been terrified.

PAUL PHILLIPS
I was terrified.
Now they had me in the hospital for-
in and out for several days.

ACTOR #10
Did they ask you questions?

PAUL PHILLIPS
Oh yes.
All kinds of questions.
They determined that I was homosexual and that there was nothing they could do about it.
And uhm
final report from Mayo's was that uhm
according to their state laws that I should be-
they should report me and have me incarcerated.

ACTOR #10
Incarcerated?

PAUL PHILLIPS
Yah.

ACTOR #10
For what?

PAUL PHILLIPS
Because I was different.

ACTOR #10
Put in jail?

PAUL PHILLIPS
In jail.
They said that since I was a uh
a- a- client of theirs
they would
not do that.
So we went back home and reported to Dad.
I might say this, that I was an-
an adopted child.
And I often used to wonder as a kid,
"What will he do when he finds it out, see?
Will he put me out or kick me out or will he

accept me?"
My dad was very understanding.
I say understanding I don't think he actually understood but he was willing to accept
I should say.
So he finally told me he says, "Well,
since they don't know what to do about it
find you a friend that you can trust
and bring him home."
He says, "I don't wantcha playin' around on the streets
or out on the country roads 'cause you never know who's gonna step up behind you y'know
        step up on you.
Bring him home.
What you do in your room is your business."
Because he didn't want me out on the street.
That helped me a lot.
At least I was loved by my father.
And 'course Mother she just
idolized me regardless.
They were renar- remarkable people as I look back I didn't think so at the time.

Typically, if an interviewer interjects once in a chosen excerpt, I replace the interjection with "[interviewer speaks]" as a direction to the actor, so that they know to perform the act of listening to whatever comment or question the interviewer offered and then continue with the character's response. In the case with "Paul Phillips" and other cases throughout Marcus's dataset, the interjections were numerous enough to necessitate including them. Some ethnodramas incorporate interview prompts as projections and voiceovers, which can serve as practical guides to help bolster an audience's understanding.

An ethnodramatist should also consider the **world of the play**, the context within which a play and its performance occur. The world of the play can reflect the historical, social, and cultural contexts of the play and its characters, and it can also refer to how the characters who inhabit the play interact with each other and with the audience. It is essential to determine whether the world of the play is literal or metaphorical, actual or fictional, because that is where the play's action takes place. The ethnodramatist should not leave those decisions to chance but should make solid choices and include written directions and descriptions in their script. Some might think that staging a play falls solely to the director, but the ethnodramatist, as the playwright and principal investigator, has the ability and obligation to establish parameters for the world of the play and performance dissemination in the scripting process. Playwrights use **stage directions** throughout a traditional play script to notate how they imagine the play's setting and how its action might unfold. Some stage directions are quite specific, while others can be more general. Playwrights also have to allow for flexibility with a play's staging, but they cannot abdicate artistic responsibility to someone else. In published plays, stage directions often describe the world of the play and how the action unfolded in its first production, reflecting staging and design choices made by the original director, designers, and actors.

Because I also direct plays, I imagine how a production will unfold as I create a script. If I have a strong image from the start, I usually begin an ethnodrama with draft stage directions that describe my initial image of the world of the play. Then, I revisit those stage directions throughout the scripting process to clarify how the play functions as the script evolves. Stage directions appear throughout the script, often cueing the actors and the director about moving the characters around the stage in performance. The stage directions also help designers understand my vision of how the play would look and sound in performance. Again, designers can make these choices, but as the ethnodramatist and principal investigator, I should offer input around disseminating these findings.

Given that I created *Making Gay History: Before Stonewall* from materials in an oral history archive, I knew I wanted to channel the look and feel of a physical archive space as part of the performance. I began conversations with a longtime collaborator, scenographer Troy Hourie, before starting the scripting process, and he agreed with this idea. He shared images of library reading rooms, bookshelves, and archive boxes that would inspire the final design for the play's premiere production. Out of his visual research, our conversations, and the rehearsal and production process, these stage directions now appear at the top of the script:

> *The rare books and manuscripts room of a large library. Think: New York Public Library—Stephen A. Schwarzman Building as an example. The space includes two large tables, one high counter, and a number of chairs and stools. All furniture can be moved and reconfigured into different positions. There are three rolling cabinets that hold archive boxes containing files, clippings, and objects related to each of the people investigated and performed in the play. Hovering above the playing space upstage is a large set of shelves spanning the width of the stage and extending down to the floor on one side. The shelves are also full of archive boxes and serve as a projection surface throughout the performance, providing the audience with images and information that help to identify each of the people performed by the actors.*
>
> *House lights go to half. The ensemble enters the playing space and faces the audience. One actor carries an archive box. They place the box on a table, open it, and begin to unpack its contents: a tape recorder, a cassette tape, Eric Marcus's books (*Making History *and* Making Gay History*), and a master list of what's contained in the full archive. The rest of the ensemble and audience watch this unpacking. The actor completes the unpacking and holds a cassette tape in their hand. They turn to face the audience.*

Notice that these opening stage directions define several physical objects and reference how lighting changes at the beginning of the play. The stage directions also offer some of the actors' initial physical activities. These directions represent what happened in the premiere production at NYU, but a subsequent performance of the play at Deerfield High School in Deerfield, Illinois, under the direction of Britnee Kenyon and designed by students, used these exact opening stage directions to create the physical world of their production.

While this image of an archive was vital for me as I began the scripting process, I have had other projects in which I arranged the interview excerpts first, and then the idea for the world of the play emerged. Regardless of the order, the articulation of the world of the play contributes to the rules of engagement. By establishing rules like the ones discussed so far, even if they shift and change, the ethnodramatist has established a solid foundation to begin arranging the interview excerpts from thematic bins into a script.

Basic Scripting Conventions: Monologues and Duets

Scripting conventions refer to the various ways an ethnodramatist can arrange interview excerpts in a script. Saldaña (2011a) splits these scripting conventions into two types of constructions. He defines a monologue as "an extended, one-person, dramatic narrative" (p. 63), and then uses "ethnodramatic dialogue" (p. 99) to name a set of constructions in which two or more characters are speaking on a particular topic. I further differentiate ethnodramatic dialogues using the musical terms *duet, trio, quartet, montage,* and *choral piece*. These terms more accurately represent what happens structurally in the ethnodrama and ethnotheatrical performance (Salvatore, 2020b, 2025). The musical terminology also acknowledges the musicality (rhythm, pitch, tempo) that lives naturally in how we speak. In ethnodramatic scripts, these multicharacter moments may emulate the actual circumstances of an interview that included more than one character, or the moment can be constructed by placing two or more characters in conversation, even though they were interviewed separately (Saldaña, 2011a).

The ethnodramatist must intentionally arrange the interview excerpts using these scripting conventions to support the script's proposed dramaturgical structure and create an effective ethnodrama. The dramaturgical structure emerges following the preliminary thought and planning discussed earlier. The ethnodramatist can work to keep the audience's attention by switching back and forth between multiple scripting conventions. They can make these choices based on what convention best fits the finding they want to present and where the finding appears in the overall script and performance. Different scripting conventions work for different types of findings and even for different moments within the dissemination process, in this case, the performance. The remainder of this chapter focuses on the monologue and duet scripting conventions, and Chapter 6 explores trios, quartets, montages, and choral pieces. The following sections offer descriptions of the monologue and duet scripting conventions, how to use these conventions effectively in the scripting–performance–dissemination process, and examples of both conventions as verbatim scored transcripts from ethnodramas I have created.

Monologue

As mentioned earlier, a **monologue** is a continuous section of an interview transcript from one character performed by one actor. The monologue can effectively introduce a particular concept or idea central to the ethnodrama, such as the definition of a term or a description of an incident. I often begin an ethnodrama with a series of two or three monologues to introduce the audience to the main ideas of the research findings and the various perspectives they might encounter. If one of those early introductory monologues also features elements like those highlighted in the earlier excerpt from Bartlett, the monologue can also be a great way to introduce one or more rules of engagement (Salvatore, 2020b, 2025). Beginning an ethnodrama with the monologue convention also helps to introduce the audience to the aesthetics of the form, as I operate from the assumption that most audiences have little experience with ethnodrama in performance.

The monologue convention also frequently depicts a participant's story that provides insights about the overarching research question grounded in personal lived experience. When selecting interview excerpts as monologues, I often look for participants' stories that include strong visual imagery and detailed descriptions of events, people, places, or things. In much the same way that a soliloquy from a play by Shakespeare includes these details, an ethnodramatic monologue also benefits from these elements.

The following monologue comes from *Whatever You Are, Be A Good One* (Salvatore & Huff, 2022), the VPL project exploring political polarization in the United States. I include the title of the interview excerpt as an example of an *in vivo* code and the time-stamp to show the length of the excerpt when delivered by the speaker during the interview. Notice that the duration of the monologue is about 2½ minutes.

Title: "People learn from that"
Timestamp: 44:27–46:59

RONALD CRUTCHER
Uh a- and then I- I'll share with you another experience I had where I did use my father's- I did
    r- remember my father's
um lesson
and that was
when I was in Texas.
(clears throat)
I was head of the
School of Music at the University of Texas.
I had gone to meet with a gentleman
to um ask him for some money for a scholarship for violin.
He was head of a foundation
but he was al- he was an oil- he was uh CEO of an oil company.
He shook my hand
and literally as I was lowering myself to my seat he looked at me and he said, "I had no idea you
    were Black."
And ini- my initial response was anger and I remember what my father- I thought, "This is-
Take a deep breath"
and rather than leaving or getting angry I just listened
and then the next sentence he said to me,
"Perhaps you can help me:
my wife and I have been going to the Aspen Music Festival for 30 years
and we rarely see any Black violinists.
Why is that?"
Great opportunity for me
(laughs) right?
And I use that- I use that-
that story as a cautionary tale with my mentees
because of course they're horrified when I tell them the story.
You know, like- "And you didn't get up and walk away" you know?
So we have a conversation, but it- it- it is-
it is-
and I- I- I use it as a cautionary tale
because I also you know I find in our society today
that young people are much

less willing to be forgiving when people make mistakes.
And-
and that's a problem if you're trying to
develop
relationships or have a conversation across
differences
because young people are going to make mistakes
and so you have to be- you have to be more forgiving more humble.
You know, okay if someone does it five or six times then you don't have to be humble you need
    to call it out, right?
But if it's one or two times you know you have to be
willing to push back
or I'll- or I'll say you know
just question the person. "Do you realize what you just said?
Let me- let me- let me parrot for you what- what you just said to me
and then explain to you why that's offensive to me."
People learn from that.

    Ronald Crutcher's monologue features the story of a specific moment that he recounts to the interviewer. Then, he goes on to illuminate how this particular story answered the central research question for the project: What are the causes of the extreme political polarization in the United States? Crutcher states that he has shared this story many times before, but the moments of disfluency notated by the scoring demonstrate that he is also constructing meaning and connection in the moment as he shares the story aloud within the context of this particular project. His response also connects to the project's second research question: What can we do to address political polarization over the next 5 years? While there was no interview prompt specifically posing that question, many participants, like Crutcher, responded to other prompts and then pointed either implicitly or explicitly to how we might address the problem of political polarization.

    A second example of a monologue comes from *Of a Certain Age*, in which a character named Marilyn recounts her experiences with microphones and rehearsal studios at various points during her career. As you read through the piece, notice how the interviewer's presence emerges both in the transcript and in Marilyn's responses.

Title: "That somehow made it wonderful"
Timestamp: 32:07–35:18

MARILYN
First of all- *Ball-*
what I-
what I really loved
when I was- was- was- was
auditioning
was that you always auditioned in a theatre.
Now they don't do that anymore
and that-
and it was- it was funny

because when I auditioned for *Ballroom*
'cause I was like 70-
I was 70
I hadda audition in a studio
and I felt very uncomfortable
but now
these kids
are used to it.
It was wonderful to audition in a Broadway theatre.

[Interviewer speaks]

Yes
and also
that's the other thing.
(she laughs to herself at the thought)
We didn't have any mics.
The mics were down here. *(points down, as if to the lip of the stage)*
So when I did *Ballroom* and I get mic-ed-
this has been seven years
I'm 77- I was 70-
I was 70 when I did it
it was the first time I was mic-ed
and everyone thought I was cuckoo.
I had never
been
mic-ed.
So it was like this thing here *(points to her face)*
and behind
uh-huh.
Even in *King of Hearts*-
now that was in 70 . . . 8 or so-
the mics were on the floor.
There were no mics.
So that-
it's like you don't have to project now.
You never-
you had to project.
If you're auditioning on a Broadway stage
and no mics-
no mics.
There's the mics down here-

[Interviewer speaks]

Yeah, you've got mics down here.
Of course
Ethel Merman

didn't need a mic!
You know?
So that
and the uh
studios
now everyone has to have a big studios
and they're-
and they're- they're air conditioned.
We had like a big fan
you know I mean
so the conditions are so much-
the kids are so comfortable now
and they complain that it's not-
So what else did you ask about that question 'cause I don't think I really fully fully

[Interviewer speaks]

Well, that's been surprising to me!
That they want
all this
wonderful studios
and this-
and the audition
and- and the dressing rooms
and they "Oh!"
Sometimes they-
a dance studio when I took a class
you had to get a key from the woman that was there and you had to go up the hill
and get the-
and go up to the bathroom
and if someone's already got the key
you're knocking on the door
to go to the bathroom
and you got a class that's going on
you're almost late for the class
I mean
it's all those-
But you know what?
That
somehow
made it
wonderful
you know what I mean?
Those things that you hadda-
(*In a worried voice*) "Oh God, I'm gonna be late for class if the girl's got the key in the
    bathroom."
Where now it's like everything is just there

you know?
It made it- it made it really kind of-
I don't know.
And the studios weren't great.
The studios weren't great
'cause that's like the old-
I don't know.
It's just-
now everything's very sterile
you know?

Marilyn's response follows the interviewer's prompt, "What is surprising to you about growing older as a performing artist?" There are two moments where the interviewer makes some kind of comment that indicates they are following Marilyn's response. In a third moment, Marilyn asks for clarification about the original interview prompt. When the interviewer replies, Marilyn responds, "Well, that's been surprising to me!" As a reminder, the research question for this project was "What are the experiences of performing arts professionals over the age of 65?" Several participants spoke about the earlier stages of their careers, so those earlier recollections became a thematic bin and one of the early scenes in the ethnodrama. Following three monologues and two duets that addressed this theme, I ended the scene with Marilyn's monologue. Marilyn's descriptions of auditioning in a studio versus a Broadway theatre, her experience being mic-ed for the first time so late in her career, and her nostalgia for rehearsal studios as they used to be, provide moments of humor and also vivid memories that help the audience to understand the stakes of aging as a performer. Marilyn's monologue served as a bridge from these early career moments into the next scene of the ethnodrama, which focused more on the challenges performers faced as they grew older.

Both monologue examples fall right around the 2- to 3-minute length I have suggested as optimal when coding for excerpts. They emulate the duration of a typical monologue in a more traditional play, and each example features a clear narrative arc. Occasionally, I encounter a longer monologue from a character that is very important to include. I spoke before about my preference for characters to appear more than once in an ethnodrama, but in the case of an extended monologue that contributes to the research findings in a unique way, I include the piece and allow the character to appear only once. In those cases, I refer to the monologue as an **aria**, again nodding to the musical terminology used in opera to describe a piece sung by a solo voice. I think of a musical aria as having an essential role in an opera's story and requiring a particular virtuosity to execute it. Similarly, an aria in an ethnodrama tends to have the same qualities and characteristics.

Duet

In a **duet** scripting convention, two related interview excerpts from two characters come together in a conversation that illuminates a particular topic or idea from different perspectives and drives home a point revealed during the data analysis. Two actors play these characters whose perspectives may agree or disagree around a particular topic. The characters may agree but offer different insights to support a research finding, or they may disagree, and their diverging viewpoints can demonstrate the complexity of multiple perspectives. Typically, the two characters featured in a duet were interviewed separately, but when the excerpts join together, the ensuing convention gives the appearance of a conversation, with both characters presented onstage simultaneously. As their "conversation" begins in the performance, it might give the impression that someone interviewed the two characters together. As the section progresses, it becomes clear that the characters were interviewed separately. There are also times when a duet comes together between two characters, and it seems they are speaking together, potentially even responding to each other. In this case, a director might instruct the actors to acknowledge each other as if they were interviewed together (Salvatore, 2020b, 2025).

All multicharacter scripting conventions rely on the ethnodramatist's ability to emulate a conversational quality between the characters' voices in the dialogue, which I refer to as **bounce**. In ethnodramatic dialogues, keeping the dialogue flowing can be challenging. A single character speaking for too long can slow the progression of the ethnodrama and, in turn, the dissemination of the data analysis, which increases the danger that an audience will lose its grasp of the research findings. Effective bounce relies on finding a rhythm that allows the dialogue's tempo to flow naturally and maintain the audience's attention. To create bounce in ethnodramatic dialogues, I break up the excerpts from each character into smaller chunks, so that the energy of the constructed conversation shifts frequently from character to character. The topic of conversation bounces back and forth between characters, creating the illusion that they are in a robust discussion about a given topic. They sometimes seemingly agree or disagree with one another, even though they were never in the same room together for their interviews. This energized approach to data presentation emulates the dialogue between characters in a more traditional play while also maintaining the energy of the performance and focusing the audience's attention on the research findings (Salvatore, 2020b, 2025).

Given that I work with interview excerpts that are 2 to 3 minutes in length, I initially look for one or two places to break up each piece. Sometimes, more moments exist, which might allow for even more bounce. That said, I work for a balance. If I break up an interview excerpt into too many pieces, it may lose meaning because of multiple interruptions to a character's thought process. When breaking up an excerpt for bounce, I consider the following possibilities:

• **A character breaks naturally as part of their sharing logic.** If the interview excerpt is a story about an experience, chances are there is a natural halfway point, a climax moment, or a pause to remember a detail. If a character shares their opinion or belief about something, there will likely be natural breaks for thought, contemplation, correction, or clarification. These examples represent possible moments where a character could pause, and another could enter with a section of their excerpt. Then, they can alternate back and forth until they come to the end of their excerpts.

• **An interviewer's voice interrupts the character's response for some reason.** Even though I recommend not asking follow-up questions, sometimes a simple verbal acknowledgment from the interviewer stops the character from speaking for a moment, and this pause could be a moment for a break to occur.

• **A character forgets what they were saying or has a verbal stumble.** Again, these moments offer natural opportunities for a break.

This bounce-creating process benefits from relistening to the interview excerpts. The scored transcript captures more nuances of speech than a flat transcript, but not necessarily the tempo at which someone speaks. Twenty scored lines from one person may take twice as long as 20 scored lines from another. Scoring is not an exact science, so creating bounce between voices requires sensitivity and an artistic sensibility. I have had multiple experiences of creating bounce for a script just from the transcripts, and then when I returned to the audio, I realized I should adjust the actual break by a few lines because the scored transcript did not fully express the moment's spoken delivery. This example serves as a reminder about the usefulness and importance of including the timestamp in the transcribing process. In most cases, I keep the length of the broken excerpts of the bounce to around the same length, so there is some sense of equity of time between the voices. The attention to equity of time helps to create a sense of symmetry within the script and performance.

Below are formulas illustrating how I might create bouncing structures for a duet conversation with two voices. A basic duet conversation between Character A and Character B might look like this:

A–B–A–B

or

A–B–A–B–A

In the first example, the two characters speak an equal number of times in the constructed conversation. In the second example, Character A begins and ends the conversation. Character B interjects their thoughts into the conversation, but Character A still has the final word. In either case, both examples illustrate possibilities with the duet scripting convention.

To further demonstrate how a duet can work, I offer an example of a constructed conversation from *Towards the Fear* between sociologists Robert Faris and Diane Felmlee. I encountered their research on bullying as I reviewed the literature to prepare for this project, and in their work, they used the term "social combat," which I had not heard before (Faris & Felmlee, 2011). I contacted Faris and Felmlee independently, and each agreed to an interview for the project. The term came up in their responses to the prompts in the interview protocol, and even though they are coauthors, they explained the term in related but different ways. For the ethnodrama, I spliced together excerpts from their interviews to highlight the meaning of the term and their particular perspectives on it. Thus, the effect is that of a constructed conversation, with both characters presented on stage simultaneously but not acknowledging the other's presence. As the conversation begins, it gives the impression that I interviewed Faris and Felmlee together. As the duet progresses, it becomes clear that they were interviewed separately. The duet followed a montage of other characters attempting to define "social combat." So, the ethnodrama first presents a nonacademic attempt to explain the term, followed by the academics who coined it.

As the duet begins, notice the convention used to introduce the characters to the audience. Each begins to speak but is interrupted by other actors onstage, who announce their identifiers, and then a pair of actors identify them as coauthors. Very early in the duet, the audience knows who these two characters are and their relationship, providing context for why I included them in the project. Again, note the title of the interview excerpt and the timestamp as each person speaks for the first time.

Title: "We're just like chickens"
Timestamp: 6:18–9:37

DIANE FELMLEE
Well
uhm
(clears throat)

ROBERT FARIS
Uhh
(lip smack)

ACTOR 1
Diane Felmlee, Professor of Sociology, Penn State University

ACTOR 2
And Robert Faris, Associate Professor of Sociology, University of California, Davis.

ACTORS 3 & 4
Coauthors.

DIANE FELMLEE
Bullying or aggression in schools
uh Bob and I argue
is
uh often the result of social fighting
social vying for position and so on
and uh a lot of bullying is due to that
and it's uhm
socially-based aggression
often motivated by uhm trying to maintain
uh a person's status or respect or esteem or to-
or to build up one's you know
standing within- within the social group.

Title: "An offhand remark"
Timestamp: 3:58–6:03

ROBERT FARIS
My- okay so that- the origin of that term
uhm
was from an offhand- it was an offhand remark

uhhh-
uhh to a journalist actually at- at CNN an' I- I just was
uhm
you know I was trying to explain this in- in
more
sort of illustrative terms an' he- annn' I just said that you know "It's almost like social
combat" and he jus'-
he saw the potential of that- I jus' was you know
tryin' ta- tryin' ta say it a little bit differently and he saw the potential that the power
of that- of that phrase
and uh
just jumped on it he said, "That's it!"
uhm and uh-

DIANE FELMLEE
So that's the argumen- argument we make about um
you know bullying or school aggression
that it's not necessarily due to what some of the people would argue uhm
or not certainly not solely due to
oh people's
poor family background or uhm
(clears throat) or their personal
uh-
uhh deficiencies something like that
that uh bullying is a social process that's the argument that I would make anyway I
don't know if
it fits with your question or not is that
uh bullying is a fundamental group process that
is likely to occur in many groups but especially in a group situation like high school where
    everybody's trapped together
can't get out
right, is there every day.

ROBERT FARIS
But what I understand it to-
to mean is it- is it-
it- it's an attempt to
uhm
put a label on the kinds of behaviors that I think kids are engaging in and not just
kids
but in our- in the- in the stuff- in the material I've studied uhm
it happens to be kids.
But it's a process of- of
attempting to climb social ladders using uhm means that are- are
harmful to others and- and that it's ver- it's intentionally very broad so
unlike the term bullying

this term is inten- which
I think
connotes
a fairly narrow range of behaviors an' if- an' it- it also has some stereotypical
aso- associations.
Uhm I think social combat is much mo- can be much more subtle
uhm an' it's uhm- *(lip smack)*

DIANE FELMLEE
You don' have other avenues for you know interaction with other people outside that group
you know day in and day out you're there with those same people and certain social group
    processes occur
and um-

ROBERT FARIS
An' it's more tactical
an' I think that uh kids
you know will often refer to it as "drama" or "talking shit" or
uhm "beef"
an' so they don't even- they don't refer to this stuff as these behaviors as
uhm
as bullying certainly.

DIANE FELMLEE
That's what I would see is going- I would say it's fundamentally uh
you know uh- uh a group process
you know part of fundamental group processes I guess I would say sociological
group processes
norm enforcement- enforcement of social norms.

ROBERT FARIS
An' uhm but I think it's all- it's all intended
to either maintain
their social status which is
you know really important or
potentially to climb the hierarchy
an' you know an'-

DIANE FELMLEE
In other words uhm
trying to
keep people in line with social expectations- people might fall outta those
uhm such as gays and lesbians perhaps that
don't seem to fit with kind of established-
some people might see as not fitting with established heterosexual
expectations
and uhm-

ROBERT FARIS
Depending on how they do it an' who they target
it can be very effective
uhm
unfortunately.

DIANE FELMLEE
And then the one that we emphasize in
I think the paper you read- the one we emphasize the most is- is social uhh vying for
social status another fundamental- you get people together and they vie for
social status- recognition.
We're just like chickens
you know chickens ha- establish picking- pecking orders my grandparents were
farmers
uhm
my mother grew up on a farm my father worked on a farm in the summers and
when you get around chickens
they establish a pecking order but we're no different as humans we do the exact
same thing
we establish pecking orders especially again if we're trapped in that same
chicken coop
together right
you know
and we start pecking on each other and a hier- hierarchy emerges
and I think that's what
a lot of the bullying going on in schools is about
you know it's about establishing that pecking order so that's what I see as the social
combat part of it, right.

The duet between Faris and Felmlee has an A-B-A-B-A-B-A-B-A-B-A-B-A structure, with Felmlee (A) beginning and ending the duet. The constructed conversation between these two researchers introduces the origin of the term "social combat" and demonstrates their unique ways of describing it. The duet also humanizes these researchers as they work to share their knowledge in more accessible terminology. Also note that the transcription captures some of their specific ways of speaking, like using contracted words and dropping consonants at the ends of words. Both characters responded outside of an academic environment, making their way of speaking more relaxed. The sizes of the chunks from each person change as the duet unfolds, but notice that they stay mainly symmetrical to each other. I chose to end the duet with Felmlee's vivid description of a chicken coop, as her imagery captures the simplicity of why the term "social combat" made so much sense to me when I initially encountered it. While this was the audience's introduction to Faris and Felmlee, both characters returned later in the ethnodrama. They shared more about their personal experiences with social combat, which further helped humanize them as scholars.

In another example of a duet scripting convention, we can see how the interviewer's voice came into play when combining two excerpts from separate interviews. This duet appeared in *Making Gay History: Before Stonewall* and features excerpts from interviews conducted by Eric Marcus with Dick Leitsch, an early leader of the Mattachine Society of New York and organizer of the April 21, 1966, "Sip-In" at Julius', a gay bar in New York City's Greenwich Village, and Sylvia Rivera, a transgender woman, activist, and participant in the Stonewall uprising of June 1969. Marcus's voice appears throughout the interviews, both of which are about the criminalization of the LGBTQIA+ experience in New York City around the mid-20th century. Actor #10 announces Dick Leitsch, as it marks his first appearance in the play, but Sylvia Rivera appeared earlier, so her announcement is not repeated. Actor #9 voices the interjections from Eric Marcus.

Title: "They had a formula"
Timestamp: 12:15–14:27

DICK LEITSCH
And they had this vice squad
it wasn't called a vice squad
something out of the police department
it was like a vice squad.
And uhm
they were like traffic cops.
They worked on
sort of commission
you know?

ACTOR #10
Dick Leitsch, organizer of the Julius' Bar "Sip-In" on April 21, 1966.

DICK LEITSCH
These cops were plain-clothes cops
they were out on the streets eight hours a day
in plain clothes nobody saw them
and there was no
n- working at a desk or putting in papers or something.
And the only way you could tell these people were working
was by the number of arrests they made.
And it came to a point where
if you wanted a promotion you'd better have a lot of arrests.

ACTOR #9
How would they entrap people? What was the-

DICK LEITSCH
Well
they had a formula
that they would ha- they would write in their notebooks
these little black leather notebooks cops carry.

And when they got to court no matter
what actually happened they would come up with a formula story.
Because they would arrest you know
10 or 20
and they'd get them all mixed up they couldn't remember Tom from Jim from John.
And so they'd just read this little formula out of their notebook.
And every once in a while
judges would start throwin' the cases out of court because, "Hey, wait just a minute.
The same thing happened to the last guy and the guy before that and in ca-
How come the same thing happens to you all the time, Mister?"
You know then sometimes they would get suspicious.

Title: "The laws back then were very strange."
Timestamp: 1:55–4:00

SYLVIA RIVERA
But no
it's um
you can sell anything out on the streets.
You can sell men
young boys
and young women.
There's
always a customer out there
and they are
the ones that are sick.
I remember just going home and just scrubbing myself in a tub of hot waters. "Oh, these people
    touched me."
I mean the sleaze.
Even if they weren't old.
They coulda been young.
I remember sleeping-
When I was 13 and 14 years old, I remember sleeping with
guys that were 20 and 21
because they were paying me.
And they had their hang-ups.

ACTOR #9
You knew what you were.

SYLVIA RIVERA
I knew I was a whore at that time.
I knew I was out
to make money.

ACTOR #9
And these guys were pretending they were something else coming to you for . . .

SYLVIA RIVERA
They came
for a fantasy trip.
That's what it was.
It was a big fantasy.

ACTOR #9
Uh huh

ACTOR #9
Wh- What was the routine?

DICK LEITSCH
Oh you know that
"He did approach me and he did touch me upon the genitals and he did invite me to go to his
        house
for sexual purposes." /
And all o' this kind o'-

ACTOR #9
So all it required was just- it was just a pickup and that was- /
ih-

DICK LEITSCH
Yeah.
Or you know alotta them were hired for their looks and they were good-looking cops.
They would go to bars a lot or they'd go like down on Christopher Street or in the bushes in
        Central Park or someplace like that
and they'd just hang out.
And sometimes people would go up
and actually talk to them or actually
touch them
and uh they're usually at a- a-
they were supposed to have
a partner in the background who could hear everything
and they always said they did whether he was around or not he might be on the next bench
        working another
number but-
you know working another arrest.
But uhm
they always said they were together.
Uh
and they would go to bars and stuff and they would
get picked up or they said they got picked up and then they'd
arrest you
and
take you to court
and ruin your life.
And a lot m-
alotta people who got arrested particularly in subway tearooms and in the park

were like
closet queens
people who were like
priests and doctors and stuff like that who couldn't hang out you know like at
Julius' or someplace
they didn't want to be seen in the gay community.

ACTOR #9
But how did they tr- how did ya say the police treat you during eh- when you were a kid and-
and out on the streets?

SYLVIA RIVERA
The first time
that I got arrested it was like,
"I'm going where?" *(laughs)*

ACTOR #9
What- What had you done?

SYLVIA RIVERA
You were a faggot.

ACTOR #9
Were you- were you dre- were you dressed in women's clothes?

SYLVIA RIVERA
Well back then when I first started out I was in
women's clothes.
It was what-
what they call right now, even right now what I'm wearing is "scare" drag.

ACTOR #9
Scare
drag?
What is scare drag?

SYLVIA RIVERA
What I'm wearing right now.
You don't have
the tits on or anything you just have a little makeup on you have your hair out you got women's
clothing on
and that's what they called scare drag.
Every time that I used to go in front of a judge:
"upper-head female impersonation."

ACTOR #9
Uh that was the charge.

SYLVIA RIVERA
Yeah.

ACTOR #9
Upper-head
female impersonation.
In other words
from the neck up.

SYLVIA RIVERA
Mmmhmm.

ACTOR #9
That's incredible.

SYLVIA RIVERA
The laws back then were very strange.

This duet between Dick Leitsch and Sylvia Rivera has an A-B-A-B structure. Given that the overall project focused on LGBTQIA+ history before the Stonewall uprising, I wanted contemporary audiences to understand the risks that members of this community faced, particularly at the hands of law enforcement officials. Leitsch and Rivera shared stories highlighting those risks, using vivid descriptions of what they had observed in others or experienced firsthand. I kept Marcus's interjections intact to maintain the original cadences of both interviews and to demonstrate how unsettling these accounts were to him as he conducted the interviews in the late 1980s.

The formatting of this duet also includes two examples of how to account for moments when two speakers may overlap. On page 136, there is the moment when Rivera and Marcus have text appearing side by side on the page, indicating that they spoke those words simultaneously. Then, in the exchange between Leitsch and Marcus, I use a slash to indicate their overlapping dialogue. The slash in Leitsch's line indicates when Actor #9 should begin to speak, and the slash in Actor #9's line indicates where Leitsch should pick back up with "Yeah." If the artist-researcher conducts interviews with more than one person and intends to reproduce them verbatim, these notations are important to establish as the ethnodramatist and then use consistently throughout the dataset and the script. A note explaining the notations should appear at the beginning of the script, so that it is clear how the lines of dialogue should sound.

As a reminder, these examples of monologues and duets represent continuous interview excerpts. I did not combine different moments from an interview to manufacture a monologue, and I only pulled sections from one point in time from each of the two interviews to construct a duet. I maintain the integrity of each excerpt, start to finish, not only because I work specifically with verbatim performance but also because I have a responsibility to the participant to honor their words as they originally spoke them. Other ethnodramatists work differently, taking more liberties with constructing their scripts. As you find your voice as an ethnodramatist, regardless of how you work with these scripting conventions, remember to be transparent with your participants about your intentions for using their words and with your audiences about how you've constructed your script.

In the next chapter, I expand on the basic scripting conventions of the monologue and duet by introducing more complex possibilities, including trios, quartets, montages, and choral pieces. These conventions continue to rely on the concept of bounce introduced in this chapter and maintain the integrity of the excerpts selected during the coding and analysis process.

ACTIVITIES

Describe the World of a Play

As outlined in the chapter, the ethnodramatist should describe at the start of their script how they imagine the world of their play. These initial stage directions guide directors and designers and help ensure that the ethnodramatist's intentions come to life in production. To practice writing these introductory stage directions, review the example from *Making Gay History: Before Stonewall* on page 121. Then, think about a favorite scene from a movie, television show, or play you've seen in the past year. Imagine the scene without any characters, focusing more on the physical space and the possible moments that could happen there. Write a physical description of the space using three to five sentences. Provide enough information that someone can understand what you're imagining, while leaving enough flexibility to inspire someone else's imagination to contribute ideas (e.g., a director or a designer). In the second paragraph, share a short description of the first piece of action in your favorite scene. Does someone enter the space? Does a cell phone ring? Is there a clap of thunder? What time of day is it? What is the mood? You can use these questions and many others to articulate the initial actions on stage for the director and actors. Your practice with writing these paragraphs will help you develop the skills to establish the world of the play for your ethnodrama.

Create a Duet

The concept of bounce is key to any ethnodramatic dialogue. This chapter shared examples of duets from two different plays. Now, you can experiment with bounce by creating a duet with the two scored transcripts of interview excerpts from *Whatever You Are, Be a Good One* shared below. Review the two transcripts and identify where each one can be broken in half. Remember to consider the suggestions for finding these possibilities outlined on pages 128 and 129. As you review the transcripts, you might decide to break them up into more than two sections. If so, note where those places might be. Create a duet between the two voices once you have the spots for potential breaks. Decide which character will speak first. Depending on the number of breaks for each piece, you can try a duet using A-B-A-B or one using A-B-A-B-A. Type up the new configuration, following the form I demonstrated in the chapter. Experiment with bounce and see if you can determine when there's not enough, too much, or when it's just right. The best way to test your duet is to read it out loud or ask two other people to do so while you listen.

Title: "You know we're making the best decisions we can"
Timestamp: 39:15–41:08

30-SOMETHING, WHITE, BLONDE FEMALE
And it's-
it's
destroyed my life
for the past two years.
Uhm
so
it's-
and I think it's very easy
to
ostracize somebody who you've never met
because of
a narrative or an idea that has been
manufactured
in the media and it really has been a manufactured idea that
people who haven't taken the shot are these irresponsible, ignorant, toothless,
uneducated,
don't-care-about-anybody people.
And in my experience because I've- I've been in a lot of support groups over the years
of people who can't get
vaccinated
and
uhm
almost everyone I've met who- who has not taken this shot has a story similar to mine.
Either their child has had an injury
or they have a condition like I have a v- very close friend with Lymes
anything that she does that changes her immune system will set her Lymes off-
has Lymes disease and
you know we're making the best decisions we can for our own selves and
when I'm denied access to my livelihood and to-
you know
eh
just-
I- I went to get a coffee the other day li- I-
I didn't have papers.
I couldn't get a coffee, right?
So like
this is what happens when that kind of polarization trickles down
and then policies are created based on that polarization and so
I share this with you
you know this is very vulnerable place for me
but I think it's super important because I th-
you know- and I'm also a clinician

I believe in science
I believe-
I believe in the vaccination programs.
But I also believe staunchly that we have to be able to make our own decisions about what we
put in our body.

Title: "People had made up their minds"
Timestamp: 9:37-11:39

BILL
Oh, the last time?
Um
well, the COVID thing certainly brought out a lot of disagreement
uh
with a lot of this-
a lot of-
well not a lot but I- I came in contact with people who had uh
kind of an opposite view of
what-
what their
individual responsibilities and
freedoms were
and kind of submitted to
authority that
in my view was not necessarily legitimate.
Yeah.
COVID brought out a lot- a lot of things in people that
kinda surprised me.

[Interviewer speaks]

(*sighs*)
How easily people just went along with things
without e-
without asking-
without critically thinking about what it is they were doing or why
or for what reason.
They just
folded.
Yeah
I was surprised that uh
the lack of
curiosity
let's just go along with it and uh
not question anything.

[Interviewer speaks]

Oh well huh.
Why are you wearing that mask?
Uh
because I was told to.
Uh do you think it works? Do you think it's effective?
Well, that's w-
they- they told me it is
and that I must wear it.
I kinda a-
after that I gave up
trying to uh
discuss
because I thought it-
it was just futile.
People had made up- well, that's the polarization.
People had made up their minds and there was going to be no
give and take it was going to be
here's my position and you're not gonna convince me otherwise.

6 Scripting

Complex Scripting Conventions, Finding an Ending, and Drafting

The previous chapter introduced the monologue and the duet as basic scripting conventions that an ethnodramatist can use to craft their script and emphasized that scripting choices impact how actors perform the script for an audience. When an ethnodramatic script relies too heavily on one or two scripting conventions, the script's rhythm becomes repetitive, which increases the chances that an audience's attention could wane. While the monologue and the duet offer a solid foundation for scripting, ethnodramatists should work to include even more variety in the conventions they use to disseminate findings. This variety in script arrangement can help keep an audience engaged and attentive to the research findings.

This chapter introduces more complex scripting conventions, including trios, quartets, montages, and choral pieces, and again provides examples of these conventions at work in scripts from my past projects. These conventions use the basic building blocks of the monologue, and the duet in particular, as they all fall under Saldaña's (2011a) category of "ethnodramatic dialogue." As conventions that emulate conversations, they also rely heavily on the concept of bounce, which I identified as crucial in Chapter 5.

After reviewing these complex conventions, this chapter offers insights into how the ethnodramatist can arrive at an appropriate ending for a script, which is one of the most challenging parts of the process for me as a writer, and how to think about titling an ethnodrama, another potentially tricky part of the process. The chapter also reviews the script drafting process and highlights the importance of reading drafts aloud and receiving feedback before redrafting and ultimately moving into production. Before endings, redrafting, and production, let's get to the complex scripting conventions.

Trios and Quartets

Trios and **quartets** follow the same basic idea as a duet, but they are more complicated scripting constructions that allow three or four characters to share their perspectives on a particular topic or idea. As in a performed duet, each actor in a trio or quartet plays only one character to ensure that the audience can follow the conversation. Adding more voices increases the possibility for different bounce combinations to occur. A duet is relatively straightforward and moves back and forth between the two voices, but the combinations can become more complex with three or four voices in the mix. Let's consider four character voices and label them A, B, C, and D. The formula for a simple trio or quartet using these voices might look very basic like this:

A–B–C–A–B–C
or
A–B–C–D–A–B–C–D

The conversations follow a basic pattern in which each character speaks twice and in the same order.

We might also see a trio arranged something like this:

A–B–C–B–A

In this case, Character A has the first and last words in this trio, Character B also offers their thoughts, and Character C only speaks once in the middle. This choice might be because C's excerpt is more challenging to break up or shorter than A's and B's excerpts. C's contribution may also include a story that illustrates opinions that A and B express in their pieces. These arrangements are not rigid formulas but offer options based on the content and delivery of the excerpts themselves.

If we add Character D's voice to the mix, we might get something like this:

A–B–C–D–B–A–D–C–A–D–B–C

Here, all four characters speak three times, but the order we hear from them changes throughout. This particular quartet arrangement demonstrates that bounce does not have to unfold in the same order for each round of the characters speaking, but the arrangement of voices and perspectives would need to make sense. I do not recommend introducing this level of complexity early on in a script, as it requires that the audience understands how scripting conventions work. As mentioned in Chapter 5, I usually begin an ethnodrama with the monologue convention. Then, I gradually introduce the audience to the different scripting conventions, so that their ability to follow the dissemination process is a scaffolded experience. Their analysis process becomes more complex and deepens as the performance unfolds.

Let's look at an example of a trio between three characters featured in *That's Not Supposed to Be Happening* (Huff & Salvatore, 2023), VPL's project about housing in New York City. The overall structure of the ethnodrama used two monologues, one duet, and two trios constructed from interview excerpts. The performances featured five actors, each performing two characters.[1] The actors facilitated three audience engagement exercises between the scripted sections to share more information about the New York City housing market and its regulations. The arranged interview excerpts and the exercises combined to address our main research question: What are the experiences of finding, securing, and paying for housing for people who live in the New York metropolitan area? Keith R. Huff, co-creator of this project, arranged a trio that featured three characters' stories about finding and maintaining an apartment in New York City. The trio bounces between 42-Year-Old Female, Beatriz, and Linda, and follows an arrangement of the interview excerpts that looks like this formula: A–B–C–A–B–C–B–A. Two actors introduce the three characters using their selected identifiers.

Title: "Who knows how long until they raise the rents for that one that we can't afford?"
Timestamp: 8:05-11:04

42-YEAR-OLD FEMALE
We are in a situation now where
our rent was raised
about 40%
postpandemic
and it was a lot.

ACTOR #1
This is 42-Year-Old-Female.

42-YEAR-OLD FEMALE
And we loved-
love this current apartment that we're in
and- but we
decided you know what?
They let us know with not very much notice
we didn't really
think about where we wanted to go after it- it was right-
kind of with the holidays coming up so we decided to stay.
Um but now we're thinking can we really afford
for subsequent years to stay in this apartment that we love
possibly having another rent increase next year?
Um and it's hard to
reconcile that because we are in walking distance to my child's school
our friends are nearby
we're near the park that he likes to go to
um so we also have to
do a little bit of searching to see if we can make it happen
to stay in our home that we really love or if we have tah
go through the process again
um and try to find another rental property
to be in there until who knows how long until they raise the rents for that one that we can't
    afford.

Title: "Chances are someone else did too"
Timestamp: 15:20-17:40

BEATRIZ
I had never had to pay over

a thousand dollars
in rent
um
in
my 5 years here.

ACTOR #2
This is Beatriz.

BEATRIZ
And
it was the first
time
that I had to like crunch numbers and be like
OK I'm trying to find a 3-bedroom somewhere that isn't ridiculously inconvenient for me to
        commute
to
or commute from
and
just
you know
again
because of-
I don't think it's just
like a lack of inventory I think
right now what's really awful is that landlords are trying to make up for their
losses during the pandemic.

Title: "Fees are too expensive and I can't afford it"
Timestamp: 8:35-11:32

LINDA
I think the biggest problem with renting in New York City are
the high rents
the need to provide residency
and um
the security deposit.
They are all d- too hard for me.

ACTOR #1
And this is Linda.

LINDA
I'm a refugee from China
and it's
hard to
find a good housing

in New York City
so
I had to share a bedroom with other people I work with.
But at least
uhm I'm good that I have a bed to rest
after all day
at work.
But now I'm uh kinda
used to it.
Uhm I no longer need a big home of my own.
Now I just hope that I can find some savings every month so
maybe I can buy a house in the US in the future.

42-YEAR-OLD FEMALE
That's OK.

[Interviewer speaks]

F- for
for-
I'm gonna put on my real estate hat now.
Um
free market apartments in New York City can be raised
up to any-
they could raise it a hundred percent if they wanted to, they could double your rent.
And
if you're living in a rent-stabilized apartment
uh there are limits to how much a landlord can raise.
Um so that's the kind of thing too as a real estate agent I have had clients say,
"Hey, I want to find a rent-stabilized apartment."
It's not as easy as- as it at is
many landlords don't broadcast that they have rent-stabilized apartments until you're in them.
Sometimes they do.
Um we can find that out ahead of time or we can also see
the history of the apartment or wh- kind of
what that-
what that rent looks like.
Um an- and people like those units and want to stay in those units a long time because it's a
    limit to how ya- much you're raised.
Free market apartments there's no cap on that.
Any landlord who has a free market apartment can raise the rent
as often and as much as they like.
Um obviously in your lease they're required to keep that- that amount- you have a signed lease
um
but
outside of that lease for when it comes to renewal they can raise your rent as much as they can.

BEATRIZ
And
most
salaries or incomes haven't had
that sort of adjustment
and
it really like
was unaffordable.
Right now
I've lucked out in the sense that
you know
my friend found a really good apartment
that happened to have a spare room
but
other- like otherwise
I would be
stranded right now I've been basically
like
homeless for two months
haven't been on the streets because I'm lucky enough to have a support network
that has offered me
rooms
couches to sleep on um

LINDA
Um-m-m
actually
I feel that
the answer to this question changes with my
age.
When I was young
and d- d-
did not choose to come to New York to live and work
I defined home as a place to live with my family
to be the place to rely on.
No matter what kind of problem I encounter
as long as I get home
all troubles will be gone
and I will uh arrange my room very neat and clean.
But um-m-m
after I came to New York my definition of home changed a lot
probably because
I- I- I
am getting older.
I would define home as a place where we can spend time to rest
after the long day working
and-

and
do not need to have too many
like decorations and something else in my room.
The reason is that
I only can sleep for
a- a few hours every day in my room.
And also
finding a new place and paying extra for rent
left me no way to save money.
Also this room provided by the restaurant.
So this is a way
to save my money
because I don't have to buy a lot of accessories
and they are good
they also provide me food.

BEATRIZ
But it really
has been
um
has been hard.
Prior to the apartment I got scammed at I applied for
one- another- a 2-bedroom
um applying
in Bed Stuy.
It was
out of my budget.
But I had a guarantor-
um a guarantor with a really good credit history
and
still didn't get it.
Um
so it's not just
um
it's not just that there's things that are hard to find is that once you find them
you know if you found that
chances are someone else did too
and
becomes competitive.

42-YEAR-OLD FEMALE
Unfortunately, my story is not unique.
I've had a lot of friends who have also had
their rents raised.
I have a friend
who

has been in their apartment for a couple of years because they got a COVID deal and now
    they're trying to figure out
where they're gonna live.
They have a child and they're like, "Maybe we can live
with our parents
in their Upper West Side apartment
and they can have a
one bedroom we can have another bedroom
and we can try to figure out for a couple years until
you know maybe we can take over their apartment if they move out of the city."
That's where we're at now
with the- with the-
the ha- dips- the peaks and the valleys of the New York City real estate market after COVID.

The arrangement of this trio allows three very different experiences to come together in one shared moment, and the audience hears their similarities and differences. All three characters mention the financial challenges of maintaining an apartment in New York City and focus on their struggles. 42-Year-Old Female shares that her child's needs and proximity to their school inform her housing decisions. Beatriz reveals that searching for an apartment has pitfalls, including scams and intense competition for a good deal. Linda, an immigrant from China, explains that her living situation is directly linked to her employment at a restaurant. Along with these personal experiences, the scripted trio also provides some tangible and practical information about securing housing when 42-Year-Old Female puts on her "real estate hat" and shares knowledge from her experiences working as an agent in the housing industry. The trio appeals to the audience's empathy and offers potentially useful information. Beyond the issue of housing, the characters also reference the COVID pandemic, immigration, and housing insecurity, thus situating their responses within an array of societal concerns that reference when the interviewers conducted these interviews: the fall and winter of 2022.[2]

The following example illustrates a quartet scripting convention featuring four voices from *Towards the Fear* (Salvatore, 2014), including sociologist Diane Felmlee, who appeared in the duet highlighted in Chapter 5. I include this particular quartet to demonstrate the convention and to illustrate how characters' voices can return later in an ethnodrama. While *Towards the Fear* illuminated the experiences of adults reflecting on childhood bullying experiences, characters also shared their thoughts and experiences around how to stop bullying and when they or others had stopped it. As a result, I gave this quartet a title in the ethnodrama: "The Fight Back Quartet." With Diane Felmlee, the quartet also includes responses from Nate, Ed, and Brian. As you read, notice how the bounce works in this particular construction.

Title: "Fight his ass back"
Timestamp: 12:18–14:32

NATE
One I'd say fight back. *(laughs)*

Um that was always my dad's advice
indirectly.
He always told me this story that he um
he- he- was at an all-boys school it was like really small and so they made fun of him because
      he was the shortest and he was
like he really- he was like 5'4"
at like this
you know
all-boys school they always made fun of him and the kid that made fun of him the most
      sat in front of him in math class
and he turned around and said something to my dad
and when he went- looked to the front of the class again my dad stabbed him in the back
      with a pencil
and that was the end of it.
So that was my dad's way- my dad would just drop that whenever I talked about bullying
      and that sort of like um
it's okay to fight back.

Title: "My protector"
Timestamp: 10:10–12:42

DIANE FELMLEE
I grew up in an all-boy neighborhood and- and this is in Wisconsin, OK?
And so you get winter like most of the year, right?
And so what we all do and I would do this too sometimes is build forts.
And so they would build forts along the way or up to school- get up early and wait
and they would
pummel me and- and other boys I'm-
uh as well- I don't pay too much attention to that I just felt that it was only me but
uhm
and
pummel me with snowballs- ice balls.
It's uhm really bad if you put rocks in them.

Title: "There aren't enough fist fights"
Timestamp: 19:14–20:40

BRIAN
On the one hand we've discovered or- or brought
to
discussion
a topic that is a problem.
Uhm and on the other hand I think
uhm
there's too much counseling and psychology and handwringing going on in
bringing up children these days.

Title: "Six-inch butterfly knife"
Timestamp: 6:24–7:21

ED
By the time I hit high school
it had escalated to the point that a lot of students
were taking it out- like I couldn't go to the bathroom without being attacked
physically.
Umm
got to the point that
I had to go to school armed
umm I- and keep in mind I'm about four foot one[3]
at the time.

NATE
But I feel like we're in this sort of
weird
turn
in
like the educational system
where
fighting
and
things like social combat are so different
and they don't see that one can cause the other.

BRIAN
I've- I said to the principal at my daughter's school one day I said to him, "Ya know the
    problem with this place is there aren't enough fist fights."
And
kids
in a lot of ways are- ir- there- there you got these zero tolerance policies in schools- one
    kid throws a punch on another kid
uh an' all a'sudden they're bringing out the school counselors and the parents and the lawyers.

DIANE FELMLEE
Oh an' I- an' I just dreaded going because I'd just be crying screaming and scared
to death cause all these boys had lined the sidewalks and stuff like that
and
it- it can sound funny but it wasn't.
I refused to uhm
go to school and my parents trying to figure out how to handle this problem and
uhm
and what they did is they arranged for a older boy
in the neighborhood
to be my protector.
Tim.

NATE
And I think that like had
I actually like fought someone hardcore had someone like
thrown like a real punch not just like tossed someone into a locker not like
the little things that happen after school but you know like you start a real fight like
it's very different
in the eyes of
an administrator.

BRIAN
And childhood
sometimes just requires some street justice
where
uhm
one kid's pushing another kid around he needs to be punched in the face
and
very often that'll settle it.
An' even if- even if the-
even if the victim of bullying is smaller or weaker he gets respect by charging (*starting to
     laugh)* in there.
Ya know even if he splats like a bug on the windshield
the bully will appreciate that.

DIANE FELMLEE
And I remember him well
because I would go to his house- they lived next door and I'm sure his mother made him
     do this or whatever.
I- I asked him- oh I'll go into that later- but anyway so an' I would go to his house and he
     was an
older boy who was still I guess in grade school but he was big and nice guy and strong
     and stuff so I would walk with him and he would protect me.
And so that kinda resolved the problem but I always wondered if my parents paid him
     off or what (*laughing)* right? You know, "Jus'
do this" but that made a huge difference in my life uhh
and so that's how that worked out.

ED
I had a friend get me a 6-inch butterfly knife
that
being four foot one was about (*laughs)* the length of my arm you know
umm and I carried it in my back pocket and the first time I got attacked in a bathroom all
     I did was flip it out.
I- I knew how to
make it look impressive anyway.

NATE
And so you know like I'd love to tell someone like

"Fight his ass back" like that's
because I want someone to feel
that they
have
(whisper) what's the word for it
um
that they have like authority over themselves
um
that they have
a chance to say that like, "This is
how I feel this is who I am" like whether it's
like whatever it is like I-
I think someone should feel comfortable enough in themselves to like say that.

DIANE FELMLEE
But I ran into Tim
this uhm
holiday.
I was back over the holiday break
in Wisconsin in my hometown and I ran into him at a coffeehouse and I said,
"Tim, do you know that you- you know saved my skin back in grade school?
Do you remember?" You know we talked about it and it was- it was really something but
interesting thing that he told me- he said- he says "Oh yeah, I remember.
Yeah, I remember I had to beat up Billy in order to keep him off your back. I remember
    that part" he said too "I had ta"
and I was thinking "Oh very interesting here's my protector and the way he's doing it is by
you know
engaging in aggression too, right?" You know so I
thought that was kinda interesting yeah
but uhm he remembered it.

BRIAN
So on the one hand we've got
you know there's some serious problems with this
but I think uh the adult world also has
uhmm
removed
the way kids
always dealt with this and adjusted to it.

ED
And I went from being that crazy kid everybody picks on
to that crazy kid with a knife.
But that meant
I had a security
at that point

that
I could relatively go through my day unmolested.

NATE
And I think
I guess if I were to say something to someone who's being bullied
I don't know if I could say like one thing.
I don't think I could say one thing.
Um
I mean honestly like I-
I don't know.
It's not something that you can like
fix.

This quartet appeared in the second half of the play, so the audience had already encountered all the characters. No other actors had to voice any introductions in this quartet. The bounce structure does not a set pattern but moves back and forth from character to character, based mainly on the content of what they offer up to the constructed conversation. The formula for the structure looks like this:

A–B–C–D–A–C–B–A–C–B–D–A–B–C–D–A

The various excerpts from each character are also of differing lengths, so I purposely broke my own rule about symmetry (see Chapter 5). In certain sections, when the excerpts are shorter and the bounce increases, the actors' delivery creates a sense of urgency in the constructed conversation. I made this choice intentionally because the arrangement represented the rising stakes around the problem of bullying. Nate speaks five times, Diane Felmlee and Brian speak four times, and Ed speaks three times. When examining the timestamps for each excerpt, it stands to reason that Ed speaks the least number of times, as his particular excerpt is about 1 minute long. You may think, "Joe broke his rule here," which would be correct. Ed's excerpt is much shorter than the 2 to 3 minutes I recommend, but it comes from a more extended section that the interviewer transcribed and included in the original dataset. As I created this scripting structure, this shorter section of Ed's more extended excerpt felt like it belonged as part of this "Fight Back" section. Hence, a quartet emerged. Ed's story of carrying a knife to school illustrates the stakes that young people face when confronted with bullying at school. Brian's call for more fist fights and "street justice" relates to Ed's story and represents a somewhat controversial approach to the issue, which he also acknowledges in his response. Diane Felmlee's response reflects her own experiences with bullying as a child and how her parents chose to deal with it. I remember being struck by the story, as I could immediately see how her childhood experiences somehow affected her later work as a sociologist focused on bullying and social combat, a direct answer to the project's original research question. Nate begins and ends the quartet because his response's trajectory demonstrates this issue's complexity. He strongly recommends fighting back when bullied, shares his father's experience and subsequent advice, and then completes his response by saying, "I don't know whether I could say one thing." Nate's response exemplifies that participants frequently construct meaning in the moment as they respond to a prompt. In this case, the construction of meaning does not lead Nate to more clarity. Rather, it complicates his understanding of his initial response and, by extension, the audience's response.

The trio and quartet scripting conventions offer these opportunities to create this complexity because of the layering of voices, perspectives, and experiences. I rely on these conventions to provide multiple perspectives, often perspectives that I both agree and disagree with because the resulting tensions represent why I do this work. If every trio or quartet in an ethnodrama features the same perspectives on a particular issue or problem, the ethnodrama misses the opportunity for dramatic tension. As the audience experiences the tension between the differing opinions, they have to sit with those opinions alongside their own, demonstrating that there is often no single easy answer to the issues we take up in ethnodramas.

The Montage

A **montage** functions similarly to a trio or quartet but features more bounce because the spoken excerpts from each character are usually shorter. There could also be more than four characters represented, requiring more than four actors to perform it. I have also created montages in which each actor portrays multiple characters, but this choice requires skilled actors who can make precise vocal changes to distinguish one character from the next. The montage offers great potential to provide insight into the complexity surrounding a particular concept or finding. Complexity could include confusion and contradiction. If an interview protocol invites participants to define a specific term, and those responses reveal various interpretations, the montage offers a scripting convention that magnifies the complexity of that finding. A montage placed early in a script prepares an audience for the issue's complexity and establishes the need for multiple perspectives on this topic. This kind of montage is a dramatic representation of a problem statement one might write in a more traditional dissertation. The ethnodramatist uses the various perspectives of select participants to illustrate the issue at hand rather than writing it themselves.

A montage can also serve as a way to disrupt the established rhythm and flow of a script composed of monologues, duets, trios, and quartets. The shorter excerpts with more bounce between characters' voices can "wake up" an audience that has grown accustomed to the other scripting conventions. In other words, a montage can help make an essential point that the ethnodrama must convey. If the actors can achieve a conversational tempo for the montage in performance, they can begin to sound as if they are contradicting or correcting one another. Through this blending of voices in the montage, the ethnodrama can also establish a sense of community and acknowledge the collective wisdom of those who participated in the interviewing process.

When placing a montage convention, the ethnodramatist should consider the audience's readiness to listen to a more complicated construction and simultaneously analyze the ideas shared by multiple voices (Salvatore, 2020b, 2025). Another rule of thumb to consider: The characters in a montage should always appear in other parts of the script. If you use a montage early, make sure all the characters in the montage appear later in the script. If you use a montage later, make sure that all of the characters in the montage have already appeared. I do not include participant identifiers in the montage text, so the audience either needs to be able to recognize who is speaking or the speakers' identities are not necessarily relevant at that particular moment in the script and performance. For example, suppose a montage comes near the beginning of the script. In that case, the actors performing it may use vocal and gestural distinctions to demonstrate something specific about each character. Then, later in the script, when the audience reencounters each character in a longer piece, they will recognize that character's particular way of speaking or gesturing from the montage.

To illustrate the montage convention, I share the "Disadvantages Montage" from *open heart* (Salvatore, 2010), an ethnodrama that explores the experiences of 15 men living in open, nonmonogamous gay relationships. Following a workshop reading of an early script draft, I received some advice to include more about the challenges individuals might face as they navigate these kinds of relationships. I had interviewed couples together and then each partner separately, and during the individual interview, I had a prompt that asked participants to discuss the advantages and disadvantages of their current relationship. Through that prompt, I tended to hear more about challenging moments, feelings, and experiences. While my primary research interest focused on how these couples made their relationships work, I also recognized, with the help of the feedback, that it was necessary to hear about the challenges. In particular, these challenges helped to complicate the narrative the audience experienced through the performance dissemination by adding dramatic tension around the idea of an open relationship. Five actors each performed three characters in the production, and this montage included all five performing one character each.[4] All five characters had appeared multiple times earlier in the play, as I placed this montage in the last third of the ethnodrama. It was the last scene before the script entered its conclusion. The characters included in the montage, ranging in age from 22 to 48, are Pony; Brendan; Male, 48; Anthony; and Tom. Pony and Brendan were a couple, but their sections in this montage are from their individual interviews.

The montage begins and ends with Pony reflecting for a more extended period than the other four characters because I wanted to ease the audience into the complexity of this convention. Allowing one character to speak a bit longer at the beginning and the ending helps to bookend the more complicated montage experience. This montage does not include the excerpt titles and time stamps, as I wanted to provide you with a sense of the flow without those interruptions on the page. As you read, notice how the excerpts from each character get shorter as the montage progresses, thus causing the bounce to accelerate and the conversation to become more complex. I allowed for this level of complexity only after the audience had become acclimated to the form through the other scripting conventions.

Disadvantages Montage

PONY
I recently went-
I went home for the holidays back to
see my parents and- and while I was there I had uhm-
I had this excruciating brunch with a lot of friends from college
that was like

horrible.

It was horrible and I was really depressed afterwards and

I came back here and I was like just depressed for weeks and then I was like, "I have to run away to Mexico" so I went to Mexico and I was like fine.

I like

fixed it

but I was really depressed because it was uhm like uh

it became apparent to me like the way that

friends from college

that I've stayed more or less in contact with like

uh but you know like they're like uh

they're living in a very different way than I live, right?

They- they're talking about like you know

buying shit for houses and buying houses and then buying more shit for houses and then buying cars and buying

uhm

shoes and-

and like this was like the entire brunch and I was just like

I-

I just-

I

have other things that I'm interested in than-

than buying shit.

BRENDAN

So a disadvantage would be

that

I uhm-

I'm challenged by him. *(laughter)*

It's also an advantage

that

his-

that he

like any lover isn't tailored to my vision of the world or our relationship and I have to make a compromise in some way.

And that's an advantage and a disadvantage

and I love that about him.

MALE, 48

Um

I would say-

yea- yeah-

disadvantages.

I think it's something you just touched on.

Like the disadvantages would be

I don't believe him

because
you know what I mean like
he's fucking lying.
Yeah
so it's that doubt too.

ANTHONY
I mean I guess the disadvantages are always- you're always testing it
and there's always that
possibility that
the other person could get that much more curious or
you know if you're in one of those cycles of the relationship where things aren't the greatest or
     you know you're getting on each other's nerves or-
I think everyone goes through that.
I think that happens over the course of relationship
several times.
Ummm
so yeah I think there's always that look or little bit of insecurity that things could change but
I wouldn't want to be with someone who didn't necessarily want to be with me.

TOM
And it's- I find it comic that
he is jealous of me
but I'm not really jealous of him.
So I try not to upset him by
telling him
maybe something that happened.
And then he gets- he feels like I'm hiding something and I say, "No I'm not hiding" but then he
     wants all the details.
And I feel slightly uncomfortable telling him the details.
Which might be my own issue of
speaking openly about
sex.

MALE, 48
You know it's gonna be that doubt.
This mother fucker think I'm stupid
you know what I'm saying?
I went for it one time but not every fucking time I'm gonna believe that shit.

BRENDAN
But I think that's to do- a do with some past
relationships
uhm where
either I haven't fully consented to like something that's going on or a partner of mine hasn't
     fully consented and they said they were comfortable with it.

ANTHONY
And I think that was kind of what happened when Tyler came back from Atlanta like it was
you know we had this sort of understanding of the relationship where he- maybe he did kind of
meet someone else or-

TOM
Like yes, I went to the-
whatever-
I went to the Eagle and I had fun with this guy and I pissed all over him and
he's a really nice guy and like
'tt was fun but-

ANTHONY
-someone also who excited him for you know two weeks or whatever it was and
when he came back maybe he didn't necessarily want me right away or he did but he felt like
        he had to- had to pay his penance or whatever it is or-

TOM
-to be questioned by-
about it
almost makes me want- put up my guards and-
"Well, I don't ask you about the guys you have sex with why do you have to
know all the details about-"

MALE, 48
C'mon you went to a club
you was fucking drunk
and- and- and- and c'mon
your cell phone was off
or- or- or- or always on the voicemail.
C'mon am I fuckin' stupid?

BRENDAN
And it was never like a
"You violated me like in a
horrible kind of way" kind of thing.

ANTHONY
-whereas I feel like people who aren't actually open people can lie really well.

MALE, 48
I'd rather you tell me the truth
or- or- or- or talk t-
I don't care but I just need to know.

BRENDAN
It was just that it-

it became apparent that we
wanted different things.

TOM
Yeah
'cause if he told me tomorrow he was leaving-

MALE, 48
I know you was drunk
or I know you was having a good time.
I know guys come on to you all the time.

BRENDAN
Because- but we weren't openly communicating about that like I would say,
"This is what I need"
and they would say, "OK well I'll meet you halfway" but really
to survive-

ANTHONY
And
if you don't have that opened communication all the time you- you can definitely-
that person's always keeping so many things from you.
It's easier for them to just move on and not tell you certain things.

TOM
-he was sick of me.
blah blah . . .

ANTHONY
I mean I think that's why so many men find it easy to cheat-

TOM
I would think-
"I'd be sad" and then I would think "OK."

MALE, 48
But c'mon just- I need to know for- you know what I'm saying? It's alright
I- you know at least that way I know.

BRENDAN
-they didn't- couldn't meet me halfway at all.
They needed their way.

ANTHONY
-because they feel like they're protecting the other person.

MALE, 48
And number one did you ah- ah- I know you used a condom.

BRENDAN
But if they had told me that
maybe we could've worked something out.
Maybe I would've said "No" maybe we could've
ended things before they got really horrible.

TOM
And I would continue with my life.

PONY
I don't know- like as I've started to get older like there's something about like a committed and
    long enduring relationship that appeals to me.
So uhm-
which is something that uh
for a long time I wasn't really interested in.
I was more interested in like
things changing and stuff like that.
I uhm-
I- but yeah so
I- I'd say that-
that now where I- where I sit now I'm starting to like have
more of a new interest in a- in some kind of like sense of permanence
and relationships.
Uhm
although
what that looks like
and
how probable that- if I don't know like-
but it's something that I've- I've-
I've started to realize that I'm more interested in than
I was before.
Uhm
yeah.
That didn't really answer the question at all, did it?

After hearing various characters discuss the circumstances surrounding their initial meetings and relationships, thoughts on fidelity and infidelity, and strategies for coping, this montage provided the audience with a new layering of ideas that revealed sadness, pain, and uncertainty. Pony begins the montage with a vivid story of his brunch with friends and establishes a level of uncertainty. Then, his current partner, Brendan, enters with his perceptions of Pony in their relationship. The montage folds in responses from Tom, Anthony, and Male, 48, discussing their partners with anger, frustration, and concern. The bouncing between the four inner montage characters creates a sense of urgency around the feelings they share. It captures how one's inner voice of doubt or anxiety contributes to difficulty navigating an open relationship if one is not fully comfortable with or honest about the arrangement.

The need for trust between partners, a finding presented earlier in the play, also emerged through this montage in performance. Tom abruptly stops the bounce with one line, "And I would continue my life," and then Pony returns with possibly his more honest reflection, stating that he might want a relationship that has more of a "sense of permanence." I chose to end the montage with Pony's question, "That didn't really answer the question at all, did it?," as I wanted to remind the audience about the origins of the material, that this is not fiction, and that even after his realization, Pony still wrestled with confusion and doubt about what he had just offered as a response. When a participant asks for confirmation about how they just answered, it reflects something important to remember about the form: The participant often wants to help the project's cause. Given that dynamic, how does a participant's eagerness to help affect how they respond to the prompts during the data collection process? By including moments like Pony's question in a script and performance, the ethnodramatist can help remind the audience about the presence and influence of the researcher.

Choral Pieces

Choral pieces, also known as "choral exchanges" (Saldaña, 2011a, p. 109), are created using short snippets or even single lines of text pulled from transcripts and then arranged to simulate a chorus of voices. The ethnodramatist can use choral pieces at the beginning or end of a script as a way to introduce many viewpoints or ideas quickly and dramatically. This convention can also summarize a collection of thoughts or ideas on a particular topic. A choral piece can also serve as an effective transition, either introducing a thematic finding that is to come or summarizing a finding just experienced. Choral pieces share similarities with montages in the following ways:

- Depending on their placement, choral pieces in the middle of a script can also change the rhythm of speech in the play, causing an audience to pay closer attention to what follows.
- Choral pieces highlight that many participants were interviewed and present the audience with a collection of perspectives on a finding (Salvatore, 2025).
- Choral pieces do not include a statement of each character's identifier before speaking because the snippets may be shorter than the identifier.
- Choral pieces only include voices from characters who appear elsewhere in the script. However, an exception to this point could be using other participants from a dataset that have not become characters in the script in any other way. This choice could include all participants' voices in the ethnodrama as a way to honor their participation in the research process (LaBonte, Mosley, Hamilton, Forbes, & McKinnie, 2023). In these cases, the ethnodramatist should make the sources of the choral piece clear to the audience.

In *That's Not Supposed to Be Happening* (Huff & Salvatore, 2023), VPL's ethnodrama about housing in New York City, co-creator Keith R. Huff worked with the project's sound designer, Megan Hayward, to create three choral pieces that we used as transitions between scenes. Once we had identified the 10 participants and completed the initial draft of the script, Keith returned to the audio recordings of the interviews. He transcribed those 10 participants' responses to three specific prompts:

1. How do you define quality housing?
2. How do you define home?
3. How much of your approximate monthly income goes toward rent each month?

Megan then recorded the actors speaking these responses in each participant's vocal cadence and had other production team members read and record the three prompts. Using these materials, Megan created three recorded choral pieces, leading with the recorded prompt followed by snippets from the responses of various participants to the prompt as voiced by the actor portraying them. Each prerecorded choral piece played as a transition into a scene that was somehow related to its content. The choral example below features five characters' responses to the prompt, "How do you define quality housing?" As you read, you will see the prompt followed by snippets from Beatriz, Brian Cunningham, 42-Year-Old Female, Linda, and Davidson.

VOICE
How do you define quality housing?

BEATRIZ
Basic human needs met so you know

BRIAN CUNNINGHAM
Paying a fair
market rate

BEATRIZ
Bathroom

42-YEAR-OLD FEMALE
Something that is free of hazards uh

BEATRIZ
Kitchen

42-YEAR-OLD FEMALE
Free of pests

BRIAN CUNNINGHAM
Sanitary

BEATRIZ
Roof over your head

LINDA
I think there needs to be uhm
supermarket

BRIAN CUNNINGHAM
Safe

BEATRIZ
Heat
during the winter

LINDA
Uhm subway station near the house

BRIAN CUNNINGHAM
And provides them
stability

42-YEAR-OLD FEMALE
Something that is livable conditions
uhm

DAVIDSON
A place that you can go to
and feel comfortable
being yourself.

The choral piece resembles a list poem in its fragmented construction and quickly identifies what matters to the five participants when asked about their definition of quality housing. All of the responses are words or short phrases, not even complete sentences, with the longest coming from Davidson, used as a button to end because he highlights that quality housing should be "a place that you can go to and feel comfortable being yourself." The choral piece played as a transition when the actors moved chairs and costume pieces into place for their next scene. In their sound design, Megan plotted the voices to come from different speakers in the theatre, giving the audience a sense of the voices coming from various locations and directions, representing the multiple locations where the interviews took place. The scene that followed this choral piece featured three characters. One spoke about how a city or state might define quality housing. The other two characters shared personal experiences about bed bugs in their apartment and elevators breaking down in a 50-story luxury apartment building. The choral construction introduced the concept, and the following scene deepened and complicated the idea by introducing more specific and personal experiences that emerged during the data collection process.

The actors could have performed the choral piece live but given the other actions they needed to perform in the transition, a prerecorded choral piece offered more efficiency and flexibility with the staging. Megan also initially asked to use the original interview recordings to execute this idea, but we did not include that request to the participants as part of the consenting process. Hence, the choice to have the actors record the responses instead. If an ethnodramatist would like to use participants' voices from the original interview recordings, they should outline that clearly as part of the consenting process at the time of the interview.

A Hint about Creating
Multivoice Scripting Conventions

Many ethnodramatists may create these multivoice scripting conventions electronically using a word processing program. I rely on single-sided printed copies of each interview excerpt and a pencil. I read through the single excerpt, mark in pencil where I think the breaks are, and then use scissors to cut the excerpt into those sections. I repeat the process with each excerpt that will become part of the constructed conversation, and then I arrange the clipped pieces of paper in the order I would like them to appear. I assign a letter to each original excerpt, and as I cut them, I write that letter in the margin. That way, I lessen the chance of confusing who is speaking as the excerpts get cut and mixed together. Once I have ordered the pieces, I add a number to each piece of paper to track the order. I stack the pieces in their order, then go to a computer and repeat the process electronically, following the order I created using the hard copies. If this step seems repetitive or tedious, work directly on the computer. Find the best way to work for you.

Ending the Script

Like many types of writing projects, finding the ending for an ethnodrama can be the most challenging part of the scripting process. Up to this point, the ethnodrama has presented various findings from the thematic bins, but there also has to be a way to bring the ethnodrama to a logical conclusion. A traditional play concludes via its **dénouement**, the circumstances and actions that unfold to resolve the protagonist's central conflict. The audience witnesses this resolution; they may experience some form of catharsis or emotional release, and then they leave the theatre. The ending of an ethnodrama functions differently because the dissemination of research findings does not necessarily follow a traditional dramatic structure. Rather than experiencing an emotional release, the audience for an ethnodrama should have the urge to engage with what they have learned through their experience of the performance. Therefore, an ethnodrama's final moments should somehow catalyze that urge for the audience.

When I arrive at this ending moment in the scripting process, I consider the following questions about how to end:

- Does the script's ending revisit the concepts and ideas explored in earlier sections to summarize the findings?

- Does the script's ending draw a conclusion about the research findings for the audience?

- Does the script's ending encourage the audience to draw their own conclusions or ask new questions about the research topic?

Given that the narrative of the ethnodrama should focus more on the audience's experience of the script rather than the characters' experiences, I consider the audience's experience as I think through my answers to these three questions. The conclusion of the play is not a place to introduce a new voice into the mix, so the ending moments always feature characters that have already contributed. I mentioned earlier that a choral piece could function as a summary of key ideas from the play, so sometimes it might make sense to pull lines from already-performed excerpts to review what the audience has heard. I typically have the scripting conventions wind down in their complexity in my work, so I rarely end with a choral piece or montage.

As I reviewed the endings of various scripts I created over the years, I have tended to go from a complicated convention such as a quartet or montage down to a duet, followed by one, two, or three monologues. The ending is a way for the audience to slowly come out of the meditation that I have asked them to engage with for the duration of the play, and ending with the solo voices allows that to happen most effectively in the script and performance. I review the thematic bins for possible excerpts that can help summarize the research findings while ensuring that the ending excerpts come from characters the audience has already encountered. Sometimes, the final monologue holds the play's title or features a character posing a question I want the audience to consider. Other times, multiple characters have offered a response that could make for a great ending. I must be extra careful in these moments to avoid creating a play that ends numerous times. An audience can sense when something is wrapping up, and if that wrapping up happens repeatedly, they are likely to stop paying attention. If that happens, the dissemination process loses its focus and momentum. The way a script concludes may also set up the circumstances for further audience engagement and participation in an experience that follows the performance. I address these potentials in Chapter 8.

I have also learned that the script's ending often emerges most clearly through a workshop reading of the script and during the staging and rehearsal process. In most ethnodramas I have made, I have waited until later in the rehearsal process to make the final determination for the ending because sometimes the full implications of the research can only present themselves once the ethnodrama becomes a more realized piece of ethnotheatre. The initial ending I crafted during the scripting process frequently changed once I heard the play out loud, and often the ending changed again as I worked through the staging and rehearsal process. I made these changes to better reflect the discoveries that emerged through data analysis and interpretation. The ethnodramatist can craft an ending for the script using their best insights and instincts, but then they should be prepared to make adjustments and changes during the drafting, redrafting, and rehearsal processes (Salvatore, 2020b).

Titles

A title for any project can be elusive and challenging to determine. I usually begin my process with a title for the project itself, as I have often had to give it a name to request funding through a grant application or in an initial pitch to a collaborator or sponsoring organization. For example, *Of a Certain Age* (Salvatore, 2018) started as "The 65+ Project," as the ethnodrama's title ultimately came from a phrase used by several participants during their interviews. The project about political polarization started as *Portraits US: Polarization*. During our second stage of the coding process, while selecting participants and excerpts to include in the script and performance, we discovered a participant named Angel who used the phrase "Whatever you are, be a good one."[5] Given that the project's second research question sought ways to overcome political polarization, this phrase from Angel's interview offered an excellent title for the project overall.

Both of these examples demonstrate my primary approach to titling an ethnodrama. Once I arrive at a drafted script, I look for a title within the script itself. I like to find a line from a character's transcript that summarizes the findings or indicates a central idea that the ethnodrama might address. This titling process mirrors the same method I use to title each of the transcript excerpts and reflects the idea of using an *in vivo* code for the title of the overall script as well. I also prefer that the ethnodrama's title come from the participants' words, as this choice centers and reinforces the importance of their experiences and what they have offered to the project.

Drafting and Redrafting

Once the ethnodramatist has a working draft of the ethnodrama, they can share the draft with others to obtain feedback. As in any writing process, an ethnodrama should move through an extensive drafting process before completion. In more traditional qualitative research projects, a researcher shares a written document with trusted colleagues and advisors and receives written and oral feedback on that draft. Similarly, an ethnodramatist can share a draft of a script, and colleagues and advisors can offer their reactions after reading it. That said, those reading should respond to the script and its potential as a piece of theatre, not just as a piece of research. Additionally, those providing feedback should have experience reading and imagining how plays come to life in performance.

Traditional plays move through a similar kind of feedback and drafting process. A playwright completes the first draft of a play and shares it with a trusted colleague, a dramaturg, a director, or a literary manager with a theatre company. Whatever the reader's role, they read the play using their imagination to hear the play's dialogue in their head and to interpret the play's stage directions to imagine how it would unfold in a live performance. Understanding how a script translates into a live performance is a specialized skill that develops with time, training, and exposure to many different styles of plays. Our general education system usually emphasizes understanding plays as pieces of literature rather than performance texts, so playwrights must seek feedback from colleagues who understand how to read a script as the roadmap to a performance. After receiving feedback, a playwright may attempt another draft. However, playwrights usually also seek opportunities to hear their script read aloud by actors because hearing the play provides more information about how it sounds. Just as a real person speaks with a unique rhythm and cadence, playwrights have distinctive ways of using language to create meaning through how their fictional characters talk.

Playwrights rarely, if ever, produce the first draft of anything they have written. Plays go through multiple drafts and sometimes years of development, including reading the play with actors sitting around a table. A script development process could also include a **staged reading**, in which actors carry scripts and execute minimal blocking developed in collaboration with a director. **Blocking** refers to the physical movements of actors on stage during a performance. They might sit in a chair at a particular moment or cross from one side of the stage to another to help emphasize a specific point. Staged readings do not include design elements such as scenery, lighting, props, sound effects, or projections. Instead, a stage manager or another actor reads some stage directions aloud to help the audience understand the play's action. A staged reading helps a playwright to begin seeing their play come to life on stage, allowing other kinds of editing to occur. The drafting and feedback process for an ethnodrama should include script readings, so that the ethnodramatist can understand how the script sounds when performed. A reading can also help determine the running time of the ethnodrama. If the ethnodrama runs longer than the desired target time, the ethnodramatist can look for ways to shorten the script.

When I complete a draft of an ethnodrama and feel ready for a reading, I assemble a group of actors for an initial read-through. Beyond the actors, I also invite the other collaborators working with me on the project. These collaborators could include a dramaturg, a co-creator, an assistant director, and possibly designers, depending on how quickly the production process will unfold. I hold the reading around a large table, so everyone can see one another as we read. I provide hard copies of the script for everyone gathered and ask them to note any observations, discoveries, or questions on the script as we go along. We read without stopping and then discuss their notes at the end of the reading. I make sure that I have the same number of actors who will eventually perform the script so that, if actors play more than one character, I can determine whether how I divided up the characters among the actors makes sense and is performable. For instance, if the reading reveals that an actor must quickly shift from one character to another, I can reconsider the character assignments or alter the order of the script.

This initial read-through with actors provides invaluable information about whether my choices throughout the scripting process have created a logical progression that effectively addresses the ethnodrama's research question. While I have a hard copy of the script on hand and make notes as we go, I try my best not to read along. Instead, I focus on listening to the script as if I were an audience member hearing it for the first time. Given my familiarity with the data, it can be challenging to pretend to hear it for the first time. However, my training as a dramaturg has equipped me to approach plays and rehearsals with a fresh perspective each time I experience them. Also, the actors and other collaborators in attendance may be experiencing it for the first time, so their impressions are paramount as I approach the redrafting process. I also time the reading to see how long it takes, as the ultimate running time is important. During the reading, I keep the following questions in mind:

- Does the script have a clear beginning, middle, and end?
- Do any sections of the ethnodrama feel redundant, and if so, where? Can sections be cut or trimmed without losing the overall effectiveness of the ideas presented?
- Are there any sections that seem out of order and should be moved to create a better overall flow?
- Is one character dominating the ethnodrama or a particular section or scene? Does this dominant character serve the ethnodrama or create an imbalance?
- Do any duets, trios, quartets, montages, or choral pieces need more bounce?
- Does the placement of any longer monologues slow down the flow of the ethnodrama?
- Is there a significant theme or viewpoint missing from the ethnodrama that was apparent in the interviewing or coding process? Can it be added? Does it need to be added?
- Does the ethnodrama have more than one ending? Developing scripts often suffer from multiple endings, and ethnodramas are no exception (Salvatore, 2020b, 2025).

Sometimes, as I approach this initial read-through, I want specific feedback on one or more of these questions, and in that case, I pose them to the group before we begin for their consideration as the reading unfolds. Otherwise, when we finish the read-through, I suggest a short break, and then we come back together to discuss initial thoughts and impressions. Hearing and receiving feedback about a new script can be challenging, especially in its early stages. I usually begin by asking for affirmations, as hearing positive feedback first always helps soften the critical feedback that comes next. After the affirmations, I ask for moments that those in attendance found confusing. I also invite listeners to identify places where their attention waned. Moments of confusion and loss of attention are strong indicators of places where I may need to do more work on the script. To assess the effectiveness of the ethnodrama as dissemination, I ask those in attendance what they learned about the topic at hand. As the purpose of the ethnodrama is to disseminate research findings, the reading should spark new evidence of learning in the attendees. Even if those in attendance are familiar with the interview excerpts, their arrangement in the script should reveal something new. Hearing what attendees learned from the reading offers perspective about whether the ethnodrama presents its research findings clearly and as intended by the ethnodramatist.

Hearing the script aloud typically helps me identify redundancies in content and character, which may mean an idea or individual has taken more time in the script than necessary to make a point. I also learn where I need to add more bounce to duets, trios, quartets, montages, or choral pieces, or I may discover that one of these has too much bounce. This initial reading may also reveal that I have arranged multiple endings. Depending on the answers to these questions and whatever else I discover, I typically need to make further revisions to the script before rehearsals begin. If the ethnodrama requires significant revisions, another reading may be necessary to determine the effectiveness of any changes I make in the redrafting process. If only minor revisions are necessary, I can make those as the rehearsal process begins with the actors who will perform the play. If the initial read-through of an ethnodrama includes actors who will perform in the actual production, I can also learn about which actors might play which characters. I can experiment with multiple configurations and combinations of actors in various roles.

One rule to remember: The ethnodramatist should hear something they have created at least three times before deciding to make a change. Sometimes, an actor might struggle with a particular moment, and then, with more rehearsal time, the moment becomes clear. Or a scripted section sounds like it's unfolding too slowly, but the actors just need more time to learn their lines and pick up their cues. Don't jump to make changes the first time a section of the script doesn't go as planned. Give yourself and your collaborators the chance to work through the moment at least three times before attempting a revision.

Previously, I mentioned that an early reading of a draft of *open heart* revealed the need to include an additional section that acknowledged more of the challenges faced by the men living in open, non-monogamous relationships. That realization emerged from hearing the play out loud and listening carefully and openly to feedback from those who attended the reading. With the initial read-through of *Making Gay History: Before Stonewall* (Salvatore, 2020a), I learned that one excerpt I had included from an interview with J. J. Belanger did not make sense when I heard it out loud and in relationship with the other pieces. I knew I wanted Belanger's voice to be part of the play because he talked about his experiences as a soldier during World War II. Belanger described his romantic relationship with a Canadian Air Force pilot and revealed that the pilot died in combat in 1944 (*Making Gay History* podcast, J. J. Belanger, Episode Transcript). I initially chose an excerpt that described the circumstances surrounding the pilot's death because the story moved me. When I heard the excerpt aloud during the reading, I felt that it reinforced a stereotype from that period in history of the unfortunate gay man meeting an untimely end. Belanger remained in the play, but I selected a different excerpt where he discussed the acceptance he and his lover experienced when they visited his lover's family as an openly gay couple in the early 1940s. Belanger's story of acceptance offered a unique narrative around familial acceptance for this particular historical moment. I felt that it better inspired the audience to consider their preconceived notions about the experiences of gay men in this period.

The initial read-through for *Of a Certain Age* included a mix of the researcher-actors who conducted interviews and other actors available for the reading, as well as the stage manager, designers, dramaturg, and Traci DiGesu, the social worker for The Entertainment Community Fund, who had commissioned the project. We read draft #3 of the script, and that experience answered several of my go-to questions. Some answers affirmed my scripting choices, while others revealed challenges to address in subsequent drafts. First and foremost, the reading revealed that the ethnodrama had a clear beginning, middle, and end, and even with its collage-like structure of various scenes depicting the findings from the thematic bins, the script had a dramatic arc that effectively communicated the findings. The reading also confirmed that the script's structure of 16 characters worked, and each actor had enough time between their different character portrayals to adjust their performances accordingly. However, specific monologues' positions needed to be adjusted to account for places where the script lost momentum. At various points during the reading, I also noted places in duets, trios, and quartets where I felt the tempo of the play begin to drag, and many attendees noted similar moments where they lost focus. I returned to the scored transcripts in those sections, looked for logical breaks that would allow me to create smaller excerpts for certain characters, and then restructured the conversations in each section to incorporate more bounce. I also found places in transcripts where a character made their relevant point earlier or later than I initially realized during the coding process, and this allowed me to trim the beginning or end of the coded transcript to help tighten the overall script and save time. These trimmed moments occurred at the beginning or the end, but never internally, to maintain the integrity of the selected excerpt. (Salvatore, 2020b).

Some of the script's restructuring continued well into the rehearsal process because staging the play revealed additional challenges and offered other solutions. For example, one quartet required multiple rewrites, including one night in the middle of a rehearsal in the theatre aisle with the dramaturg and the assistant director, until we finally arrived at a playable version for the actors. The quartet editing that continued into the rehearsal process created stress for all of us, most notably the actors because my edits caused them to relearn the quartet each time I changed it. Generally, I recommend setting a hard deadline of 2 weeks before a new play's first performance to finalize all script changes. This deadline allows actors to feel secure with their lines and find the rhythm and pacing of the play in performance. As described earlier, the script's ending often clarifies as all elements come together, so the actors and creative team must remain flexible.

I mentioned that, during our initial reading for *Of a Certain Age*, we read draft #3 of the script. Ultimately, the actors performed draft #12 for an audience. The redrafting and rehearsal processes revealed the version of the script that best presented the research findings, but I had to exercise a lot of patience to get there. I also benefited from working with dramaturg Sarah Bellantoni during the redrafting process, as she helped to sift through the feedback from the initial read-through and discoveries that continued to emerge through the rehearsal process.

Initial readings can also reveal how an ethnodramatist's bias might affect what they think should emerge from a dataset. Again, the process for *Of a Certain Age* offers an excellent example. After listening to the reading, Traci DiGesu, who commissioned the project, asked me, "Where's the sadness?" Based on her experiences as a social worker at The Entertainment Community Fund and our ongoing conversations during the data collection, we had hypothesized that older performing arts professionals would share sad stories about growing older. The ethnodrama included unpleasant, unfair, and difficult memories and experiences related to growing older and encountering ageism, but the script also offered positive takes, filled with warmth, humor, and gratitude. After hearing Traci's response, I wondered whether we, as an interviewing team, had missed something in our data collection and analysis processes. The team members knew that Traci and I wanted to educate our audiences about the experiences of growing older to combat ageism. We trained the interviewers about aging and ageism and instructed them to code for participants' responses that answered the research questions. Still, stories of sadness did not emerge as a recurring pattern in their conversations with these participants (Salvatore, 2020b).

This experience reminded me of an essential rule for ethnodrama or any research process, and I keep repeating it because of its importance. We cannot force data to say what we want or think they should say. We can only present what emerged through the data collection and analysis processes. With *Of a Certain Age*, we discovered that when we interviewed our participants, a particular group of older performing arts professionals, they spoke more optimistically than we expected. And that was a finding we presented to our audiences for their consideration (Salvatore, 2020b). Because theatre relies on conflict as a central driving force, ethnodramatists can sometimes feel pressured to search their dataset for moments highlighting problems, high-stakes emotions, or overly dramatic revelations. If those types of findings do not exist in your coding of a dataset, do not go looking for them. We may enter a project with a hypothesis (or worse, an assumption) about what we think we might discover, but a hypothesis differs from a finding. Don't manipulate the dataset to confirm a hypothesis or assumption; embrace the discoveries that emerge, which include the possibility that you might have been wrong about what you thought you would find.

An ethnodramatist's script drafting and redrafting process relies on a delicate balance of instinct and experience, and an ability to take in and sift through feedback from various actors, team members, and trusted colleagues. With time, energy, and patience, the ethnodramatist arrives at a workable draft of their script and then can confidently enter the rehearsal process for an ethnotheatrical production, a three-dimensional embodiment of a project's findings. New discoveries and changes may continue to emerge through rehearsal, but a solid working draft provides an excellent foundation to build upon.

ACTIVITIES

Experimenting with a Montage

An ethnodramatist can use the montage scripting convention to illuminate various perspectives on a particular topic, using shorter excerpts from interviews than one might use in a duet, trio, or quartet. In Chapter 5, I shared the duet between Robert Faris and Diane Felmlee, the sociologists who coined the term "social combat." I also mentioned that before their duet in the script, I had placed a montage of other interview participants attempting to define the term in their own words. Below, you will see the four interview excerpts I used to construct that montage from Boston Area Female, Brian, Ed, and Jeff. Notice that Jeff's excerpt is longer than the others, which gave me an indication of how to proceed. Using these excerpts, see if you can create a montage that demonstrates different perspectives on what social combat might mean. Begin by splitting Jeff's piece into four sections, then decide where to insert Boston Area Female, Brian, and Ed. I present the excerpts here alphabetized by name. Feel free to shift the order of the other three. Once you've created your montage, find some collaborators to read it aloud so you can experience your arrangement and its bounce.

BOSTON-AREA FEMALE
I'm not sure I know what that is I did read Joe's email and I assume it has something to do
    with bullying
um
and maybe it's the new word for bullying
because it emcompasses a lot of different kinds of bullying including maybe
uh cyber-
cyber bullying.

BRIAN
I don't think I've ever heard that term.
Uhm
I have no reaction I've never heard it it's a new one to me.
I'm- I'm shocked actually 'cause
like I keep up with things.

ED
I'm going to assume it refers to what happens when
two or more people
get into a hostile situation with each other
but not a physically hostile situation- emotional, psychological things like that.

JEFF
Social combat
uhhh
wow

I don't know- I don't know that I am familiar with the term.
Umm
I mean I guess I could-
I could make a conjecture as to what it means.
Umm
social combat
there is combat
there is fighting going on
social combat
like
seems like
uh-
I don't find that
um
bullying is about combat
because it's-
that implies that it's-
that you have
um
perhaps equal forces
um
when in fact bullying to me seems to be more about
um
an unequal playing field as it were.
Combat implies that there is
a force back
because there are equal forces
not necessarily equal
but there are forces
and I-
in my experience of bullying it was very much about
um-
um
an aggressor and a victim.
So
anyway
so
my two cents.

Trimming for Length

The initial reading of a new ethnodrama can reveal much information for an ethno-dramatist, including places where a character may speak for too long. When these moments emerge, the artist-researcher should not cut the section entirely, but instead look for ways to trim from the transcript's beginning or end. Others may advocate for internal cuts to a transcript excerpt, but remember that I prefer to maintain the integrity of the participant's way of speaking. Looking for ways to trim at the beginning or end can help to achieve that goal. Below, I've included a transcript from Lulu, a character in *That's Not Supposed to Be Happening*, the project about housing in New York City. Lulu's monologue appeared first in the play in the version I've shared below. However, let's imagine that I wanted to trim this monologue to cut some time from the overall running time of the performance. I've come to you as the dramaturg on the project to ask for your assistance in determining where we can make some trims. Review the transcript in its current form and decide where to trim from the beginning, end, or both while retaining the relevant and theatrically compelling parts of Lulu's response.

Title: "I really remember that was a big change in the city"
Timestamp: 5:34-7:57

LULU
Well that's-
OK uh
it's gonna go historic.
First of all
if some people know the Lower East Side Tenement Museum
as like, "Oh, that's the way New York was" I lived that.
My grandparents'
uh
apartment was a tenement apartment.
And it was a community of
uh in East Harlem.
And all the doors were open and people were welcoming and the doors were open too to get
     air
into the tenement apartment.
My earliest childhood apartment was on uh-
let's say on a hundred and fifteen street it was a-
y- I guess you could call it a brownstone it was a small building
and then we moved
around the corner to Third Avenue
uh
on a hundred and sixteen street and that was what was called a railroad apartment
where you went through all the rooms.
But what also was outside our window was the Third Avenue L.
So I got to see
the
trains going by and what I don't recall- I read this later that they stopped at 6 o'clock.
I don't remember that and we sort of were used to that.
And I remember when the Third Avenue L wa-
was uh
demolished and I got to see the last car go by.
But in terms of New York City and the landscaping of the city
uh

that was a big revelation to me because I saw the change
because of the removal of the L.
If you see those old film noir movies
the L
created shadows so there were a lot of bars underneath
sort of what we i- if you're an old New Yorker you know the like Blarney Stone bars
uh
which I can still remember the smell of.
I used to go in there with my father.
Anyway what really
uh
what I noted was
that after that
especially going down on Third Avenue say to the 60s
where Bloomingdale's is
the change
in that neighborhood-
and that was when a lot of
what you call 1960 high rises with the white brick
happen.
So I really remember that was a big change
in the city uh
and let me tell you the Third Avenue L was a fun ride.
If you got in the first car it went to Chinatown it was like a roller coaster.

NOTES

1. The acting company for *That's Not Supposed to Be Happening* included Anabel Anisfeld, Annie Abramczyk, Elijah Reyes, Ellen Mimi Schlecht, and Nicole Mercedes.

2. The interviewing team for *That's Not Supposed to Be Happening* included Taylor Beckman, Nicole Borbone, Susana Bustamante, Averil Carr, Wansu Ding, Wanshan Du, Lydia Funke, Tamara Geisler, Davor Golub, Qichuan Jiang, Melania Krych, Jen Lee, Zhihan Li, Isabella Lucia Maitino, Elizabeth Nguyen, Molly-Ann Nordin, Martina Novakova, Victoria Ostroumoff, Lauren Palmeri, Xiao Peng, Lily Plummer, Olivia Qian, Beitong Qu, Michael Roberts, Blake Salesin, Kristen Schwarz, Laura Silva, Erin Smith, Zeyuan Tang, May Tashiro, Shivani Thanneer, Melanie Torres, Margaux Trexler, Ari Weiss, Serena Wolman, Shihan Wu, Xinyi Zhang, and Yuqing Zhao.

3. Notice that I spell out *four foot one* to represent a height here in Ed's transcript, but in Nate's transcript that begins the quartet, I used 5'4" to represent a height. I transcribe exactly what the participant says, which means that these kinds of variations will occur.

4. The acting company for *open heart* included Chris Bresky, Stephen Donovan, Daryl Embry, Nick Lewis, and Karl O'Brian Williams. *open heart* received funding support from an NYU Steinhardt Research Challenge Grant in Arts and Culture.

5. Many people, including Angel, attribute this quotation to Abraham Lincoln, but our research revealed that the actual source is unclear.

7 Production

Moving from Ethnodrama to Ethnotheatre

Once the ethnodramatist arrives at a performance-ready draft of their script, the ethnodrama can move into rehearsals to become a piece of ethnotheatre. As a reminder from Chapter 1, ethnotheatre refers to the theatrical production of an ethnodrama that disseminates the investigation's findings to an audience and then engages them in an additional data collection process to further explore the ethnodrama's research question and assess its impact. The rehearsal and production process follows the aesthetic framework established by the script while also taking into account the unique dynamics introduced by live performance.

Ethnotheatre often uses **reader's theatre** to present an ethnodrama to an audience. In reader's theatre, actors do not memorize their lines but simply read the play aloud using vocal inflection to bring the play to life. The actors usually sit in chairs with their scripts in binders or stand at music stands. There is no blocking or movement in the presentation and no design elements. While this is an economical and efficient way to present an ethnodrama, reader's theatre is deceptively tricky due to its lack of staging and theatrical dynamics. Without other elements to help convey the research findings, the burden of dissemination lies entirely on the script and the actors reading it. Unfortunately, some practitioners assume anyone can perform reader's theatre because of its perceived simplicity. On the contrary, actors for a reader's theatre presentation must be highly skilled, particularly when portraying multiple characters.

I advocate for a more fully realized ethnotheatrical production of the ethnodrama because disseminating the research findings benefits from this presentation style. When creating ethnotheatre, Johnny Saldaña (2011a) reminds all of us to "stop thinking like a social scientist and start thinking like an artist" (p. 37), and I take his advice to apply to all the elements of a produced ethnodrama. I have discussed the importance of a dramaturg throughout the process, and their role should continue as the script becomes a piece of ethnotheatre. Given the dramaturg's proximity to the scripting process, their presence throughout rehearsals can help to maintain the ethnodramatist's intentions as more voices with more ideas engage with the data. The creative process for ethnotheatre should also rely on trained actors, directors, and designers, specifically those who understand that this theatre style has a greater purpose than simply to entertain. Not every actor, director, or designer should work in ethnotheatre. Throughout my time making plays in this style, I have learned that intellectual curiosity, generosity of spirit, openness to experimentation, and flexibility are all great qualities to look for in ethnotheatre collaborators. Given the collaborative nature of theatre as an art form, one might assume that anyone working in the theatre would have those qualities. Unfortunately, that has not always been my experience.

In particular, I have found that most trained directors have minimal experience working with plays constructed from qualitative data. Directors typically receive training in script analysis and interpretation, leading them to develop their own conceptual orientation to the play that helps make their production unique. We call this a **director's concept**. Think about Baz Luhrmann's 1996 film *Romeo + Juliet,* starring Claire Danes and Leonardo DiCaprio. It's a great film and an excellent adaptation of Shakespeare's original play; not the play as written, but a movie featuring Luhrmann's high-concept interpretation of the original. We see these kinds of conceptual productions of Shakespeare's work all the time in an attempt to make the plays more accessible to a contemporary audience. In the case of an ethnodrama (and any new play, for that matter), the director should not lay their concept on top of the play. Answering the ethnodrama's research question should be the focus of its production; the director of an ethnodrama needs to understand this. Because of the need to commit to the research question, I usually direct the ethnodramas I create, so the remainder of this chapter includes my perspective and practices as a director. Playwrights usually enlist a director to help craft the production of a play, so if you choose to do this, make sure that the director understands the form and agrees that the primary purpose of the ethnotheatrical production is to disseminate the research findings. If the ethnodrama is part of your dissertation project, confirm the director's role in your research and dissemination process. This conversation should happen with your dissertation chair and committee members as early as possible to avoid misunderstandings about methodology and process.

I wrote in Chapter 1 about the importance of theatrical training when working with ethnodrama, and as an ethnodrama enters its production phase, this training becomes even more critical. Background and experience in playwriting, dramaturgy, directing technique and theory, and design will help to lay a strong foundation for the team charged with creating ethnotheatre. An ethnodramatist also benefits in this transition to production from having completed reading and viewing of other ethnodramas. Understanding how other ethnodramas have moved from script to performance can be helpful as the ethnodramatist's own rehearsal and production process unfolds.

This chapter illuminates the production process for a piece of ethnotheatre, beginning with an explanation of performance phenomenology as it relates to this specific form and highlighting German playwright and director Bertolt Brecht's concept of *Verfremdung* as a technique to engage audiences in their analysis of the research findings. I offer particular attention to a style of performance that actors can use in ethnotheatrical productions and the implications this has on casting. The chapter also demonstrates how staging and design elements such as movement, costuming, lighting, scenic elements, sound, and projection can contribute to the overall aesthetic presentation of an ethnodrama and increase the effectiveness of dissemination.

Performance Phenomenology

A play takes place within a particular world, which has its own logic. For example, in a piece of American musical theatre, such as *RENT*, the character Roger suddenly breaks into the song "One Song Glory" because his circumstances so move him that singing is the only way he can express the scope of his feelings. The simple act of speaking is no longer an option. This breaking into song does not happen for most of us in real life, but it happens in American musical theatre. In a play by Shakespeare, characters turn and speak directly to the audience, taking them into their confidence. In his famous soliloquy at the start of *Richard III*, the title character reveals his devious plan to take the crown, saying he is "determined to prove a villain." The audience then watches as Richard's plan unfolds during the performance. There is no doubt about his actions because he has clearly communicated his intentions. In Lorraine Hansberry's play *A Raisin in the Sun*, the audience watches the Youngers, a Black family living on Chicago's South Side in the 1950s, struggling to find their individual paths to the American Dream. The audience sits in the dark in silence and witnesses the family's life unfolding in a too-small apartment that reflects their socioeconomic status. Each actor becomes the person they are portraying, and they never acknowledge the audience's presence until the end of the performance, when they take their final bows. The audience suspends their disbelief and invests in the idea that these actors are actually the Younger family. These examples from very different kinds of plays all describe elements of the logic of their unique and specific worlds.

Creating any live performance requires an awareness of **performance phenomenology**, which, for our purposes here, I define as the relationship between the audience, the performers, and the material being performed. This relationship helps define and maintain the world of a play as a performance unfolds. In a typical theatre experience, like any of the aforementioned performances, an actor performs a character for an audience. The performance phenomenology of the event takes the form of a triad: actor–character–audience (Olf, 1997) (see Figure 7.1).

In staging these more traditional plays, a director must consider the relationship between these three elements and make choices that support this triad. The relationship is different for each one and thus demands a different approach to performance. For example, Hansberry's play is an example of American Realism and requires a particular realistic acting style. The actor transforms and becomes the character, and the audience only sees the character in performance; the actor's identity disappears. A director guides the actor to make choices through rehearsals and performances that reinforce this particular actor–character–audience triad. An actor playing Beneatha in Hansberry's play

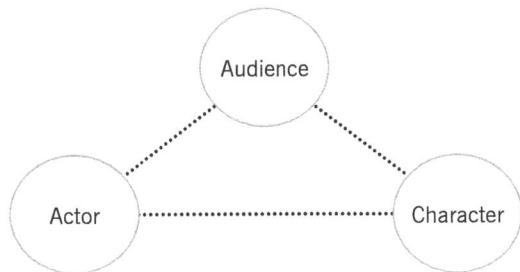

FIGURE 7.1 The performance phenomenology of a traditional theatre experience: the triad.

should not directly address the audience, as that choice would not align with the logic of the world of the play (Salvatore, 2025).

An ethnotheatrical production must consider performance phenomenology and its effect on an audience's ability to interpret the presentation of findings through performance. In ethnotheatre, the performance phenomenology is more complex and better represented by a pentagon: interview participant–artist-researcher–actor–character–audience (see Figure 7.2).

An interview participant speaks with an artist-researcher, who then transcribes and codes the interview text. Those choices become part of a larger dataset analyzed for recurring patterns. Those

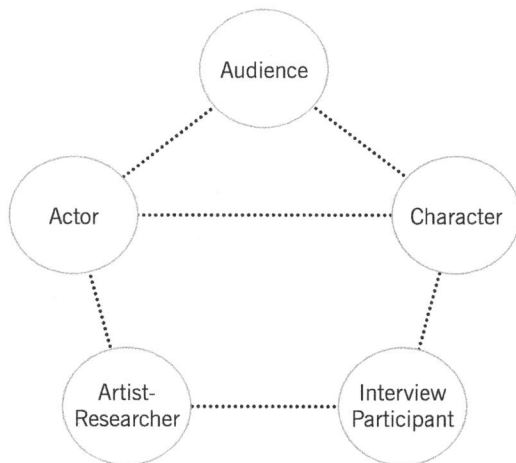

FIGURE 7.2 The phenomenology of an ethno-theatre production: the performance pentagon.

patterns become findings arranged into a script, then learned and interpreted by/as an actor and performed for an audience. The "by/as" distinction for the actor considers that the artist-researcher could be the actor or not; even if it is the same individual, they process the data differently depending on the role in the pentagon. Because of this performance pentagon, the ethnotheatre production must somehow acknowledge the research process, data analysis, script construction, and the portrayal of findings through the voicing and embodiment of characters. The pentagon also helps us to remember that the play's characters are directly related to the participants who spoke those words initially. The audience then interprets their experience with the data, leading to their own conclusions about the phenomenon explored by the ethnodrama. The director of ethnotheatre must utilize performance aesthetics to highlight this pentagon, so that the audience remains engaged in the interpretive process. While audiences make interpretations of material in any theatrical experience, the audience's responsibility to interpret data and draw conclusions increases significantly in ethnotheatre (Salvatore, 2025).

To facilitate this audience awareness and engagement in meaning making, an ethnotheatrical production benefits from embracing theatrical conventions that remind an audience that they are watching a piece of theatre. These reminders help to raise the audience's critical consciousness and focus them on the research discoveries presented by the ethnodrama. A director of ethnotheatre should consult the theoretical writings of the German playwright Bertolt Brecht for guidance with this process (Salvatore, 2025). Brecht was born in Augsburg, Germany, in 1898 and began his writing career during the Weimar period. He continued producing plays through World War II, eventually leaving the world with 26 plays when he died in 1956. He and other literary figures of the Weimar period dealt mainly with "urban life and all the social, psychological, and political tensions associated with modern urban society" (Pinson, 1966, p. 459). Brecht wrote and directed plays that looked at the world in a specific way to assist his audience members in understanding the social and political forces around them. By shedding light on these forces, Brecht hoped that his audience members would leave the theatre with an urge to change their world (Haus, 1991). Brecht is most associated with *The Threepenny Opera*, which includes music by Kurt Weill, *Mother Courage and Her Children, Galileo, The Good Woman of Setzuan*, and *The Caucasian Chalk Circle*.

Throughout his career, Brecht also developed and wrote about several techniques for staging his plays, coining the term *Verfremdung* to describe how he sought to raise an audience's critical awareness. This term does not have an exact English equivalent, but for many years, translators have substituted the word "alienation" when writing about Brecht's ideas in English. The scholar Meg Mumford (2018) identified that Brecht did not want to "plunge spectators into a state of alienation" but rather "sought to challenge a condition of alienation through a theatre of empowering observation" (p. 62). Mumford translates *Verfremdung* as "defamiliarization" in English because she believes that word "conveys more clearly the fact that Brecht regarded *Verfremdung* as political intervention into the (blindingly) familiar" (pp. 60–61).

Brecht (1992) described his concept in the following way:

[*Verfremdung*] consists in turning the object of which one is to be made aware, to which one's attention is to be drawn, from something ordinary, familiar, immediately accessible, into something peculiar, striking and unexpected. What is obvious is in a certain sense made incomprehensible, but this is only in order that it may then be made all the easier to comprehend. (pp. 143–144)

To achieve this *Verfremdung*, Brecht used various techniques, including a more presentational acting style, projections, placards, music, and singing, all as ways to interrupt an audience's cathartic response, so that they would instead think critically about the external forces that affected his characters and caused the events of his plays to unfold (Brecht, 1992; Mumford, 2018). Brecht's (1992) theatrical approach places the audience in a mindset of analysis and interpretation, so they can come to informed conclusions about what they have just experienced and then take action using their new knowledge. Brecht's audience maintains an awareness that they are experiencing a theatrical event, which helps avoid an emotional catharsis from overtaking a more analytical approach. Ethnotheatre should have a similar goal of disrupting an audience's emotional response to its material, so that they intentionally engage in analyzing and interpreting the research findings presented through the ethnodrama.

However, the performance dissemination must balance aesthetic engagement and entertainment with analysis, interpretation, and critical thought. An ethnotheatre director can achieve this balance by making intentional choices with various theatrical elements: acting style, casting choices, staging techniques, design elements, multimedia, and other art forms. These elements combine to create textures in a performance that can contribute to achieving this balance of aesthetics and analysis, ultimately leading to full audience engagement with the research findings.

Acting Style for Ethnotheatre

The actor's approach to portraying a character in ethnotheatre differs from that used in a more traditional play, and a director must understand and support this approach throughout the rehearsal process. Through her work as a researcher-actor on *Towards the Fear* and for her ethnodrama, *The Space Between Us All: Playing with Dissociation*, drama therapist Darci Burch (2019) coined the term "ethno-actor" to describe the unique acting approach required for an actor performing a piece of ethnotheatre. She writes:

> The actor coaching and character creation [in ethnotheatre] varies so vastly from traditional theatre that the role of "actor" is changed. I propose a new term, *ethno-actor*, to encapsulate the role. The ethno-actor is challenged to create a portrayal that maintains the dignity of and respect for the interviewee while maintaining room for new discovery of knowledge and understanding. They must be conscious in their choices to avoid caricature, misrepresentation, or falsehood in their performance. The ethno-actor is charged with the ability to have empathy for the person/role they perform in order to truthfully render the performance of the individual. Adding to the complexity of the ethno-actor's experience is the potential for the person they embody on stage to be audience to the performance. With this possibility, empathetic as well as ethical considerations come to the forefront of the ethno-actor's performance. . . . While the writer of an ethnodrama must consider how to sculpt the play to best represent the interviewee's words, the ethno-actor must continue that process in the development of vocalization, physical portrayal, movement, and acting intent. Unlike traditional pieces of theatre with fictionalized characters and speech, the ethno-actor creates verbatim or composited presentations of real people and real stories, thus adding to the responsibility of the authentic performance. (p. 29)

Burch's description uses words like "dignity," "respect," "discovery," "understanding," "empathy," "embody," "ethical," and "authentic," all of which relate to the level of care for participants that I call for at every step of an ethnodrama's creation and that the **ethnoactor**[1] and the director must maintain with the performance dissemination. I encourage ethnoactors to think about the process of performing characters as gift giving. The gift is allowing someone to experience themselves differently through the careful and attentive retelling of what they shared during their interview.

Typically, when an actor rehearses to perform a fictional character created by a playwright, the actor reads the play carefully and analyzes it to identify the character's given circumstances. The term **given circumstances** comes from the theoretical writings of Russian director Konstantin Stanislavski (1863–1938), whose Method of Physical Actions has deeply informed and influenced Western acting and actor training for the last century. In *An Actor's Work*, Stanislavski (2008) defines "given circumstances" as

> the plot, the facts, the incidents, the period, the time and place of the action [of the play], the way of life, how we as actors and directors understand the play, the contributions we ourselves make, the mise-en-scène, the sets and costumes, the props, the stage dressing, the sound effects, etc., etc., everything which is a given for the actors as they rehearse. (Stanislavski, pp. 52–53)

At first glance, this description of given circumstances implies everything an actor can learn from a close study of the play. However, the description also includes how the actors and director understand the play and the interpretive contributions they make through their creative process. For decades, theatre artists have interpreted these two elements of Stanislavski's description as meaning that the actor creates a fictional character by starting with the self, asking questions like "How am I similar to this character, and how does that inform my interpretation and performance?"; "If I were in this same situation, how would I behave?"; "What experiences from my personal life are similar to this situation, and how do I use my memories of those experiences to inform my performance of this character?" When creating a fictional character, these can be relevant questions because the character is not real.

However, as Burch (2019) points out, the ethnoactor crafts a performance of an actual person, so they have the added responsibility of delivering a performance that is authentic to that individual. Consequently, the preparation for the ethnoactor resembles an investigation, and I use that term to describe it. For this investigation, the ethnoactor should have access to the selected interview transcripts, the complete recording of the original interview, and the field notes gathered at the time of the interview. In my process, those field notes would come from the Participant Characteristics and Physical Surroundings Survey. Similar to how an actor working on a traditional play utilizes the script to identify the given circumstances, the ethnoactor working on an ethnodrama uses the available data to determine the given circumstances. For example, in a **verbatim documentary theatre** project, where the ethnoactors have access to the audio or video recordings of the interviews and to the collected field notes, the ethnoactor learns the spoken words of the character as they would in any other production, but they have the advantage of a scored transcript and a recording as a reference. Both pieces of data indicate speech patterns and provide insights into how the interview participant initially delivered the material. The field notes capture additional physical attributes and mannerisms of the participant, and those characteristics can assist in crafting the authentic portrayal of the participant.

When performing ethnotheatre, I ask ethnoactors to use verbatim performance as their technique for dissemination. As review from Chapter 3, verbatim performance is "the precise portrayal of an actual person using their exact speech and gestural patterns as a data source for investigation, literally word for word and gesture for gesture" (Salvatore, 2023; Vachon & Salvatore, 2023). My understanding and practice of this technique emerged after my introduction to Anna Deavere Smith's work in 1995. While I never studied with Smith directly, I studied and read her work extensively and saw her performances on video and in person. As a result, I developed a methodological approach to creating verbatim performance using the knowledge and insight gained from those experiences. From 1995 through 2016, this practice manifested through working with data culled from interviews that I or a team of interviewers conducted. Since 2016, my practice has expanded to include work with found media artifacts, which refer to video or audio clips of important contemporary or historical moments. The initial project that spawned this expansion is *Her Opponent*, a verbatim performance of excerpts from the 2016 U.S. presidential debates with gender-reversed casting, wherein a woman portrayed Donald Trump and a man portrayed Hillary Clinton. I co-created that piece with Maria Guadalupe, Professor of Economics at INSEAD (Guadalupe & Salvatore, 2017).[2] Although working with found media artifacts and interview-based data yields different kinds of ABR projects, verbatim performance provides a technique that encourages ethnoactors to investigate and perform the words and gestures of real people with a high level of specificity and accuracy, which leads to the authenticity that Burch (2019) calls for in her description.

An ethnoactor approaches a verbatim performance much like a musical theatre actor approaches a song. Like a singer first studies and learns the melody of a song, the ethnoactor must first study and learn to perform the patterns of speech and physicality for the character, including all of the breaks in those patterns—pauses, stumbles, stutters, changes in direction or focus—as Anna Deavere Smith (1993) believes that "the break in pattern is where the character lives" (p. xxxix). Again, these patterns are part of the character's given circumstances, but they are not fictional. After the ethnoactor can perform the character's words and gestures with technical precision, they then work with a director to explore *why* the character's breaks in pattern occur in particular moments. The ethnoactor considers what the character says and how they say it, then employs more traditional acting techniques based on Stanislavski's system. These techniques call upon the ethnoactor to use their imagination to create reasons for the character's pattern breaks. As Burch (2019) identifies, the ethnoactor cannot rely solely on traditional acting techniques used with fictional characters because honoring the authenticity of the interview participant's way of speaking and moving is fundamental. However, employing these techniques as a second step in ethnotheatre character creation can foster a more nuanced interpretation that captures the character's essence while avoiding a one-dimensional caricature, a frequent criticism of verbatim documentary theatre performances (Salvatore, 2020b, 2025). Verbatim performance can achieve a greater level of authenticity, a deeper level of understanding, and a higher standard of care because of the specificity required for the ethnoactor's investigation and performance.

Most ethnotheatre does not use verbatim performance, but instead relies on the actor to make choices as they usually would when acting as a character in a more traditional play. While I understand that approach, particularly when considering Saldaña's (2011a) reminder to ethnodramatists to think like artists rather than social scientists, I wonder about the ethical implications of performing someone's story differently than they shared it at the moment of their interview. For example, I might read a transcript from a participant and connect deeply with something they shared, so much so that I choke up as I read it. Using a traditional actor-centered technique, I would then use my emotional response to inform my portrayal of the character. But what if the participant delivered that story without choking up? What if there was anger in their voice? Or what if they offered their story with nervous laughter rather than the choking up it caused in me? How will a participant feel when they experience my portrayal of that moment if I've not honored their behavior at the moment of the interview? If, as an actor, I decide that my interpretation is more "appropriate" for the moment than the participant's original response, what am I saying about the participant's lived experience? For me, an ethical problem arises when actors freely interpret the words and gestures of real people. I use verbatim performance to disseminate the research findings in ethnotheatre to reduce that problem.

Other arts-based researchers will argue with my assertions here, and I welcome that discussion (Vachon & Salvatore, 2023). Even though I have clear preferences, I appreciate other ways to approach ethnodrama in performance. Most importantly, I advocate for transparency at each stage of the process about how data will be performed so that participants, ethnoactors, and audiences have clarity as they enter the process and engage with the ethnodrama. Vachon, Hossain, Ramsay, Moore, and Milo (2019) share a series of recommendations for ethnotheatre productions working with actors and one of Vachon's key suggestions is that there is "[a]n articulated understanding regarding the actors' and director's latitude in making artistic choices (character, aesthetic, tonal, etc.)" (p. 128). In other words, ensure everyone is on the same page about how the production will present the data from the get-go, then remain consistent and faithful to that decision throughout each step of the process.

When working with an ethnodrama that includes composite characters, more complications arise because a composite character is a work of fiction. While the composite character emerged through combining the actual words of more than one participant, I would not use verbatim performance to portray a composite character. Jumping from one way of speaking to another would not make sense for a character constructed as a single individual. The ethnoactor charged with portraying a composite character should work with the ethnodramatist and the director to identify a vocal quality that considers a detail from each participant that makes up the composite. If the composite comes from three different participants, this could be a specific way of saying a particular vowel from one, a way of upgliding from another, and the tempo of speaking from the third. Then, using those three speech characteristics, the ethnoactor can fabricate a manner of speaking that emulates something from each of the three participants yet is a fictional interpretation of the composite character. As stated in Chapter 5, the ethnodrama and, by extension, its production, should find a way to acknowledge the presence of composite characters, so that the audience understands what they are experiencing through the dissemination. Compositing is part of a project's research methodology, which should be transparent.

Casting Ethnoactors

My casting process for ethnotheatre has evolved over the years to embrace a workshop model, similar to a blended audition (Kronenberg & Ricardo, 2022). This model invites interested actors for a 90-minute session that introduces the ethnodramatic form and performance style used in the ethnotheatre production, followed by an interactive component working with interview transcripts. I teach actors how to read a scored transcript; then, I ask them to interact with pieces of data I have selected to become part of the ethnodrama. The actors read their assigned excerpts of scored transcripts aloud, placing them into a conversation with other excerpts assigned to different actors. Then, I listen to hear how attentive each actor is to the scoring and observe how they work together with others throughout the session. I may also ask the actors to perform a short nonverbal story set to a piece of music to assess their ability to identify gestures that convey meaning.

I have learned that not all actors are best suited for the ethnoacting required by a piece of ethnotheater. Burch (2019) discusses the importance of the ethnoactor's empathy for the person they are performing. While some argue that any acting relies heavily on the ability to empathize, an ethnoactor must be more sensitive to its importance. Actor training within a Western context tends to center the actor on the self, encouraging actors to apply their lived experiences to the characters they portray. The audition workshop process described earlier has helped to identify actors who can move away from centering themselves and shift their focus to the investigation and performance of another. The workshop's text-based exercises also help assess an actor's ability to navigate text presented in another person's speech pattern. Over the years of working in this form, I have identified that actors with strong voice and speech training, experience performing verse plays, particularly Shakespeare's plays, and musical training all demonstrate an affinity for performing as ethnoactors, primarily because they understand the importance of rhythm and specificity. This affinity becomes amplified once the actors gain access to the recordings of the interviews and can use those to help develop the performance of each participant.

As discussed in Chapter 5, the rules of engagement for an ethnodrama should encourage the audience to engage critically with interview data. By seeing ethnoactors first as themselves and then witnessing the process the ethnoactor undergoes to become the character they are portraying, the audience maintains an awareness of the investigative and analytical intentions of the performance (Salvatore, 2023). Remember that avoiding an emotional catharsis in ethnotheatre helps keep audiences more critically engaged and analytical; therefore, we want to remind them that they are watching ethnoactors perform data.

That reminder can be reinforced through a type of casting choice that asks ethnoactors to engage in **portraying across identity**, meaning that they portray someone of another race, ethnicity, gender, gender identity, age, ability, or orientation different from their own (Salvatore, 2023; Vachon & Salvatore, 2023). A basic example would be that a female-identifying ethnoactor portrays a male-identifying character; she initially appears to the audience in an expected way, but then her physicality and vocal choices as the male-identifying character create an unexpected experience for the audience, thus achieving Brecht's *Verfremdung*. The audience is surprised and intrigued by the cross-gender portrayal and listens more carefully to the content of the character's comments, which helps in their data analysis. The audience stays more connected to the content of what a character says because they have experienced cognitive dissonance that "shakes them awake" and out of their preconceived notions and implicit biases. They have experienced an unexpected difference, and

> [d]ifference is a central idea for Brecht's theatre. It allows the audience to compare one thing with another and speculate of how the two relate to each other. . . . Difference is concerned with discontinuity and interruption. The theatre is no longer about stability, but change, and by highlighting difference in its many forms, Brecht is trying to prevent the easy consumption of the material on stage and asking spectators to confront contradiction. (Barnett, 2015, p. 81)

When the audience experiences the difference and the contradiction of a cross-identity portrayal, it disrupts their consumption and slows their processing of information. The audience can then work to construct their meaning from the data as the production unfolds.

That said, *ethnotheatre does not require actors to portray across identity*. An ethnodramatist could decide that their project would benefit from casting actors who share the same identities as the participants, which is certainly valid. Some ethnodramatists might be concerned about how an audience might respond to actors portraying across identity. Again, I respect and share that concern, particularly if actors have minimal experience with ethnoacting. So I advise any ethnotheatrical production team that wants to cast across identity to think carefully about why they are using it and to what end. I have used this casting convention from the beginning of my work in this form, primarily inspired by Anna Deavere Smith's portrayal of her interview participants in her one-woman performances. Smith plays all interview participants selected for inclusion in her script, so she frequently portrays across identity. Traditional theatre practitioners might refer to this as "casting against type." I refer to it as portraying across identity because of how Smith (1993) wrote about her own choices and their relationship to the spirit of theatre and the potential of the actor:

> If only a man can speak for a man, a woman for a woman, a Black person for all Black people, then we, once again, inhibit the *spirit* of theater, which lives in the *bridge* that makes unlikely

aspects *seem* connected. The bridge doesn't make them the same, it merely *displays* how two unlikely *aspects are related*. These relationships of the *unlikely*, these connections of things that don't fit together are crucial to American theater and culture if theater and culture plan to help us assemble our obvious differences. The self-centered technique [of acting] has taken the bridge out of the process of creating character, it has taken metaphor out of acting. It has made the heart smaller, the spirit less gregarious, and the mind less apt to hold on to contradictions or opposition. (pp. xxviii–xxix, original emphasis)

Smith's metaphor of the bridge inspired me to adopt the phrase "portraying across identity," as I envision the ethnoactor's process as starting in one space of awareness and crossing a bridge through performance to another. This investigation of another person's experience becomes a potential pathway for an ethnoactor to empathize with someone else's perspective, thus expanding their worldview. Gaining empathy for someone's perspective does not mean suddenly agreeing with them or having more positive feelings toward them. However, an ethnoactor might gain additional awareness, sensitivity, or understanding of another person's perspective. The ethnoactor does not become an expert on that person's experience, nor can they suddenly proclaim to speak for that person. However, portraying across identity can potentially expand the ethnoactor's views about a perspective different from their own. When an audience witnesses the ethnoactor's expansion, they may also experience an expansion in their own worldview (Salvatore, 2023).

An ethnotheatre director does not have to cast ethnoactors to portray across identity for every character in a play, but it is essential to identify how the casting choices function in the ethnodrama's production. Typically, in my projects, ethnoactors play more than one character; frequently, they play one across identity and one closer to self. Additionally, I include language and information about this casting in the participant recruitment and consenting processes. Each participant can mark on their consent form whether they understand and agree to an actor of a different identity playing them in a performance or prefer to be portrayed by an actor more closely matched to their own identity. The interviewer also reviews portraying across identity with the participant during the interview protocol (see Chapter 3) to further ensure they understand the casting possibilities should their interview become part of the ethnodrama. I honor the participant's choice around casting based on their responses during the consenting and interviewing processes. I also include an additional step: I offer potential participants an opportunity to view an example of a cross-identity portrayal to increase their understanding of the performance process. Blayne Welsh, First Nations performing artist and scholar, Wailwan people of North West New South Wales, Australia, inspired this addition to my process through his cross-identity verbatim performance work sharing the stories of the survivors of the Kinchela Boys Home (personal communication, February 15, 2023).

Rehearsing an Ethnodrama: Coaching and Staging

A rehearsal process can begin once the director has cast the ethnoactors. The length of that rehearsal process depends on whether the script will be fully produced or presented as reader's theatre. A rehearsal process for reader's theatre will be much shorter, since it does not require that ethnoactors memorize their lines. From here, I describe the rehearsal process and the design elements I would use to mount a fully realized ethnotheatrical production. A reader's theatre process can benefit from the sections below about rehearsing with ethnoactors.

As I begin work with any company of ethnoactors embarking on a rehearsal process, I ensure that the ensemble members develop empathy for the characters they will portray by moving them through an exercise like the one I described in Chapter 4 for researcher-actors conducting interviews. Each ensemble member interviews another member and prepares a 2-minute selection from the interview for presentation to the group. They use the interview prompts from the data collection process for the particular project to experience how participants may have felt as they responded during their interview. If we are using verbatim performance as the acting style, the ethnoactors perform their fellow ensemble member verbatim. Each time I have facilitated this exercise with a new group, the ensemble members see and hear each other and themselves in new ways, building trust, understanding, and empathy within the company. This attitude then informs the portrayal of the characters, laying a solid foundation for a respectful and rewarding experience for the performers, the interview participants, and the audience (Salvatore, 2025).

Rehearsing ethnoactors for ethnotheatre requires a process different from that of a traditional play. Actors come together more often to rehearse a conventional play, as their interactions are usually more realistic and depend on their ability to play off each other in various situations. In ethnotheatre, much of the ethnoactor's work requires their own investigation and study of the characters they will portray. Given that the ethnoactor typically learns pieces of interview transcripts as monologues or parts of constructed conversations, the rehearsal process for ethnotheatre often requires more time dedicated to one-on-one ethnoactor coaching sessions.

The ethnoacting company typically comes together for an initial read-through of the current draft of the script, which serves as an introduction to the play and can help to determine whether the casting choices make sense in the current script configurations. If casting needs to change, I can make those adjustments immediately, preventing anyone from learning unnecessary material. The read-through also provides an opportunity for questions from the ethnoactors about the script and the process. The rehearsal process then moves into a two-pronged approach: coaching sessions and staging rehearsals.

Coaching the Ethnoactors

A coaching session allows an ethnoactor to work with a director or an acting coach to investigate their assigned interview excerpts for each character they perform in the ethnodrama. Using the scored transcripts, the audio/video recordings, and the field notes for each interview, the ethnoactor and the coach can read and listen/watch together to begin to identify similarities and differences between the ethnoactor and the character. I hold at least three one-on-one coaching sessions with each ethnoactor for each character they portray. If the ethnoactor portrays more than one character, I coach each character in each session so that the ethnoactor grows accustomed to switching between the different portrayals. Their ability to differentiate their characters is crucial for effectively disseminating research findings during the performance. Given the verbatim performance style of acting that I use, the ethnoactor begins by learning the speech and gestural patterns for each of their characters, including all of the breaks in those patterns. In the coaching sessions, we listen to the character's interview, paying attention to things like unique ways of saying certain words, the tempo of speaking, and the rise and fall of the pitch and volume of the voice. If video is available, we may watch for specific gestures and behaviors exhibited during the interview. The ethnoactor notes these observations on their scored transcript as a form of **gestural coding**. Then, they use these notes to continue memorizing the words, speech patterns, and behaviors. When an interview was only audio recorded, we rely on the Participant Characteristics and Physical Surroundings Survey to provide information about gestures and behaviors (Salvatore 2020b, 2025). In cases where other ensemble members conducted interviews for a project, I invite them into the coaching session for the interview they conducted so they can share their experiences and observations with the ethnoactor portraying that character. In the case of *Making Gay History: Before Stonewall* (Salvatore, 2020a), Eric Marcus regularly attended our coaching sessions because he had conducted all the interviews. He provided invaluable recollections of how the interviews unfolded and how some participants behaved during their interviews.

As coaching progresses, I eventually bring together ethnoactors who may be in the same duet, trio, or quartet to help them learn the places in their interview excerpts where I have made breaks to create bounce in a constructed conversation. Since these interview excerpts are continuous sections, the ethnoactor can initially learn the section as a monologue and then integrate the breaks later in the process. That said, different ethnoactors learn lines differently; some prefer to learn the bounce breaks from the start of their process. I remain open and responsive to the ensemble's needs throughout the rehearsals. In cases like *open heart* (Salvatore, 2010) and *Making Gay History: Before Stonewall*, both datasets included interviews with couples or pairs, some of which found their way into the scripts. Then, it became even more important to schedule coaching sessions with those ethnoactors earlier in the process, as their interactive conversations had actually happened and required more rehearsal to achieve the accuracy, specificity, and timing needed for the verbatim performance approach.

Staging the Ethnoactors

Earlier in Chapter 6, I referenced the theatrical term **blocking**, which refers to the actors' movements on stage. The blocking of the actors is part of the **staging** of a play. Staging refers to how a director presents a play to an audience and, more specifically, how the play's production looks, moves, and sounds. In this section, I focus on the staging of ethnotheatre with ethnoactors, then discuss design in detail in the following section.

When I think of staging ethnoactors in ethnotheatre, I think about how to position the ethnoactors in ways that can offer aesthetically pleasing stage pictures for the audience that do not distract their attention from the research findings. Simply put, the staging of ethnotheatre needs to reinforce the data's dissemination, not overpower it. I hold staging rehearsals with the company of ethnoactors once or twice a week as we move through the rehearsal process, and we experiment together to arrive at the staging for each scene or section. That said, I subscribe to some general rules of thumb regarding staging.

Scripting conventions, performance style, and intentional casting can stimulate audience awareness of the research and analysis process inherent in ethnodrama and ethnotheatre, and the staging choices can reinforce this process as well. While I do not characterize ethnodrama as theatrical Realism, I do work to maintain some authenticity in the physical representation of the character during the participant's interview. The staging often involves the ethnoactor sitting in a chair or standing in one position for their portrayal. Rarely have I interviewed someone who moved around while we were speaking, so

I avoid using too much movement of the ethnoactors in my staging. As seen in Figure 7.3, I do take artistic liberties with sitting and standing to compose different stage pictures, using various configurations of chairs and stools on stage to illustrate connections and contradictions between characters, especially during dialogues (Salvatore, 2025).

In ethnotheatre, the performance style should reinforce the performance pentagon and motivate the audience to remain critically engaged with the material. The way an ethnoactor performs can draw the audience's attention to the data by clearly acknowledging the ethnoactor's presence. In a more traditional theatre production, the actor merges with the character, and the audience believes they have become that person. In this case, the audience's first encounter with the actor onstage is in their role as the character. Through watching the character within the world of the play, the audience becomes invested in the character's plight, which usually leads to an emotional catharsis. In ethnotheatre, the actor should not merge with the character. Instead, the audience should first encounter the ethnoactor as themselves and then see them working to present data through their character portrayal. The ethnoactor's process of bringing the character's words and gestures to the stage should be transparent for the audience.

This process begins with the ethnoactor taking on the character's role in full view of the audience in a presentational and highly theatrical way. An article of clothing or hand prop present during the interview symbolizes each character in the performance. I refer to this symbol as the character's **talisman**, representing the character each time an ethnoactor performs them for the audience. We select each talisman by referring to the field notes collected and recorded on the Participant Characteristics and Physical Sur-

FIGURE 7.3 Seated ethnoactors Rai Arsa Artha (l.) and Megan Conway (r.) perform a duet from *Of a Certain Age*. Ethnoactors witnessing left to right: Sherill-Marie Henriquez, Suzy Jane Hunt, and Hayley Sherwood. Photo credit: Saskia Kahn.

roundings Survey as part of the interviewing process. Examples from past projects have included a blazer, a pair of glasses, a hair band, a large necklace, a hat, a purse, a scarf, a coffee cup, and even a bag of potato chips. An ethnoactor never exits the stage to put on or take off a talisman; this change occurs in full view of the audience. The ethnoactor "puts on" the character by putting on the talisman in front of the audience so that they remain fully aware that the ethnoactor is performing a role and presenting a finding. The ethnoactor "takes off" the character in the same way, by removing the talisman in view of the audience. The putting on and taking off of the talisman also happens with a breath, so there is a ritual-like quality to the process. Because a talisman serves a symbolic purpose and breath links directly to speech, I also think of the process as a channel that helps to bring the character into the theatrical space for the ethnoactors and the audience. This presentation creates a highly theatrical, ethnoactor-driven performance meant to continually maintain the audience's critical consciousness and awareness of the research process and remind them that part of their job is to analyze what they are experiencing (Salvatore, 2020b, 2023, 2025).

To remind the audience of the ethnodramatic form, I also include the presence of a **witness** on stage throughout the performance. The witness initially emerged out of necessity to identify each character as they appeared in the performance. In my early ethnotheatre productions, another actor announced the identifier for any new character the audience encountered for the first time. In Chapter 5, I identified this announcement as a scripting convention, and it resurfaces here as a staging consideration. As I incorporated the witness's presence into more of my works, I realized the technique also functioned as a visual metaphor for the interviewer in the original interaction between the artist-researcher and the interview participant. By mimicking that relationship in the staging choices, not literally, but by simply having another ethnoactor or the entire company present to hear what a character says, I provide a visual reminder about the origins of the material and ethnodrama as a form. The witness(es) can stand or sit, but their main job is to direct their full attention to whoever is speaking onstage. The presence of the witness also mirrors the audience's experience of watching and listening and further highlights ethnotheatre's performance pentagon (Salvatore, 2025).

Regarding text delivery, I instruct the ethnoactors to use direct address and speak out to the audience. Brecht often employed direct address when staging his plays to maintain the audience's critical engagement, and the choice works equally well in ethnotheatre. Direct address may seem the obvious choice for monologues, but I also tend to use it in ethnodramatic dialogues. Even though those scripting conventions may include constructed conversations, I like the ethnoactors to deliver directly to the audience whenever possible to emulate the interview experience. Sometimes, the connections between characters' responses can be so synchronous that I may experiment with having the ethnoactors acknowledge each other's presence onstage and make eye contact. The interaction appears more like an actual conversation, albeit a fictional one. These choices usually emerge through rehearsal, and I experiment with them in real time before making any final decisions. A dramaturg or an assistant director can be very useful in these moments to help determine if the choice aligns with the logic we have established for the world of this play.

Another staging convention that often emerges during rehearsal involves ethnoactors voicing other individuals who might appear in a character's story. When a person shares a story involving others, they frequently repeat what those others said in the situation they are recounting. Embodying these individuals and their voices on stage adds another layer of theatricality to the performance. I usually introduce moments like these after the audience has become accustomed to the ethnodramatic form. For example, we can look at a piece from *Of a Certain Age* (Salvatore, 2018). This piece appeared as part of a trio in the script and performance, but I present it here as a monologue to clarify the additional voices. The piece features Yolanda, a 70-year-old Black actress and singer, and she conveys a story about a particular moment when she faced ageism as a performing artist. As you read, you will encounter two other ethnoactors voicing characters in Yolanda's story.

"Do you drink blood?"
Timestamp: 18:05–20:55

YOLANDA
Yeah but
as I said like down in Saint Tropez down in- in the other countries
especially uh- some of the uh
private events that I used to work
or the boutique hotels that I would work in-
uh
I worked at one six years
and then I
didn't work there anymore
and uh the guy invited me about four years late- he invited me to a
party
but
he didn't
tell me that he wanted me to sing and I thought I was just invited.
So when I got there
he was behind me but he didn't know I was there-
he didn't know I was there and so he said,

ACTOR 1
"Uh-
oh uh-
we uh- uh-
we don't have a singer."

YOLANDA
And so his uh- uh manager said,

ACTOR 2
"Yes, but you invited Yolanda ya know you said she was a great singer."

ACTOR 1
"Uh yes but she's very old right now. I don't know if she can sing or anything."

YOLANDA
I was
standing right there
but he was standing behind me- didn't know I could hear
and so I turned around I said, "Hello" and he said,

ACTOR 1
"Oh there, you can sing some song for us?"

YOLANDA
And I thought, "Well I don't have any backtracks, I don't have a band."
But they had a DJ
and he made me mad about what he said about "Oh, she must be older by now
and can't do it."
I went up I kicked ass.
I got three standing ovations.
I didn't even have music I just made it up
because it's- you know it's house music you just go and-
it doesn't have a bridge it doesn't have any
construction to it so you can make it up.
When I got off that stage
that guy had a bottle of champagne
he had all his friends-

ACTOR 1
"You look fabulous but uh- uh- wh- what do you- do you drink blood?
You uh-"

YOLANDA
(laughter)
And when I used to work for him long time ago he was like so cute and everything.
Now he had no hair la la la so he was aging.
You know French people are very superficial on how you look
you know.
But it made me mad that- that he would just automatically
uh put out- he had not seen me in four years
but I came back like
nothing had happened.
So it was kinda cool like that, you know what I mean? It's like
I don't like people-
I don't- ya know I don't look in the mirror and say, "Oh, you're old."
Everybody's old.
Each
day
you get older
ya know so that shouldn't stop you from what you have to do.
And uh as far as contracts are concerned I- I gotta tell you the truth.

If I

send a contract- this is especially before uh internet and all that where people could see you
        actually see you-

I would always take ten years off.

I would tell 'em I'm 50 when I was 60 and I'm 70 now tell 'em I'm 55.

I will lie until they throw dirt in my face and tell me to lay down.

I will lie.

My son is 50.

I'm telling everybody I'm 50 so I told my son, "Look we both can't be 50.

We both-

Somebody gotta take it."

"Yeah," he says. "OK you be 50, Ma." I said, "OK thank you, Honey,"

and that's it.

That's it.

That's it.

Yolanda's story already had a lot of life and vivid imagery, but the additional presence of the two ethnoactors embodying the voices of the club owner and manager helped to enhance the staging of the moment in the performance. The two ethnoactors spoke to each other as the characters in Yolanda's story, and the ethnoactor playing Yolanda continued to deliver the story directly to the audience. These staging choices emerged from experimentation during a rehearsal. Through trial and error, the ethnoactors located the correct rhythm and pacing for the added voices so Yolanda's delivery could continue without awkward interruptions. I did not add another ethnoactor to voice Yolanda's son because the delivery of that exchange had a uniqueness of its own. I kept that moment in her voice as portrayed by the ethnoactor.

Texture and Design

While the content of the ethnodrama and the theatricality of watching ethnoactors shift into and out of their performances may be compelling for an audience, ethnotheatre still runs the risk of becoming visually static and repetitive. Since participants usually sit for their interviews, a director must establish a balance between honoring the moment of the interview and avoiding an entire performance of seated actors reciting text. Saldaña (2011a) reminds us that "a play is not a journal article" (p. 36), and I would add that a production of a play can be more than simply text and actors. Ethnotheatre does not exist without those two essential elements, but beyond asking an audience to watch and listen to the ethnoactors, I also try to introduce other ways of sharing information that diversify the ethnotheatrical experience. I think of this as introducing other **textures** that provide multiple connection points to the research findings. In classroom teaching, we think of this process as differentiated instruction. In ethnotheatre, we can think of it as **differentiated dissemination**. Because my particular approach to ethnodrama includes collecting field notes using the Participants Characteristics and Physical Surroundings Survey, designers have access to details about the physical appearance and behaviors of the interview participants and the actual locations where the interviews took place. While I don't advocate for designers reproducing all of these observations literally on stage, the observations can undoubtedly serve as an essential source of information and inspiration for designers working to develop the physical world of the play.

Saldaña (2011a) identifies scenic elements, props, costumes, makeup, media (e.g., video and projections), lighting, sound, and music as potentially effective techniques to enhance ethnotheatrical staging. A director of ethnotheatre should use these possibilities carefully and with specific attention to their aesthetic impact on an audience. No single theatre artist can realistically have expertise in all these areas, so one of the first steps an ethnodramatist and their director should take is to assemble a team of designers with training, experience, and the capacity to work with the form. Similar to what I look for in ethnoactors, I seek designers who recognize that the purpose of ethnotheatrical production is to share research findings with an audience. In initial conversations with a potential collaborator, I listen for interest in the research topic and curiosity about the form and the process. I look at or listen to their past projects to see if there are aesthetic similarities to how I might want this new ethnodrama to unfold in performance. While demonstrating great skill in their design area, a strong potential collaborator will also express interest in learning how their skills can contribute to this ABR format.

Maintaining simplicity in staging and design allows the ethnodrama's research findings to emerge. To achieve this simplicity, I suggest including these different textures like a chef might add seasonings to a recipe. The ingredients and preparation have already combined to create something delicious, and the seasonings should enhance and bring out certain flavors without overpowering others. Too much seasoning, and we lose the essential flavors and their originality. Ethnotheatre works the same way.

While the previous section focused on how staging with ethnoactors can enhance an ethnotheatrical performance, the following sections provide examples of how movement and design areas such as scenic elements, costuming, lighting, projections, and sound can add textures that contribute to differentiated dissemination for an audience.[3]

Movement

In several pieces of ethnotheatre, I have incorporated choreographed movement pieces created in collaboration with ethnoactors to introduce a different texture to the audience. In *Towards the Fear* (Salvatore, 2014), we created three different movement pieces. One responded directly to the academic article that formally defined "social combat" by using frozen images that the ethnoactors created with their bodies to symbolize specific words and phrases plucked from the article's text (as seen in Figure 7.4).[4] We then ordered those frozen images and created movement transitions between them. A second movement piece used a similar technique but focused on the personal experiences that company members had with bullying. The third movement piece, created in collaboration with choreographer Ryan VanDenBoom, was inspired by a section of an interview highlighting the need for connection to combat bullying, social combat, and aggression, and it concluded the performance. None of the ethnoactors identified as dancers, so we built the pieces using simple devising exercises and pedestrian movement (Salvatore, 2025). Composer Eddie Bean created original music to accompany all three movement pieces, and this music became part of the sound design for the production. This example illustrates how two or more textures, in this case, movement and sound, can complement one another aesthetically and contribute to differentiated dissemination.

In another example, I used movement linked to a specific task to end a performance with an element of theatrical magic. *The Class Project* (Salvatore, 2008) explored the perceptions of class and socioeconomic status among people living and/or working in New York City. Nine ethnoactors portrayed 18 characters who shared their thoughts on the topic at a surprisingly relevant moment: the stock market crash in the fall of 2008.[5] We staged the performance in a black box theatre with audiences in raked seating on two sides looking down onto the floor of the playing space. After a final monologue closed out the spoken portion of the performance, all ethnoactors grabbed a piece of chalk and moved to the floor. Together in a choreographed unison movement, they traced a map of New York City's five boroughs based on the MTA subway map's depiction of the city. Then, one by one, they inscribed the identifiers of the 18 characters on the floor map close to where the participant lived or where the interview had taken place (see Figure 7.5). In the same way that ethnoactors had honored the integrity of the participants in their spoken performances, I wanted to visually honor their participation in the data collection process by leaving a mark on the stage. The magical appearance of the map and the signatures represented accumulated knowledge obtained by the company and then conveyed to the audience. It also meant that the audience exited the performance space by walking across the installed map, another added layer of experience meant to connect directly to the theatrical event and the research topic.

TIPS FOR MOVEMENT

✓ Use movement to share an abstract representation of a research finding, as this approach encourages audiences to bring their own interpretations to the performance.

✓ Find ways to incorporate movement as a palette cleanse, providing the audience with another kind of experience in between significant scenes that reveal different research findings.

✓ Allow ethnoactors to generate movement possibilities, so they emerge organically rather than using a choreographer to impose movement upon the ensemble. After the ensemble has created the movement, a choreographer can join the process to help refine the movement work.

Scenic Elements

Theatrical production requires an understanding of space and its possibilities, regardless of whether a performance occurs in a traditional theatre, a site-specific location, a conference room, or a classroom. The style of performance used in an ethnotheatrical production also affects the kind of space that an ethnodramatist might use to present their findings. A traditional theatrical space often begins as an empty space, allowing maximum potential for a fully mounted production. In this scenario, scenic elements can establish a unique and specific environment for performance dissemination.

A director and scenic designer can collaborate with the ethnodramatist to make choices about defining the environment in which the ethnodrama unfolds. A scenic designer may also collaborate with a props artisan to create various elements that the ethnoactors interact with during the performance. **Scenic elements** usually refer to large structural elements, including furniture pieces, that help define the playing space and the world of the play, while **props** refer to elements that the ethnoactors handle and carry. Scenic designers can often source ideas from the Participant Characteristics and Physical Surroundings Surveys used in the data collection process. Inspiration for scenic design

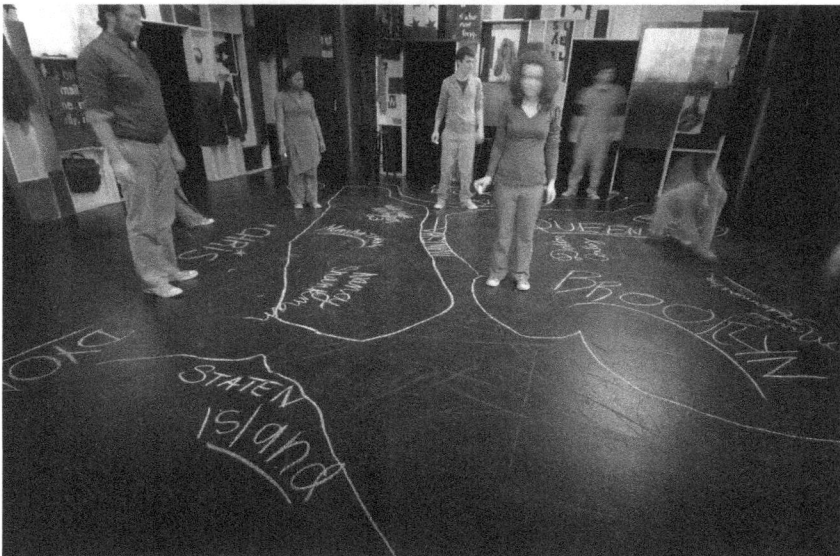

FIGURE 7.5 The final moment of *The Class Project* as the ethnoactors chalk the floor with the characters' names they performed and the five boroughs of New York City, where the interviews took place. Pictured left to right: Karl Leone, Carolyn Burke, Tyler Johnson Grimes, Sarah Misch, Robert Keith, and James Webb. Photo courtesy of NYU.

choices can come from the description of the environment where an interview took place and the objects a participant used.

For *Of a Certain Age*, scenic designer Andy Hall created a design mimicking a neutral art gallery space that allowed the ethnoactors to install visual elements as the performance unfolded. I wanted the scenic design to include a dynamic visual component because the performing arts rely on visual communication with an audience. I also wanted to symbolically represent data coding onstage as a nod to the process of creating an ethnodrama. Andy designed a large box that contained many pieces that fit together like a puzzle onstage. As the audience entered the theatre, they discovered a space with white walls and a light brown floor, almost like an empty art gallery, but with the large, neutral-colored box on stage (as seen in Figure 7.6).

At first glance, the box resembled a large packing crate used to ship a sculpture. As the performance began, the ensemble of ethnoactors entered the playing space and took the large box apart, revealing over 30 different pieces (as seen in Figure 7.7).

Some of those pieces functioned as storage containers for costume pieces, chairs, and hand props used by the ethnoactors, but most served another purpose. Each of the 16 participants whose stories became part of the script and performance had a dedicated box that contained a visual collage representing different moments from their entire interview. Under the supervision of Andy and the props artisan Sven Nelson, the ethnoactors created and assembled the boxes for each character they portrayed (examples of which are shown in Figure 7.8).

FIGURE 7.6 A large box greeted the audience entering the theatre for *Of a Certain Age*. Scenic design by Andy Hall; lighting design by Daryl Embry and Lee Cohen. Photo courtesy of the author.

FIGURE 7.7 The large box was dismantled and spread across the stage, and the ethnoactors performed among its many pieces. Pictured left to right: Hayley Sherwood, Keith Morris, Megan Conway, Sherill-Marie Henriquez, Josh Batty, Amalia Adiv, Rai Arsa Artha, and Suzy Jane Hunt. Scenic design by Andy Hall; costume design by Márion Talán de la Rosa; lighting design by Daryl Embry and Lee Cohen. Photo credit: Saskia Kahn.

FIGURE 7.8 Examples of the boxes that represented each character in *Of a Certain Age*. The ethnoactors created these boxes with the guidance of scenic designer Andy Hall and props artisan Sven Nelson. Photo credit: Saskia Kahn.

During the performance, when a character spoke for the first time, their box was revealed to the audience by another ethnoactor, who also announced their identifier. So, as these boxes flipped into view during the performance, the otherwise neutral playing space became dynamized with bright colors and three-dimensional textures for the audience. After a character spoke for their final time in the play, an ethnoactor installed their box on the large wall at the back of the stage (see Figure 7.9).

The large, multipart box that Andy designed to begin the performance represented the stack of interview transcripts we had to analyze and code to create the play. When the ethnoactors dismantled the box in the first moments of the performance and spread those pieces out on stage, it represented my process of spreading transcripts all over the floor to make sense of them and their patterns. And finally, the reconfiguration of the characters' boxes on the wall (shown in Figure 7.10) represented the emergence of the ethnodrama through the scripting process. Although the meaning of this symbolism was not explicit for the audience, the act of researching, as metaphorically represented onstage, provided layers of additional texture beyond the words spoken by the ethnoactors.

The scenic design for *Of a Certain Age* created a playing space grounded in the symbolism of the research process used to create the ethnodrama. For *Making Gay History: Before Stonewall*, scenographer Troy Hourie developed a playing space based on a more easily identifiable environment: an archive in a library. As mentioned in Chapter 5, Troy and I discussed very early in the scripting process that the performance should occur

FIGURE 7.9 Ethnoactors installed a character's box into the back wall of the playing space after they spoke in the play for the last time. Pictured left to right: Suzy Jane Hunt and Amalia Adiv placing boxes; Josh Batty, Sherill-Marie Henriquez, Hayley Sherwood, and Megan Conway. Scenic design by Andy Hall; costume design by Márion Talán de la Rosa; lighting design by Daryl Embry and Lee Cohen. Photo credit: Saskia Kahn.

FIGURE 7.10 Ethnoactor Sherill–Marie Henriquez placed the final character box on the back wall to complete the onstage installation for *Of a Certain Age*. Scenic design by Andy Hall; costume design by Márion Talán de la Rosa; lighting design by Daryl Embry and Lee Cohen. Photo credit: Saskia Kahn.

within an archive-like environment. Troy's design, shown in the context of a performance in Figure 7.11, ultimately included two large wooden tables, a high counter, and a set of chairs and stools that one might find in a library, along with three large rolling cabinets that contained archive boxes for each character featured in the piece.

Each archive box contained an image of the character, documents, and other hand props related to the stories they shared in the performance. These elements emerged from the boxes and became part of a larger collage of materials that accumulated on each table as the performance unfolded. The collages grew in size and complexity as new characters emerged (see Figure 7.12).

Above the stage, higher up on the back wall of the theatre, Troy also designed a large surface that looked like it contained shelves and shelves of archive boxes. We used this surface to project images throughout the performance (see Figure 7.13).

The ethnoactors also each carried a notebook throughout the performance. Given the archival environment of the play's scenic design, I asked the ethnoactors to invest in their role as historians and archivists, listening to the play carefully each time they performed it and making notes in their notebooks as new discoveries emerged. As the performance concluded, each ethnoactor placed their notebook in an archive box to symbolically represent that their research process of investigating and performing these characters also contributed to the archive.[6] Troy's scenic design provided a fictional container for the play and a logic for the ethnoactors as they performed it within this fictional world. The

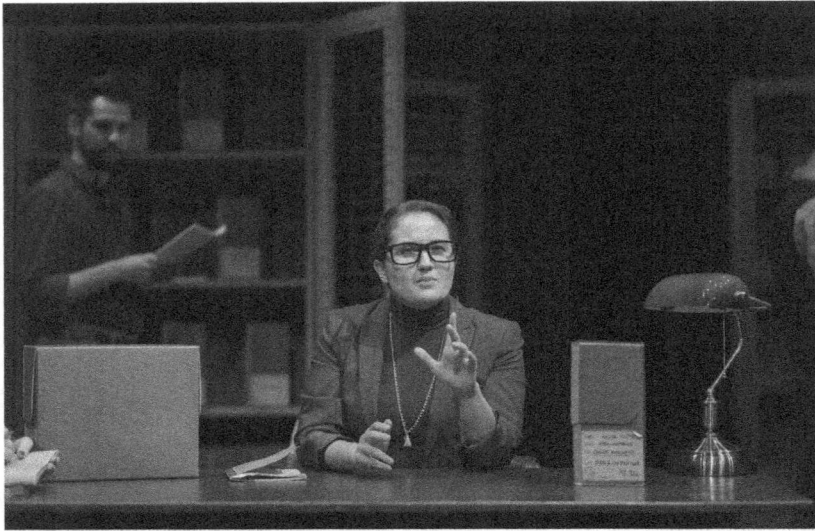

FIGURE 7.11 Ethnoactor Saya Jenks performing on the archive-like scenic design created by Troy Hourie for *Making Gay History: Before Stonewall*. Aaron F. Bratemen is pictured in the background. Costume design by Márion Talán de la Rosa; lighting design by Daryl Embry. Photo credit: Michael Abramyan.

FIGURE 7.12 Photos and documents from the archive boxes accumulated on the tables as the performance of *Making Gay History: Before Stonewall* unfolded. Pictured foreground left to right: Mak Morin, Anvita Gattani, and Andy Borda Cordova. Pictured in background left to right: Andrea Ambam, Callum Fedele, Aaron F. Brateman, Kevin Qian, Cordelia Driussi, and Kate McCreary. Scenic design by Troy Hourie, costume design by Márion Talán de la Rosa; lighting design by Daryl Embry. Photo credit: Michael Abramyan.

FIGURE 7.13 Throughout the performance of *Making Gay History: Before Stonewall*, images were projected above the stage on a large surface designed to look as if it contained shelves of archive boxes. Pictured left to right: Andrea Ambam, Kevin Qian, Andy Borda Cordova, Kate McCreary, Cordelia Driussi, Saya Jenks, Anvita Gattani, Callum Fedele, Aaron F. Brateman, and Mak Morin. Scenic design by Troy Hourie, projection design by Adam J. Thompson; costume design by Márion Talán de la Rosa; lighting design by Daryl Embry. Photo courtesy of the author.

visual messaging also helped to remind the audience that the play featured the stories of real members of the LGBTQIA+ community who had made historical contributions often overlooked by society at large.

TIPS FOR SCENIC ELEMENTS

✓ A recognizable environment can help ground a performance for an audience, allowing them to focus on listening, analyzing, and interpreting the data presented.

✓ Keeping the actual floor of the playing space open allows for greater flexibility when creating stage pictures. These stage pictures can help illustrate the relationships between characters' stories, especially when working together in ethnodramatic dialogues.

✓ Know your audience and how to reach them. And know your playing space and how to be efficient. For example, if you plan to present your ethnodrama at academic conferences, keep your scenic design simple. Chairs can be your best friends.

Costuming

I have worked with Márion Talán de la Rosa as a costume designer for most of my ethno-drama projects over the past 17 years, and she has developed a costuming aesthetic that focuses the audience's attention on the ethnoactor and the process they undergo to portray each of their characters. In her ethnotheatrical designs, Márion establishes a unified base costume for the ensemble, working with each ethnoactor to select a clothing silhouette that matches their personal style. Her choices help to reinforce the idea that the audience should experience each ethnoactor first and foremost as themselves, then as the characters they portray.

Márion has designed different base costumes for various projects for the ensemble members. In *The Class Project*, she dressed the ethnoactors in gray pants and tops. For *Of a Certain Age*, she selected casual looks for each ethnoactor: jeans on the bottom and shirts and blouses from a soft color palette of blue, green, white, gray, and beige on top. In approaching *Making Gay History: Before Stonewall*, Márion worked closely with each ethnoactor to define a base costume that reflected how they might dress if they worked in an archive. In each project, Márion established a visual unity for the ensemble and created a "blank canvas" effect that encouraged the audience to project their impressions upon the ethnoactors when they added a talisman and spoke the words and replicated the gestures of the characters they portrayed (see Figure 7.14).

Costume designs for any ethnotheatrical production benefit from the field notes compiled using the Participant Characteristics and Physical Surroundings Survey. Even when a video recording of the interview exists, the survey can provide a quick summary for a costume designer of the essential elements that stood out about what a participant wore or handled during the interview. What an interviewer remembers and records on the survey after the interview represents what is important about how the participant presented during the interview. These elements offer the best possibilities for the talisman an ethnoactor uses in their performance of a character.

FIGURE 7.14 Ethnoactor Kevin Qian wears his base costume for *Making Gay History: Before Stonewall* in both images: a dress shirt and trousers. On the left, Kevin adds a black tie as his talisman to perform Paul Phillips, and on the right, he adds a cardigan sweater to perform Herbert Donaldson. Costume design by Márion Talán de la Rosa. Photo credit: Michael Abramyan.

Márion guides the selection and design of the talismans for each character in a production. In our collaboration for *Whatever You Are, Be a Good One* (Salvatore & Huff, 2022), Márion identified 50 different talismans for 50 characters and then fitted and matched each of those talismans to the ethnoactor portraying each character (see Figure 7.15).

Ten ethnoactors each had five talismans, one for each character they performed. Márion consulted all 50 Participant Characteristics and Physical Surroundings Surveys and reviewed 50 video recordings of the interviews. In a few instances, she determined that it would be easier for the ethnoactor to remove a part of their base costume to reveal a talisman underneath, like a particular T-shirt worn by an interview participant. Márion also remained open to the idea that a talisman could be an object the participant used or handled during the interview, like a coffee mug, a large headset, or a writing utensil. Márion collaborated closely with the ethnoactor, the director, and the props master to identify when objects made more sense than articles of clothing, and the props master secured those items. She then worked with the stage manager and the director to ensure that each talisman had a specific location onstage where the ethnoactor could find it during the performance. As with any project that features portraying across identities, Márion worked through adaptations for talismans, especially when a particular clothing silhouette or hairstyle did not easily translate to an ethnoactor of a different identity.

The talismans play a central role in the performance style, as the ethnoactors use them to indicate going in and out of their portrayals. The unified base costumes allow the talismans to "pop" when the ethnoactor dons them in performance. The physical transformation with the talisman requires an ethnoactor to experiment to find the most efficient

FIGURE 7.15 Costume designer Márion Talán de la Rosa sourced 50 different talismans for the characters performed in *Whatever You Are, Be a Good One*. We stored the talismans onstage during the performance, hanging visibly behind the ethnoactors on each side. Pictured left to right wearing base costumes and talismans: Noah Jackson, Devin Joyner, Averil Carr, and Michael Roberts. Video design by Adam J. Thompson. Photo courtesy of the author.

sequence of movements. Márion regularly attends rehearsals to observe the ethnoactors as they integrate the talismans into their performances. Working with the director, Márion coaches the ethnoactors through the movements to use each talisman, identifying the simplest and most elegant ways to transform themselves into the character. These collaborations between the costume designer, the ethnoactors, and the director help ensure the performance style's clarity and the dissemination of research findings.

TIPS FOR COSTUMING

✓ Base costumes should function as a neutral palette so that audiences see the ethnoactors move in and out of portraying characters as they add or remove their talismans. Neutral does not mean without color.

✓ A talisman must read for the audience, which means audience members must be able to see the piece on stage from where they are seated. Avoid selecting small pieces of jewelry or small hand props as talismans.

✓ Make sure an ethnoactor can quickly put on and take off a talisman. Articles of clothing that go on and off over the head can be challenging.

Lighting

Theatrical lighting design can serve many functions in a production. Lighting can help set a mood for a particular scene, and it can also help focus an audience's attention on where to look on stage. The cueing of lighting moments can also influence a production. How lighting cues change in performance from one quality of light to another and the amount of time it takes for that change to happen can affect the tempo of a performance. If a scene finishes, and the lights quickly change to another look, called a **bump**, that bump in lighting can signal an abrupt change or shift to another research finding in an ethnotheatre production. A scene could also finish with the lights slowly changing from one color to a different color, called a **fade** or **crossfade**. That type of lighting change can signal a relationship between the ideas presented or indicate the need for additional time for the audience to process what they just experienced. The point here is that lighting is a potent tool in ethnotheatre, as it can contribute much to production and dissemination (see Figure 7.16 for a striking example).

When *open heart* (Salvatore, 2010) premiered at the New York International Fringe Festival in 2010, lighting designer Emily Stork received limited time for a technical rehearsal in the theatre to create the various lighting cues for the production. She and I met in advance of that rehearsal slot, discussed each scene, and made some initial decisions about the color and direction of the light for various moments based on the **repertory lighting plot** provided by the festival. Theatres hosting festivals establish a repertory lighting plot offering basic lighting coverage for all areas of the stage. All productions in that theatre use that same plot, and the designer works within the confines of that plot without changing the lighting instruments' positions or colors. Within the allotted rehearsal time, Emily worked quickly to create the lighting cues to highlight moments when an ethnoactor spoke alone as a character or conversed with others. She used a combination of lighting cues that illuminated the entire stage and cues that isolated individuals or pairs, depending on a scene's content and the tone of what the characters shared. We also learned through this process that fewer lighting changes made the performance dissemination

FIGURE 7.16 Lighting designer Daryl Embry used different lighting colors and intensities to indicate two worlds, reality and memory, in this scene from *Making Gay History: Before Stonewall*. In the foreground, a character recounts a memory to those listening, and in the background, three other ethnoactors reenact the memory. The different qualities of light distinguish the two different worlds on the same stage. Pictured foreground from left to right: Andrea Ambam, Kate McCreary, Andy Borda Cordova, and Saya Jenks. Pictured in the background from left to right: Cordelia Driussi, Callum Fedele, and Kevin Qian. Scenic design by Troy Hourie, projection design by Adam J. Thompson; costume design by Márion Talán de la Rosa. Photo credit: Adam J. Thompson.

easier to follow. In some instances, we had planned to have the lighting cues follow the bounce of a particular duet, trio, or quartet, but that choice became distracting. Instead, we maintained the lighting on all parties involved in the dialogue and relied on the performances of the ethnoactors to draw the audience's attention and focus. I have used this invaluable lesson learned from Emily in subsequent projects to maintain the focus on the research findings rather than distracting away from them with a design element.

Lighting can also help to signal tonal shifts in a character's story. Lighting designer Daryl Embry has created multiple designs for ethnodrama projects with me over the last 10 years, and he has excellent instincts about how to use subtle changes in color and intensity to affect an audience's experience with a particular piece of data. In Chapter 5, we looked at a piece of text from *Of a Certain Age* in which Marilyn shared her stories about auditioning in a studio rather than on a Broadway theatre stage and her experiences rehearsing in less-than-stellar studio facilities (see pages 124–127). During her interview, as she completed the story, she grew nostalgic "about how things used to be," and her vocal quality reflected that nostalgia as she spoke. The ethnoactor portraying Marilyn conducted the interview and incorporated Marilyn's emotional shift in tone in her portrayal. When Daryl and codesigner Lee Cohen watched a rehearsal in preparation to complete their design, they immediately picked up on the tonal shift. They developed a specific set of lighting cues that helped to highlight the moment. Marilyn's monologue began with the stage fully awash in light, with several other ethnoactors positioned as witnesses. When Marilyn's storytelling shifted to a more reflective tone, Daryl and Lee started a subtle and slow fade of the lighting that had created the whole stage picture and transitioned into a lighting cue that highlighted the ethnoactor portraying Marilyn in a warmer light. In contrast, the lighting on the ensemble members as witnesses faded down. The focused lighting that emerged on Marilyn over time functioned like a closeup in film, pulling the audience's attention even more intensively on Marilyn and her story as the tone shifted. This moment remains one of my all-time favorite examples of how lighting design can enhance a finding without overpowering a character's story.

> **TIPS FOR LIGHTING**
>
> ✓ Keep the lighting cues simple. Too many changes in lighting can become distracting.
> ✓ Use lighting to focus the audience's attention.
> ✓ Choose the color and intensity of lighting cues carefully, as they can subconsciously affect how an audience experiences the performance.

Projections

Projection design has been the fastest-growing theatrical design area over the past two decades. More and more professional productions have integrated projection in various forms as this theatrical design discipline has become more common. Projection design can include film, video, animation, graphics, still images, and text, all of which can help to enhance the dissemination of research findings. A traditional academic conference presentation now often includes a projected slide deck that helps illustrate a speaker's research findings. These slide decks often include text, charts, graphs, still images, and video clips. Given the projected image's role in our contemporary culture and our famil-iarity with it as a means of communication, it only makes sense to leverage its power to convey meaning to audiences in various contexts. With ethnotheatre, projection can take on a greater aesthetic sensibility than in a conference presentation or classroom setting.

For *open heart,* the primary visual element of the production came from a projec-tion design by Blake McCarty. Blake's design included video montages that functioned as transitions between each scene or section of research findings and also started and ended the overall production. We also used projection to illustrate the identifiers for each char-acter. Rather than witnesses speaking the identifiers onstage, we projected the identifiers as text the first time each new character appeared. Blake also represented each character with a video clip referencing something they spoke about in their interview. For example, one character referenced eating pancakes rather than eggs for breakfast, so Blake sourced a video clip featuring a giant pancake flipping. He then created a "scrub" of that clip. The scrub moved forward and in reverse like the "boomerang" function on Instagram, but more slowly. The first time that character appeared, the audience saw this video to represent the character. Blake also incorporated collections of these scrubs into various transition videos between scenes and sections of the performance.

Given that *Making Gay History: Before Stonewall* featured excerpts from interviews conducted in the late 1980s and early 1990s, we wanted to include images of the original interview participants to bring their historical significance to the forefront. The projec-tion designer, Adam J. Thompson, created a design that included photographs of the par-ticipants Eric Marcus interviewed for the project. As an ethnoactor began to perform an interview excerpt, that character's photograph appeared projected above the stage (as seen in Figure 7.17). The picture stayed visible for about 20 seconds and then slowly faded away.

This convention repeated throughout the performance each time a character spoke. As discussed earlier, each character had an archive box, which included their photograph that the ethnoactor could remove and see, plus other images and objects related to the participant. As ethnoactors removed materials from the boxes and laid them out on the tables, Adam used two overheard cameras to provide the audience with a bird's-eye view of the tables' surfaces as the objects accumulated (see Figure 7.18). The audience could see the unpacking of an archive on stage and on the screen above the stage. This layering of photographs and images, stage action, and live-action projection again provided a visual representation of a literature review, gave the audience information about what the characters looked like as compared to the ethnoactors portraying them, and provided a closer and more detailed look at the materials in each archive box.

Each of these examples demonstrates the powerful possibilities projection design can provide in ethnotheatre. The ethnodramatist and director should always consider that projection design requires a careful balance between the action unfolding onstage and the projections. Our eyes draw naturally to moving images, so projection design can also

FIGURE 7.17 As ethnoactor Kevin Qian begins to perform Paul Phillips in *Making Gay History: Before Stonewall*, an image of him appears on the projection surface above the stage. Pictured from left to right: Kevin Qian, Anvita Gattani, Callum Fedele, Mak Morin, Aaron F. Brateman, and Cordelia Driussi. Scenic design by Troy Hourie, projection design by Adam J. Thompson; costume design by Márion Talán de la Rosa; lighting design by Daryl Embry. Photo courtesy of the author.

FIGURE 7.18 Projection designer Adam J. Thompson used cameras mounted above the stage to capture live-streamed images of the table tops as more archival materials accumulated throughout the performance of *Making Gay History: Before Stonewall*. Pictured from left to right: Mak Morin, Andrea Ambam, Aaron F. Brateman, Kate McCreary, Saya Jenks, and Callum Fedele. Scenic design by Troy Hourie, costume design by Márion Talán de la Rosa; lighting design by Daryl Embry. Photo courtesy of the author.

distract from the action playing out onstage. A projection design used thoughtfully and judiciously can offer an efficient way to provide the audience with important information that helps to enhance the dissemination of the research findings. Production teams should also be mindful of obtaining permission to use projected images or videos if they are not original creations for the production. An experienced projection designer should already have this awareness through their training. Additionally, researching the rules for fair use of copyrighted material can help guide this area.

TIPS FOR PROJECTION

✓ Ensure that the projections reinforce the live action happening onstage rather than disrupt it.

✓ The locations and positions of the projector and the projection surface affect many other choices. Consider locations carefully and ensure that lighting choices do not wash out or dim the projections.

✓ Remember that we are a "screen culture," so our eyes quickly go to screens. Think about that carefully as you integrate projection into your production.

Sound

Because ethnotheatre relies so heavily on an audience's ability to listen, analyze, and interpret, an ethnodramatist and director might resist adding additional sounds that could distract from the primary data sources. However, like other textures discussed, sound design can help set the tone for certain moments within a production, assist with making transitions from one research finding to the next, and help to maintain the tempo of the dissemination. A skilled and experienced sound designer can collaborate with the ethnodramatist and director to enhance the dissemination process rather than distract from it.

For *Making Gay History: Before Stonewall*, sound designer Megan Culley created sound cues to help create a clear transition from one moment of data presentation to the next. In our early discussions about what these transition moments might sound like, Megan and I both felt drawn to the possibility of hearing the original voices of the interview participants. Eric Marcus audio-recorded all of his interviews and obtained consent from each participant, allowing him to use the audio recordings fully. Because Eric had the record of these signed releases and granted his permission, Megan could use the original audio recordings to create the sound transitions. The project also featured ethnoactors playing across identity, so we wanted to reinforce the audience's awareness of that choice through the sound design. When the performance moved from one scene or section to another, Megan created sound collages featuring the participants' voices. Sometimes, Megan selected a snippet from an interview with a character we would hear in the upcoming section. Other times, she selected a section of the interview that we did not hear in the forthcoming section. In either case, including the voices of upcoming characters helped foreshadow who would be speaking next and what they might share about their experiences. In many instances, the audience would hear a section of text in the voice of an older person, the original participant, and then that same section of text would be voiced in performance by a much younger ethnoactor. The difference in vocal quality created a cognitive dissonance for the audience, keeping them more critically engaged and aware of the content and potentially more thoughtful about the causes of the participant's circumstances.

For the play about housing in New York City called *That's Not Supposed to Be Happening*, Megan Hayward felt drawn by certain sounds of New York City that interview participants had described during their interviews. As part of their design process, Megan generated a list of potential sounds that might emerge as the ethnoactors performed their interview excerpts. As creators and directors, Keith R. Huff and I listened to those choices and then worked with Megan to select which sounds could effectively enhance the performance dissemination. The play began with a story from a character identified as Lulu, who described her childhood experiences living near the Third Avenue elevated subway line. Megan identified that hearing the sound of a subway train passing could help enhance the audience's ability to imagine the environment and the experience that Lulu described. Megan used the sound of a subway train to underscore two points during the performance of Lulu's interview excerpt. Megan set the volume of the sound loud enough for the audience to hear it but not so loud that it overpowered the ethnoactor's voice as they spoke. The sound cue gave the impression of a memory floating into and out of Lulu's consciousness, which is how she delivered the moments during her interview. Megan struck an excellent balance with these cues in this project, but as with other design areas, overusing sound, particularly when ethnoactors are speaking, can distract an audience's attention from the data analysis.

TIPS FOR SOUND

✓ Use sounds to help establish the rules of engagement and the world of the play for an audience.

✓ Listen for the optimal balance between sound cues that support and enhance the dissemination of findings versus sound cues that overwhelm or distract. Sometimes, the volume level of the sound makes the difference between enhancing and distracting.

✓ Original interview recordings can be excellent sources for sound design. If you are interested in using audio from your interviews, include that option as part of your consenting process. Hence, participants know before agreeing to an interview that an audience may hear their actual voices.

As evidenced by these examples of texture and design, ethnotheatrical productions of an ethnodrama can benefit from intentional staging and design choices. When a creative team carefully considers these choices, they can effectively introduce and reinforce research findings from the ethnodrama and help cue the audience to remain in an analytical mindset throughout the performance experience.

A Note on Resources and Budgets

As I stated earlier in this chapter, I advocate for creating ethnodrama and ethnotheatre with as much theatricality as possible, which means that various designers and design elements play a crucial role in my work. All of these additional collaborators and their materials come with significant costs. I work in an environment in which every 2 or 3 years, I have access to a theatre space, the staff members to operate it, technical equipment and support, and a budget to help pay for a project I want to produce. That access has allowed me to create many of the projects I share throughout this book. However, sometimes an idea strikes, and it's time-sensitive. Without the predictable resources I can access every few years, I have had to develop ways to produce ethnodrama and ethnotheatre without all those supports. I have applied for and received funding from internal sources within my university and school that help to cover some of the production costs. I also consistently search for external funding sources, particularly those that privilege innovation in research methodology, theatrical form, dissemination strategies, and cross-disciplinary collaboration, as ethnodrama and ethnotheatre meet these criteria. Also, I look to the social sciences, health sciences, and humanities, as those disciplines often use qualitative methods in their research and scholarship and can be open to experimentation with form and content.

When I have limited resources, I use a simpler form of ethnotheatre and still preserve the integrity of the project and its research findings. For example, when I mount a production outside of a traditional theatre space or with a limited scenic design budget, I use chairs to define a playing space and then craft different configurations of those chairs for various sections of the ethnodrama. The varied arrangements create compelling stage pictures and reveal meaning about the relationships between the characters and the research findings.

I described fully realized projects in this chapter to demonstrate the possibilities of higher-level production support. Ethnodrama and ethnotheatre deserve the resources needed to produce them as fully realized theatrical productions. However, disseminating research findings through performance can also happen in a simple room with chairs and a group of committed ethnoactors. If you have limited resources, simplicity can be your greatest asset when disseminating your research findings.

ACTIVITIES

Experimenting with Staging

In this chapter I have discussed the various possibilities an ethnotheatre director can use when staging an ethnodrama. Now, it's time to give some of those possibilities a go. You had the opportunity to create a duet as part of the activities at the end of Chapter 5 and a montage at the end of Chapter 6. Choose one of the scripting conventions you created and use it to experiment with staging. Find an empty room and have a few chairs to use. Whether you're using the duet or the montage, consider how you want to arrange the chairs for ethnoactors to perform the script. It is even better to find a few friends to occupy the chairs and read your arrangement out loud, so you can hear it. As mentioned, hearing something out loud impacts our understanding of a script arrangement's effectiveness, and seeing it performed increases awareness. When you arrange the chairs, consider the following:

- Are the characters speaking to each other or talking to the audience? Remember, these choices will also affect the performance phenomenology and the dissemination of the findings.

- Do the ethnoactors begin in the chairs? Or do they start standing somewhere else onstage and arrive at the chairs? Or do they begin sitting and then leave the chairs? How might their different movements amplify or interrupt an audience's analysis of the research findings?

- In the case of the duet, imagine that it's the first time the audience meets both characters in the play. Where would you place the announcement of their identifier in the text, and where might you put the witness doing the announcing onstage?

- For the montage, consider how the ethnoactors might use their talismans. Will they all put on their talismans together and then begin, or will they put them on one at a time? How will they remove them?

In each of these instances, experimentation is vital. You will gain valuable information about your script arrangement and staging choices by exploring different possibilities. The experimentation helps to determine your preferences as an ethnodramatist and ethnotheatre director.

Using Field Notes to Inform Production

The following activities provide some practice using field notes from the Participant Characteristics and Physical Surroundings Survey to inform choices for an ethnotheatical production. In Chapter 3, I shared an example of field notes for a participant I interviewed for *Whatever You Are, Be a Good One*. Use those field notes to complete the next two activities.

NAME THAT TALISMAN

A talisman is a costume piece or hand prop representing an interview participant when embodied as a character in a performance by an ethnoactor. A talisman can be an article of clothing, a personal effect, such as a pair of glasses, or a hand prop, such as a coffee mug. A costume designer works with the director and the ethnoactor to identify a character's talisman from the field notes reported by the artist-researcher who conducted the interview. Read the Physical Description of the interview participant from the Participant Characteristics and Physical Surroundings Survey example on page 77. As the costume designer for this production, what options can you identify from the description as potential talismans for the ethnoactor portraying this character? Remember that the ethnoactor's transformation should happen in full view of the audience, so they must be able to put on and remove the talisman easily. Also, consider how ethnoactors of various identities might need to approach this talisman selection differently. Make a list of possibilities, gather them, and then practice using them yourself as the ethnoactor. Experiment with different ways of using the talisman to enter and exit the performance of the character. Practicing in a mirror can help you to find the most efficient way to use the talisman. And after you've finished this exercise, set the talismans aside. Look at yourself in the mirror. What are you wearing? What might an interviewer notice as possible talismans if they interviewed you today?

WHAT CAN A GESTURE REVEAL?

For this next activity, consider the description of the same interview participant's Physical Behavior during their interview for *Whatever You Are, Be a Good One*, outlined on page 77. Identify three distinct gestures using the details outlined about the participant's behaviors. Once you have those three gestures, practice each one individually, repeating it slowly 10 times. As you repeat each gesture, notice what thoughts and feelings come to mind. While we cannot know if your thoughts or feelings match the participant's at the time of their interview, you may discover that replicating certain gestures reveals exciting possibilities for you to consider if you were to play this character in a performance. Embodying gestures taps into a different way of understanding a character beyond what they are saying.

NOTES

1. Burch uses a hyphen between "ethno" and "actor." I use one compound word to align it more closely with the terms *ethnodrama* and *ethnotheatre*, which are not hyphenated.

2. *Her Opponent* premiered in January 2017 at NYU's Provincetown Playhouse, then moved to an Off-Broadway run at The Jerry Orbach Theater in New York City. The cast included Daryl Embry, Rachel Tuggle Whorton, and Andy Wagner. The production was nominated for an Off-Broadway Alliance Award for Best Unique Theatrical Experience (2017). An archival recording of the project can be viewed at *www.heropponent.com*.

3. The productions discussed in the following sections of this chapter were produced by various entities. *The Class Project, Of a Certain Age, Making Gay History: Before Stonewall,* and *Whatever You Are, Be a Good One* were produced by the Program in Educational Theatre, Department of Music and Performing Arts Professions, NYU Steinhardt. *open heart* was produced as part of the New York International Fringe Festival/FringeNYC.

Towards the Fear was produced by the Program in Drama Therapy, Department of Music and Performing Arts Professions, NYU Steinhardt. *That's Not Supposed to Be Happening* was produced as part of the Festival of Voices, Institute of Performing Arts—Drama, NYU Tisch.

4. The acting company for *Towards the Fear* included Kyla Blocker, Darci Burch, Liane Tomasetti Byrne, Yulissa Hidalgo, Wanning Jen, Arielle Sosland, Nikolai Steklov, and Dennis Yacobucci.

5. The acting company for *The Class Project* included Carolyn Burke, Tyler Johnson Grimes, Katie Issel, Robert Keith, Karl Leone, Sarah Misch, Rachel Shapiro Cooper, Gabriela Tejedor, and James Webb.

6. The acting company for *Making Gay History: Before Stonewall* included Andrea Ambam, Andy Borda Cordova, Aaron F. Brateman, Cordelia Driussi, Callum Fedele, Anvita Gattani, Saya Jenks, Kate McCreary, Mak Morin, and Kevin Qian.

8   Evaluating Ethnodrama

The concept of evaluation tends to raise anxiety and concern, as it often determines value, indicating a judgment of something's worth to others. That assigned value may also imply something about creation and presentation, leading to binaries such as right versus wrong, good versus bad, and so forth. From the beginning of this chapter on evaluating ethnodrama, I want to dispense with the idea that an evaluative process is definitive and has to determine whether something is good or bad, successful or unsuccessful. Instead, let's think about evaluating ethnodrama as another step in the research process, another way to generate data that can lead to a deeper understanding of a project and its goals. Evaluating any work of art is inherently subjective, and this subjectivity continues as we consider how to evaluate ethnodrama as a form of ABR. While a traditional evaluation might embrace a more positivist approach, I prefer to lean into the subjectivity inherent in ABR and explore ways to harness an inquiry-based approach to evaluation.

An ethnodrama's ultimate purpose is to convey research findings, and there are unique opportunities to evaluate those findings with three different constituencies: the audience, which could be general or specific to the ethnodrama; the research participants interviewed during the data collection process; and the team of artist-researchers and creatives charged with creating the ethnodrama and the ethnotheatrical performance. For Sallis (Sajani, Sallis, & Salvatore, 2019), "it is the audience(s) who decides whether or not the ethnodramatic piece has succeeded in fully realizing its aims" (p. 84). While I agree with Sallis's assertion, we should not limit an evaluative process to only the audience. We can also evaluate the effectiveness of the ethnodrama's creation process through discussions and exercises with the artist-researchers, creative team members, and research participants involved with the project.

This chapter begins with an overview of how other scholars suggest evaluating ABR. Then, I use their recommendations as source and inspiration to outline an inquiry-based approach that posits five questions for consideration when evaluating an ethnodrama. The chapter then explores ways to gather feedback from audiences, research participants, and creative team members, all in service of answering the evaluation questions.

Evaluating ABR

Scholars have identified the complexities of evaluating ABR projects and, more specifically, the tensions that exist when those evaluations attempt to apply metrics used with more traditional forms of research (Barone & Eisner, 2012; Chilton & Leavy, 2020; Leavy, 2020b, 2023). In their description of assessing ABR, Barone and Eisner (2012) identify the difference between *standards* and *criteria*, stating that "standards are indeed measures of quantity. And as such, they can, more or less, be easily applied to and used universally" (p. 147). Universal standards do not work well for ABR given that the research may use various artistic genres. Each different ABR project may require a unique combination of metrics to help measure the project's effectiveness; therefore, it is difficult to standardize an approach to evaluation. As a result, rather than immovable standards, Barone and Eisner advocate for criteria, as they are "much more slippery" and "demand judgment regarding significance or value" (p. 147). The evaluation criteria should be dictated by the project, not vice versa. Nonetheless, Barone and Eisner understood that "a part of the mark of expertise is having available a variety of criteria that suit a variety of performances or works" (p. 147) and thus identified six general criteria for judging the quality of ABR outlined in Table 8.1. Barone and Eisner offered these criteria as a common starting place while simultaneously advocating for "criteria that are idiosyncratic to the work itself" (p. 155).

Leavy (2020b) amplifies what Barone and Eisner have offered, suggesting that each genre within ABR may need its own set of evaluation criteria, potentially adapting or clarifying those general criteria to the genre used in the research project. She offers seven overarching criteria for evaluation, as outlined in Table 8.2, and divides most of these larger categories into subcategories that help tease out a project's various nuances, depending on its genre. She also recognizes that evaluating ABR "puts us in a messy terrain," but she advises artist-researchers to "accept and indeed *embrace* that messiness" (p. 297, author's original emphasis).

Criteria for Evaluating Ethnodrama

Artist-researchers using ethnodrama as their primary methodological tool will benefit from clearly defining their evaluation criteria. Specifically, doctoral students should com-

TABLE 8.1. Barone and Eisner's Criteria for Judging the Quality of Arts-Based Research
• Incisiveness
• Concision
• Coherence
• Generativity
• Social significance
• Evocation and illumination
Note. Based on Barone and Eisner (2012, p. 148).

TABLE 8.2. Leavy's Evaluation Criteria for Arts-Based Research
• Ethical practice
• Methodology
• Usefulness, significance, or substantive contribution
• Public scholarship
• Audience response
• Aesthetics or artfulness
• Personal fingerprint or creativity
Note. Based on Leavy (2020b, p. 295).

municate with the members of their committee and their chair about the metrics for evaluation and include those in their proposals. Junior faculty should engage in similar conversations with senior colleagues as they enter a faculty position and approach evaluation for tenure or promotion. Given that the nature of ABR and ethnodrama defies typical standards, the artist-researcher should proactively articulate the criteria used to evaluate their research.

The criteria Barone and Eisner (2012) and Leavy (2020b) suggested for evaluating ABR and their recognition of its uniqueness inspire me to offer an evaluation system for ethnodrama but presented in a nontradi-

TABLE 8.3. Key Questions for Evaluating an Ethnodrama

- How has the ethnodrama answered the project's research question(s)?
- What observations have emerged about the aesthetics of the ethnodrama from reading the script and experiencing it in performance?
- What is the ethical orientation of the ethnodrama?
- How does the ethnodrama consider a diversity of viewpoints and perspectives?
- What learning has occurred from the ethnodrama and its creation process?

tional way. Rather than outline a set of criteria against which to measure an ethnodrama, I offer five overarching questions for consideration when evaluating an ethnodrama's effectiveness and accomplishments, as shown in Table 8.3.

I suggest these questions based on my own experiences creating and teaching ethnodrama and what I have come to value about the form when I've experienced it at its most potent. I offer questions rather than criteria because questions generate conversation and deliberation. In my mind, the best evaluation experiences unfold as inquiry-based discussions, rather than one-sided declarations of whether something meets a standard. In working to answer these questions, the artist-researcher and the evaluators can rely on data collected following experiences with the ethnodrama and the ethnotheatrical production. Let's look at these key questions in more detail, including additional suggestions for prompts to stimulate further conversations between the artist-researcher and evaluators.

How has the ethnodrama addressed the project's research question(s)? While this question may seem obvious, I lead with it to ground the evaluation process in what matters most: the generation of new knowledge about the topic at hand via this particular research methodology. An artist-researcher can produce an outstanding, sold-out production run of an ethnodrama, but if the script and performances do not answer the research question, something has gone awry. Similarly, ethnodrama also offers an artist-researcher the opportunity to expand the possibilities of creation and dissemination. When doctoral students approach me with a potential research project using ethnodrama, I ask them if they want to become experts in their topic of interest, research modality, or both. How they ultimately respond to that consideration often influences the research questions for the project. The ethnodrama's script and performance should demonstrate how they have addressed the project's research questions. Some examples of specific ideas to consider related to the research question(s):

- What has the ethnodrama offered to the topic of interest and the field of study?
- What has the ethnodrama offered to the research modality?
- How has the ethnodrama demonstrated innovation through its creation and dissemination?

What observations have emerged about the aesthetics of the ethnodrama from reading the script and experiencing it in performance? As we're in the last chapter of this book, it should come as no surprise that aesthetics would play a significant role in my evaluation framework. An artist-researcher using ethnodrama must consider the project's aesthetics as a script and a performance. Any evaluation must consider aesthetics and the legibility of the artist-researcher's choices in all project areas. Some examples of specific ideas to consider related to aesthetics:

- Does the ethnodrama have a clear beginning, middle, and end?
- How does the ethnodrama establish clear rules of engagement for the audience?
- Is there a clear dramaturgical logic that carries across the script and the performance?
- Does the script provide clear stage directions that help define the world of the play, the aesthetics of performance, and casting? How are these areas realized in performance?
- Does the script follow a consistent structure and readable format?
- Can someone without theatrical knowledge or experience read and follow the script?
- How does the performance style embodied by the ethnoactors encourage the audience to engage in their own data analysis?
- How are characters identified for the audience?
- How does the performance engage with other theatrical textures such as movement and design elements?

What is the ethical orientation of the ethnodrama? Ethical orientation refers to how an artist-researcher integrates ethical practices into creating and presenting the ethnodrama. I have emphasized the importance of ethics and care throughout the creation and dissemination of the project; therefore, the artist-researcher's ethical orientation should be evident to a reader or viewer. Some examples of specific ideas to consider related to ethical orientation:

- How does the ethnodrama make the origin of the source of the material clear for the audience?
- How do the ethnoactors exhibit care in their performance of the characters?
- How does the audience respond to the content of the ethnodrama, as a script and as ethnotheatre?
- What ethical questions arise for an audience following an experience with the ethnodrama?
- If interview participants choose to experience the ethnodrama, how do they respond?

How does the ethnodrama consider a diversity of viewpoints and perspectives? As described in Chapter 1, one of the main strengths of ethnodrama is its ability to bring together multiple viewpoints on a particular topic or question and create a "conversation" across those viewpoints. All drama requires conflict to exist, and in the case of ethnodrama, the conflict emerges when contrasting viewpoints and experiences coexist. If an ethnodrama only offers one angle or perspective on its topic, it will lack dramatic tension and risk losing an audience's attention. Similarly, suppose all perspectives come from participants of the same demographic, and that was not the artist-researcher's intent or a clearly stated delimitation. In that case, the uniformity of that demographic may produce less interesting and insightful results. This latter point depends on the purposes of the project, but the artist-researcher must be aware of their sample demographic throughout all phases of the project. Some examples of specific ideas to consider related to diversity of viewpoints and perspectives:

- Does the ethnodrama seem driven by the artist-researcher's agenda?
- How does the ethnodrama amplify multiple perspectives?
- Does the ethnodrama privilege one perspective on an issue? If so, why? Is this purposeful or accidental? Did this single perspective exist as a delimitation at the top of the research process, or did it emerge during data collection or analysis?
- How does the ethnodrama address the demographics of its participant pool? Does this affect how the audience experiences the ethnodrama?
- Does the ethnodrama simplify or complicate the topic it seeks to explore?

What learning has occurred from the ethnodrama and its creation process? The main goal of generating new knowledge drives any research process, so the evaluation of an ethnodrama should reflect on what learning has taken place. The inquiry about learning extends across the artist-researchers, creative team, research participants, and the audience. Some examples of specific ideas to consider related to learning:

- What new information does the ethnodrama reveal about the topic?
- How does the ethnodrama activate thought, reflection, and dialogue amongst the various contributors, participants, and audiences?
- How does the creative process inform learning?
- How does the ethnodrama surprise?
- What new questions does the ethnodrama raise about the topic?

These five main questions can serve as a starting point for a formal or informal evaluation process. So, how can an artist-researcher begin to answer these evaluation questions? The next section of this chapter outlines ways to evaluate an ethnodrama's effectiveness by gathering evidence from audiences, research participants, and creative team members. An artist-researcher may gather feedback from one or all of these groups, generating a secondary dataset that contributes to answering the evaluation questions.

Gathering Audience Feedback

Traditional theatre productions often engage audiences in a conversation following a performance, commonly called a **talkback**. In these instances, the talkback is usually optional, meaning that the audience experiences the performance and then chooses to stay for the discussion or to leave. Some productions plan for a talkback as an audience engagement experience included in the overall event, but those happen with less frequency. More often, the talkback functions as an add-on to the performance, making it feel like an after-thought. An ethnodrama process benefits from intentionally planning around audience engagement at the project's initial conception. As discussed in Chapter 2, a project can sometimes have more than one research question: one that the data collection and analysis process seeks to answer and another that gets answered through the audience's engagement with the ethnodrama as a piece of ethnotheatre.

In the case of a new play or a play in development, a creative team might use a talk-back to elicit feedback from an audience about what they experienced to help improve the next version of the play (Brown, 2015; Fisher, 2014). The team might ask the audience to respond to specific questions, or they may take questions from the audience. This talk-back style requires a skilled facilitator, as sometimes audiences begin to offer thoughts and feedback that can derail a new project in process. A facilitator should focus a talkback on gathering the feedback that a creative team wants and needs rather than allowing the audience to determine what they want to share. Choreographer and community-engaged artist-choreographer Liz Lerman (Lerman & Borstel, 2022) developed a technique for critical response that uses a highly structured framework led by a facilitator who moder-ates the process between the artists and the audience.

Another style of talkback, usually employed with finished productions, focuses on providing the audience with opportunities to ask questions of the actors and creative team about their process and the content and themes of the play. These talkbacks can unfold with just a playwright or director, or they might include a panel that comprises cast and creative team members. A moderator hosts the event, fields questions from the audience, and helps to make connections between the play, the production, and the audience's com-ments. Rather than providing the artists with feedback, this talkback style assists the audience with understanding the production process and sharing their responses to the finished production.

A third talkback style uses an invited guest or panel of guests with expertise related to the play and its content and themes. These guests see the performance with the audience, and then share their impressions afterward. A moderator facilitates the conversation and usually also takes questions from the audience for panelists to discuss. This talkback style focuses on enhancing the audience's experience of the play and production and providing a broader understanding of how the play fits within a larger historical or contemporary context.

When using any of these talkback styles to evaluate an audience experience with an ethnodrama, the artist-researcher should consider who the audience is, why that audience might be attending a performance of the ethnodrama, and what that audience might gain from the experience. Depending on the ethnodrama and its purpose, its audience may be general and, as a result, quite diverse in perspective and viewpoint, or it might be more specific, with a well-developed awareness of the topic at hand. Understanding these potentials for audiences can help to inform the design of an evaluation experience.

When I create an ethnodrama, I tend to have a general audience in mind unless someone has commissioned me to make a play that must speak to a particular audience demographic or group. Similarly, as I think about evaluating the impact of the ethno-drama, I consider what questions I might ask the audience that can provoke the kinds of responses that would help me understand whether the ethnodrama has caused any learn-ing to occur. If an audience can identify moments of learning, then the ethnodrama has achieved one of its goals: dissemination of research findings.

A talkback could provide space for an audience to discuss their learning, but over the years, I have observed how standard talkbacks privilege those who feel comfortable speaking up in a high-focus situation. I'm more interested in learning about the experiences and observations of audience members who are less likely to speak up in a public forum like a talkback, so I have developed a model of audience engagement that allows individuals to select how they would like to participate. By differentiating the engagement, I have gathered a more comprehensive range of perspectives, which helped to deepen the evaluation of the experience.

In general, I am interested in an audience's answers to the following questions:

- What moments from the performance were memorable for you? What moments will you remember two weeks from now?
- What did you learn from experiencing the performance?
- What new questions do you have about the topic of the ethnodrama?

The third question draws inspiration from my colleague and mentor, Judith McVarish, who insightfully noted that new questions that arise from an experience are significant evidence of learning (Milne & McVarish, 2014). I embrace this concept in my teaching, research, and creative projects, as I understand and value the vital role that new questions play in the learning process. If I conclude an experience without any new questions, I realize I haven't learned much. In contrast, when I have new questions after an experience, they take me into uncharted territory, requiring further inquiry. I learn more from that further inquiry and then develop more new questions. This never-ending learning loop keeps me intellectually curious and striving for new knowledge. I want to stoke that same curiosity for audiences.

Sometimes, I engage an audience with these three questions as I've written them here and, other times, I ask variations, as there might be something more specific that I want to surface about the audience's experience with a particular topic. These engagements usually happen immediately after a performance concludes and offer multiple ways for the audience to participate and respond. These differentiated ways of participating in the evaluation process build upon the concept of differentiation in dissemination, which I mentioned earlier in Chapter 7.

When a performance ends, the company of ethnoactors assembles for a bow as the audience applauds their work. Then, one designated ethnoactor invites the audience to participate in a postperformance activity. While the ethnoactor explains the activity, other company members transform the playing space to allow the activity to unfold on stage and inside the theatre. The activity could also occur outside the playing space in a lobby area, separate studio, or classroom. Still, I prefer to engage the audience in the space where they experienced the performance dissemination. The ethnoactors also remain in the playing space to converse with the audience. The final instruction identifies that the lighting will change and some music will play as a way to shift from the performance experience to this postperformance engagement. Audience members then choose how they might like to engage in the activity. They can join the ethnoactors on stage, remain in their seats and speak to other audience members around them, or they can exit the theatre and move on to their next event or activity. Providing these options allows each audience member to maintain their agency and autonomy over whether they participate. Audiences should not feel trapped by a discussion and forced to participate. The postperformance activity usually offers up to three prompts for the audience to consider, and the stage setup typically includes at least one flat, table-like surface and writing materials for the audience to write their responses. The setup also uses a container to collect the responses so that audience members can deposit them anonymously. I have used this model of postperformance engagement to evaluate the effectiveness of some of the projects discussed in this book. I outline examples of variations in this model below.

As described in Chapter 7, *Of a Certain Age* (Salvatore, 2018) featured a boxed visual collage representing each character, and those boxes and each of the talismans came together to form a visual installation on the upstage wall and the stage left wall of the playing space. The audience witnessed these installations coming together throughout the performance, so as part of the engagement, we invited them onstage for a closer look. This invitation to the stage to learn more about the production by seeing the design up close and speaking to the ethnoactors incentivized participation in the evaluation process. Below is the text we used to begin the postperformance facilitation. I offer it here as one example of an approach, but each ethnodrama will require a unique invitation to an audience.

> *Thanks, everyone. My name is [ethnoactor's name], and I'm a member of the acting company for* Of a Certain Age. *Thanks so much for being with us for this performance this evening/today.*
>
> *As you can see, throughout the performance, we've created an installation on the upstage and stage left walls, and we'd like to invite you on stage to get a closer look at the various pieces. We just ask that you refrain from touching any boxes on the upstage wall.*
>
> *We've printed visual guides for both walls so you can link the boxes or costumes to the character they represented in the play. My castmates are also setting up two stations on stage. We invite you to share your responses to the show on these costume tags on the table at the right and then place them in the box on your left. We're particularly interested in what you learned from experiencing this performance.*
>
> *Now, we'll transition into some gallery light here on stage and in the house and turn on some music. Feel free to join us on stage to view the installation, ask us questions about our process, stay seated to observe or talk, or you can exit through the lobby to move on to your next engagement. Whatever you choose to do, thank you again for joining us for* Of a Certain Age.

We then coded and analyzed the data collected from the evaluation process to determine the ethnodrama's effectiveness in disseminating the research findings to an audience. In this particular project, we were most curious about what the audience learned as it related specifically to our second research question: How can gaining a clearer understanding of the experiences of older performing arts professionals help to combat ageism within the population at large? If an audience member chose to leave a written response, they deposited them in the box onstage. As referenced earlier, we used large cardstock tags that a costume designer might use to label the clothes hanger for a costume piece (Salvatore, 2020b). We wanted to link the data collection instrument to the performance content somehow. After the run of the performance, two members of the ensemble, Hayley Sherwood and Amalia Adiv, reviewed and coded the responses into four categories:

- Direct quotations or references from the performance
- Aesthetic or artistic commentary about the production (i.e., "loved the scenic design")
- Self-awareness of the artist
- Perspective shifts

A closer inspection of the responses in these four areas revealed that multiple audience members reported shifts in perspective related to the presence and prevalence of ageism and the concept of invisibility for those who are aging. Audiences also expressed a greater appreciation for the commitment it takes to be a performing arts professional of any age. As evidenced by the first of the four categories, some audience members cited direct quotations from specific characters, acknowledging that their words stayed with them after the performance. Several audience members also acknowledged ethnodrama as an effective way to convey information about aging and ageism to the larger community (Salvatore, 2020b). All of these audience responses helped to identify that the project had answered both research questions guiding the project and, more specifically, had allowed the audience to hear and analyze the data and consider how that experience might affect their lives going forward.

Following *Towards the Fear* (Salvatore, 2014), we invited audiences to reflect on their past experiences as aggressors, victims, and bystanders with bullying and social combat. Audience members who joined the ethnoactors onstage could write down the first name of a person who came to mind. This name could represent a person who bullied them, someone they bullied, or someone they witnessed being bullied. After writing the name on an index card, the audience member installed the card on the upstage wall of the theatre or deposited it in a box for a cast member to install. Over the run of four performances, we created a visual collage of names that kept growing to acknowledge the power and importance that these moments of aggression played in the lives of our audience members. After the last performance, we photographed the installation to document the audience's collective experience over the performance run (see Figure 8.1).

In the case of *That's Not Supposed to Be Happening* (Huff & Salvatore, 2023), we coupled scenes featuring characters with scenes that we called "activations," where the ethnoactors engaged the audience in activities to educate them about finding housing in New York City. After the play concluded, the ethnoactors invited the audience to add their responses to the performance to a graffiti wall set up in the theatre's lobby. We hid the wall from the audience's view as they entered the theatre to prevent any preconceived ideas from emerging before seeing the performance. As audiences exited, they encountered a whiteboard functioning as a graffiti wall and containing the following prompts:

- What are you carrying away with you after the performance?
- What will you share with someone else about this performance?
- What is something you learned that you will put into action after this performance?

Audience members used markers and sticky notes to leave their answers to these prompts on the wall, and their responses accumulated over the performance run (see Figure 8.2). The graffiti wall responses helped us measure the impact of the interview

FIGURE 8.1 The installation of names left by audience members after experiencing *Towards the Fear*. Audience members wrote the name of someone who came to mind as they watched the performance on a card and then placed the card on the back wall of the theatre. Photo courtesy of the author.

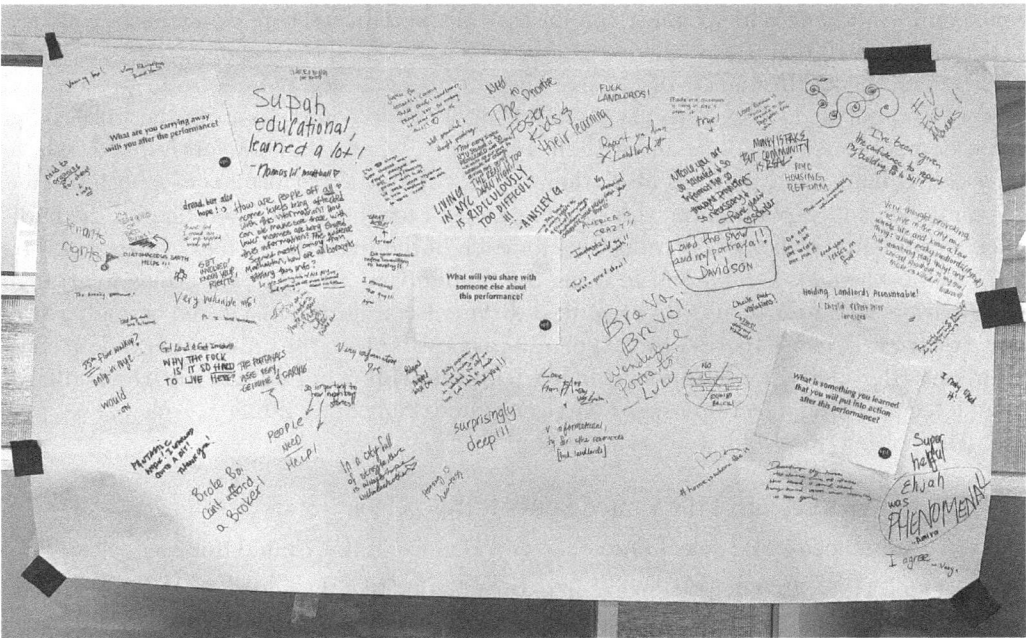

FIGURE 8.2 A graffiti wall of the audience's responses to the Verbatim Performance Lab's production of *That's Not Supposed to Be Happening*. Photo courtesy of the author.

excerpts and the audience activation pieces, as audience members commented about specific moments from the characters' stories shared by the ethnoactors and policies and procedures they learned about during the audience activations.

Artist-researchers can also track audience responses to an ethnodrama in real-time as a performance unfolds. In VPL's production of *Whatever You Are, Be a Good One* (Salvatore & Huff, 2022), we created an interactive experience for the audience, allowing them to respond in real-time to the performance using the online software Poll Everywhere on their smartphones. As discussed in Chapter 2, we created this project to investigate two questions: What are the causes of the extreme political polarization we are currently experiencing in the United States? How can we address this political polarization over the next 5 years? The project also considered how geographic location influences opinion on issues of national importance and the assumptions that audiences might make about where someone comes from based on their views.

In Chapter 4, I described how the binning round of analysis for this project yielded 50 excerpts: 10 excerpts from each of the five geographical regions of the United States: Northeast, Southeast, Midwest, Southwest, and West. For the performance dissemination, we assigned these excerpts to 10 ethnoactors, each learning five different characters' selections, one from each geographical region. Each performance featured five ensemble members, so the company of 10 ethnoactors rotated performances as two smaller ensembles. The project had eight performances live at the Pless Hall Black Box Theatre at NYU, October 20–30, 2022. NYU-TV broadcast four live performances, allowing the event to reach online audiences in 40 states, the District of Columbia, and 17 countries beyond the U.S.[1] (Salvatore, 2023).

Before the performance began, we invited all audience members (in person and online) to use Poll Everywhere via their smartphones to complete an initial poll asking basic demographic questions about their age range, where they currently lived, where they called home, and political affiliation. At the top of the performance, a host greeted the audience and explained the rules of engagement for the event, then tapped the audience to randomly select 10 portraits, two for each of the five ethnoactors to perform. The ethnoactors then worked backstage using the randomized audience selections to arrange the portraits into four scenes that featured different configurations: a solo, a duet, a trio, and a quartet. Because there were 50 portraits as possibilities, the number of random combinations offered a different performance each time. Following each scene, the audience completed a polling question using Poll Everywhere (Salvatore, 2023).

The polling questions were as follows:

- Solo: What region of the United States is this person from?
  - Audiences could select one of the five regions of the United States.
- Duet: How often do you engage in a conversation like the one you just experienced?
  - Audiences could select Daily, Weekly, Monthly, Yearly, "I avoid it like the plague."
- Trio: Which of these three people do you agree with the most?
  - Audiences could select a character's name or "I don't agree with any of them."
- Quartet: Which of these four people would you like to grab a coffee or drink with?
  - Audiences could select a character's name (see Figure 8.3 for an approximation of this polling exercise).

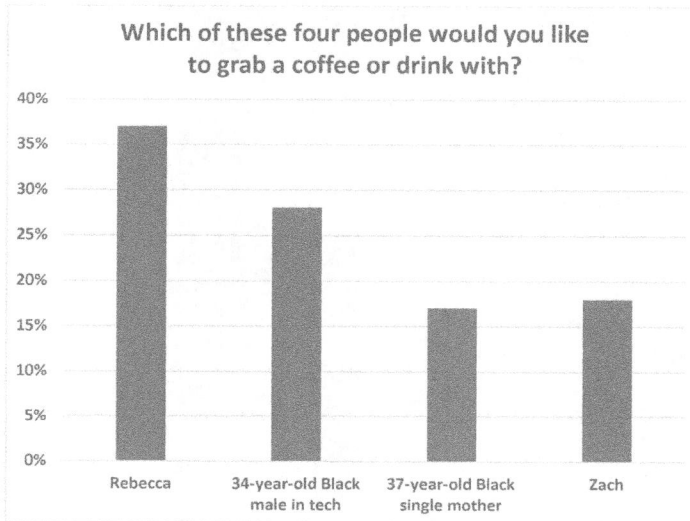

Which of these four people would you like to grab a coffee or drink with?

FIGURE 8.3 An example of a bar graph representing audience responses to a polling question in Poll Everywhere.

We crafted these questions with a general audience in mind and to generate a discussion following the performance. Additionally, between the trio and quartet scenes, the host revealed the polling results of the demographics of the particular audience for that performance.

Following the four scenes featuring the interview excerpts, the event shifted to a town hall format. During the performance, a team of three data processors worked in real time backstage to prepare the data for dissemination at this moment in the event. Using screen projections of the results of the polling questions listed earlier, the host facilitated a conversation with the audience about what they had experienced (see Figure 8.4).

The ethnoactors also joined the town hall conversation to offer insights and reflections about the process and their observations from that particular performance. In the final moment of the town hall, the host invited the audience to complete one last polling question that specifically addressed our second research question about what we could do to combat political polarization over the next 5 years. We asked audiences to consider three words they would carry with them from their experience of the event and then enter those into the Poll Everywhere application. The application converted the audience's real-time responses into a word cloud (a similar but distinct version of which is seen in Figure 8.5), where the more times audiences entered a word, the larger it appeared in the cloud. We projected these word clouds onto the screens in the theatre and into the broadcast, leaving the audience with a final image of potential learning and an answer to our question. Words like "listen," "listening," "empathy," "patience," "understand," "understanding," and "compassion" appeared the largest in each word cloud, indicating that the audience shared those words the most in their responses.[2] The polling data collected using Poll Everywhere provided information about how the audience experienced the interview data via the ethnotheatrical performance and demonstrated how they might work to disrupt the polarized political climate in the future (Salvatore, 2023).

FIGURE 8.4 Audiences for *Whatever You Are, Be a Good One* were polled throughout the performance via the Poll Everywhere platform on their smartphones. The host then used the polling data to engage the audience in a dialogue immediately following the performance. Photo courtesy of the author.

Share 3 words you'll carry with you as you leave this experience.

FIGURE 8.5 A word cloud generated by Poll Everywhere reflected the audience's responses after a performance and town hall discussion for *Whatever You Are, Be a Good One*.

In each of these examples of audience engagement, the performed dissemination of the interview data generated another opportunity for data collection to evaluate the efficacy of the ethnodrama. An artist-researcher could also evaluate their ethnodramatic work based on whether audience members change their positions or beliefs in some way after their experience of the play. The researcher can gather quantitative data via pre- and post-performance surveys and ask audiences to respond to various statements using numerical scales to measure agreement or disagreement on a continuum (Nichols, Cox, Cook, Lea, & Belliveau, 2022; Snow, Segalowitz, D'Amico, & Mongerson, 2023). These numerical data can signal whether a change has occurred, as they quantify an audience member's attitudes and beliefs before and after experiencing the ethnodrama. The comparison of these quantifiable measures provides validity for some researchers and research sponsors and can reinforce qualitative evidence. I'm most interested in how audiences become more aware of why they think or believe the way they do. Therefore, I primarily use qualitative measures to evaluate an ethnodrama's impact on the audience.

Another method of gathering qualitative data is to email audience members after the performance and ask them to complete a survey that addresses similar ideas to those I introduced in these examples of immediate postperformance engagement. I prefer to engage the audience in the evaluation process while their experience remains fresh in their minds, but delayed surveying could measure whether an ethnodrama has a longer-lasting impact. Delayed surveying via email a few days after a performance also allows audience members to complete an evaluation at their convenience. However, I have experienced a significant drop in surveys completed using this delayed technique. Hence, I prefer to solicit feedback immediately following the experience.

As an alternative to formally surveying an audience following a performance, the artist-researcher could consider using social media platforms as an informal way to obtain feedback on an ethnodrama. Social media also allows for a wider audience beyond the theatrical performance to engage with the performed interview data. In VPL's *Portraits US: COVID-19* project, ethnoactors created video portraits of interview excerpts, which we posted on our website (2021). VPL intern Anna Gundersen then posted moments from selected video recordings to our Instagram account with an attached polling question. That platform includes a simple polling function, so users can respond quickly and efficiently. The polling questions typically asked for the viewer to consider where the original interview participant was living at the time of their interview, and the resulting responses helped us to understand viewers' perceptions of specific opinions on COVID based on their geographical biases (see Figure 8.6 for an example).

We tracked the number of engagements with the post and the polling ques-

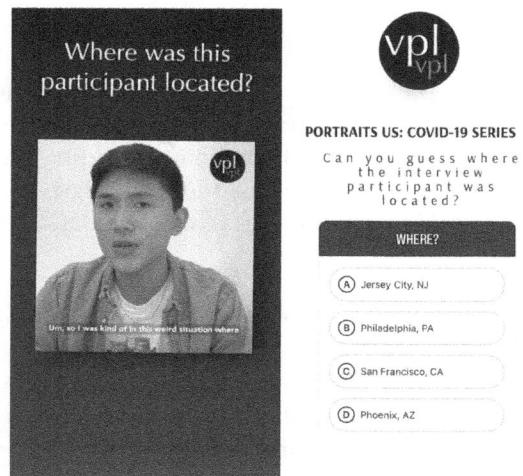

FIGURE 8.6 Example of the Verbatim Performance Lab's *Portraits US: COVID-19* series on Instagram using polling questions to collect viewer reactions. Pictured: Charles Hsu.

tion, and we cataloged the comments left on each post, again, as a way to track viewers' engagement and responses. We also tagged each post with #covid19 and #ethnodrama to reach new viewers not already following our social media. While social media allow the performed data to reach a larger audience, the artist-researcher also has much less control over who is seeing the data. Also, the artist-researcher's followers may only see the post. In that case, the artist-researcher must also account for potential bias if they plan to use the data collected from social media for formal evaluation of an ethnodrama's efficacy. As in so many instances, social media can be a powerful tool, but we must continue experimenting with its role in this kind of evaluation.

Gathering Research Participant Feedback

The evaluation of an ethnodrama may also include gathering feedback from research participants after they have experienced a performance. I have made it an essential part of my practice to invite anyone who sits for an interview to experience the ethnodrama in performance, regardless of whether an excerpt from their interview becomes a part of that particular script. If a participant invests time and energy to share their thoughts and experiences, I have an obligation to offer them the opportunity to experience the research outcomes. More traditional dissemination through an academic journal article or conference presentation can sometimes be inaccessible to lay and public audiences. Because ethnodrama uses performance as dissemination, the potential to share the outcomes with wider audiences, including the interview participants, expands (Cox & Belliveau, 2019; Leavy, 2020b; Mienczakowski & Moore, 2008). Of course, this also depends on the format of the performance dissemination. An ethnodrama's live performance allows participants to attend based on their proximity to the venue. A live stream of the performance increases the possibility of attendance for those who live farther away. An audio or video recording of the performance further increases the likelihood that participants can experience the dissemination of the research findings, particularly if the artist-researcher can upload the recording to an online host like SoundCloud, YouTube, or Vimeo.

If a public audience can attend or experience the performance dissemination, I contact participants approximately 2 weeks before the first performance or screening. I email each participant an invitation, reminding them of their participation in the project and how they can experience the resulting performance if interested. When a participant's material has become part of the script and performance, I use the following language:

> *Hello,*
>
> *Thank you for completing an interview for [project name] back in [month year of data collection]. As a reminder, this project is exploring/investigating [the project topic and/or a variation of the project's research questions].*
>
> *We've completed the scripting process and have started to rehearse the resulting new play called [title of play—may be the same name as the project or different].*
>
> *I'm writing to inform you that portions of your interview have been selected for inclusion in the play. An actor will perform sections of your interview as part of a production set to take place at [name and location of venue].*
>
> *To thank you for sharing your thoughts with us, I would like to offer you two complimentary tickets to see a performance of the play. Performance dates and times are as follows:*

[list the dates and times available]

Please reply to this email by [deadline date] with the date/time when you would like to attend and whether you would like one or two tickets. I will then follow up with a confirmation email.

Again, thank you for taking the time to share your thoughts and stories with us. We're very appreciative and look forward to sharing this new work with you.

All best wishes,

[Your name]

[Your role on the project]

I offer two complimentary seats to participants whose material is included in the ethnodrama because I want to encourage them to bring along a guest to provide support as they experience their material in performance. As I have described in earlier chapters, seeing and hearing one's interview performed by another can be unsettling, but it can also be a great gift when handled with care. It is difficult to describe to a participant what that experience will feel like as it unfolds or predict how each participant may react. Hence, the invitation to bring a friend or loved one along for the experience.

Over nearly three decades of creating ethnodrama and presenting the findings in performance, I can count on one hand the number of times I have had a participant express feeling upset about a performance they attended. On the contrary, participants typically respond positively to the sharing of their thoughts and stories. Still, I carry these few examples of participants feeling upset into every new project. I use those moments as a reminder about the level of care and intentionality I need to bring to this work as an artist-researcher. I have also come to accept that even with all that care and intentionality deployed, I cannot always anticipate how someone will receive themselves when performed by another. The consenting process for participants strives to make the ethnodrama creation process as clear and transparent as possible, especially because I use verbatim performance for the ethnotheatrical dissemination. I also look to all members of the creative team and the ethnoactors to openly express thoughts and concerns about the arrangement of material in the script and its presentation through the staging and performances. I take that feedback seriously and implement as much of it as possible, while also working to balance the dissemination of the findings.

Suppose an artist-researcher encounters a participant who responds negatively to the overall performance or their portrayal by an ethnoactor. In that case, it is essential to hear that person's response and to embrace whatever feedback they are willing to share at a time and in a space mutually agreed upon by the participant and the artist-researcher. Some questions or points to guide that feedback process include the following:

- Allow the participant to describe what about the experience upset them.
- Acknowledge that feedback and accept it.
- Do not negate the participant's experience. While your intention might have been sound, recognize and accept the impact on the participant.
- If the participant is interested and open to hearing, describe the steps taken to create the play, how and why you selected their interview excerpt, and its importance as a research finding.
- Describe the process by which the ethnoactor prepared their performance.

- Ask the participant what they would have liked to happen differently.
- If the ethnodrama's performances will continue, consider whether you can make any changes to address the participant's concerns, including removing their excerpt from the script and performance.

This follow-up conversation with a participant might not change their feelings about their experience with the performance. However, allowing them to express their concerns and suggesting possible modifications can help to remind the participant of the artist-researcher's original intentions, even if their experience differed. Given that the last point above implies that the artist-researcher may need to remove a section of the play, they should clearly outline this possibility for the ethnoactors as the rehearsal process begins.

For every participant who sits for an interview but whose material does not become part of the script, I also offer them a chance to see the performance. Typically, I offer these participants one seat each, but if they ask for more seats and I have them available, I grant the request. The language of their invitation looks very similar but with relevant modifications:

> *Hello,*
>
> *Thank you for completing an interview for [project name] back in [month year of data collection]. As a reminder, this project is exploring/investigating [the project topic and/or a variation of the project's research questions].*
>
> *We've completed the scripting process and have started to rehearse the resulting new play called [title of play—may be the same name as the project or different].*
>
> *Because of space and time, we could not include your interview in the performance script, but your thoughts and stories have certainly contributed to our understanding of this topic. We are most grateful for your time and contributions to this project.*
>
> *To thank you for sharing your thoughts with us, I would like to offer you one complimentary ticket to see a performance of the play. The production will take place at [name and location of venue].*
>
> *Performance dates and times are as follows:*
>
> *[list the dates and times available]*
>
> *Please reply to this email by [deadline date] with the date/time when you would like to attend. I will then follow up with a confirmation email.*
>
> *Again, thank you for taking the time to share your thoughts and stories with us. We're very appreciative and look forward to sharing this new work with you.*
>
> *All best wishes,*
>
> *[Your name]*
>
> *[Your role on the project]*

Participants whose material does not become part of the script frequently attend a performance. They are curious to learn more about what the project has revealed about the topic, and they want to understand more about the uniqueness of ethnodrama as a form. Conversely, sometimes, participants want to know why I did not select their interview for the script. I have received that question in person, by phone, and by email. The conversation is not necessarily easy, but when I explain more about the analysis process, the repetition of ideas that emerge as a result of that process, and the limitations around the length of the script and time of the performance, participants usually understand. I also emphasize that their interview continues to exist as part of the archive for this project and that future performances with the data are possible. I can revisit the data to create another ethnodrama informed by that particular moment, my shifting point of view, or another research question altogether. My experience with Eric Marcus's dataset for *Making Gay History: Before Stonewall* exemplifies this idea.

If the performance of the ethnodrama occurs live in a theatre, participants arrive on their own and watch the performance. I do not let the ethnoactors know whether or when specific participants will attend, as knowing when a participant is in the audience can create concern and nervousness for the ethnoactor, adversely affecting their performance. Additionally, I want to maintain the confidentiality of the participant. If the participant chooses to identify themselves after experiencing the performance, that is their choice. That said, when ethnoactors also conduct interviews for a project, they may recognize participants sitting in the audience. The same holds true if the ethnoactors viewed the videos of interviews as part of their preparation and rehearsal process.

When I used an audience engagement activity like the ones described in the previous section, participants frequently took that opportunity to approach the ethnoactor who portrayed them and introduce themselves. Or they approached me to identify themselves. I have read about other ethnodrama projects where the participants are more featured, seated in a particular location in the theatre, and acknowledged as present before the performance begins. Some projects feature participants as guests in a talkback with other audience members and the actors. While this kind of attention might seem like a positive thing to do to acknowledge and thank the participants for their contributions to the project, it sets up a questionable dynamic. Suddenly, there may be a direct comparison between the participant and the ethnoactor who portrayed them. Audiences might expect participants to speak or comment on the performance dissemination when, in fact, they may not have participated in the analysis and rehearsal steps of the process. Participants may not want to speak about their experience or elaborate beyond what they shared during their interview. Placing participants in this kind of high-focus position assumes they want to be in that position; I do not make that assumption. If that high-focus potential was not outlined at the start of the process when gaining their consent, then expecting participants to attend and participate in conversations about the work may be an ethical overstep.

When participants self-identify following a performance, an opportunity emerges to hear their responses to the ethnodrama, and these responses can become part of the evaluation process. In past projects, participants expressed gratitude that their stories were shared publicly and stated that they felt seen and heard in ways they had not experienced before. Participants often want to meet the ethnoactor who portrayed them, and I have seen them request a picture with the ethnoactor. Participants have self-identified to other audience members around them, expressing pride at being part of the production. In some cases, participants have asked to touch, hold, or try on the talisman the ethnoactor used to represent them in performance. This particular response speaks to the talisman's strength as a symbol for the participant and the importance of the ritual of moving in and out of the portrayal. The process of putting on and taking off the talisman endows the object with meaning, and the participants who have wanted to engage with the talismans have understood that and their importance.

These examples come from my anecdotal observations and interactions or experiences that ethnoactors have described to me following the performances of multiple projects. They are also all positive responses to performances, which raises questions about their trustworthiness as evaluative evidence. Other participants could have attended these same performances and chosen not to identify themselves for positive or negative reasons. All artist-researchers must be mindful of the potential bias that could emerge from positive feedback through participants who self-select.

Ethnodrama projects can benefit from an evaluation process that casts a wider net to reach all participants who choose to attend a live performance or screening of an ethnodrama. Surveys sent via email reach those participants who attended, or depending on location and proximity to the participant pool, an artist-researcher could conduct a focus group. In both cases, allowing a few days or a week for the participants to process their experience of the ethnodrama before asking for their feedback may foster deeper observations and reflections as part of the evaluation process. I suggest the following open-ended prompts as possibilities for a survey or focus group discussion:

- What did you learn about the topic through the performance?
- What did you learn about yourself and others?
- How did you feel about how we shared your contributions as part of this project?
- What do you now know or recognize about yourself after attending the performance?

A survey instrument can collect responses using a Google form or Qualtrics, but in the case of a focus group, recording and transcribing the conversation alongside a running record of observations and anecdotal statements can help to collect data for an evaluation process. Depending on how the artist-researcher intends to use the data collected from a survey or focus group, the process may require an ethics committee review and a separate consenting process. Alternatively, the artist-researcher can include this evaluation process in the overall project design and manage it during the initial ethics committee review and participant consenting process.

Gathering Creative Team Feedback

An ethnodrama's creative team, including artist-researchers and ethnoactors, the director, dramaturg, and designers, can also provide important insights for an evaluation process. Theatre practitioners can be particularly sensitive to the human condition, contributing to their evaluative sensitivity. With ethnodrama, the engagement with actual people's words creates an opportunity for the ethnoactors and other creative team members to leverage their sensitivities in ways that can reveal deep insights into the topic at hand and the accompanying research question(s). By design, a rehearsal process fosters long-term immersion in the data. It facilitates ongoing data analysis through deep listening and embodiment by the ethnoactors, with close attention from the director and the designers. An evaluative process helps to gather the creative team's learnings and insights. I collect qualitative data for the evaluation process, as those data tend to be the most revealing and present thicker descriptions of each team member's experience.

The evaluation with creative team members can use a series of related prompts in a preinvestigation and postinvestigation surveying process to ascertain what they learned and how they learned it. In particular, ethnoactors who embody the stories of the interview participants may have much to offer about their discoveries as they speak and perform the words of another. The ethnoactor comes the closest of any creative team member to gaining new understanding and empathy for a different perspective through their encounter with another person's words. Because of this potential, I encourage ethnoactors to remain open to what they might discover about the character they are investigating and performing and what they might learn about themselves, their preconceived notions, and their implicit biases (Salvatore, 2023).

An ethnoactor should begin their engagement with the creative process by establishing a baseline of their understanding of the ethnodrama's topic and the characters they will play. This baseline allows for a point of comparison at the end of the process to identify discoveries. As an ethnoactor enters the rehearsal process and receives their character assignments, the lead artist-researcher can administer a preinvestigation analysis survey for each character the ethnoactor will portray. Potential preinvestigation analysis survey prompts can include the following:

- What do you currently know and understand about the topic of this ethnodrama?
- What do you currently know and understand about each character you will investigate and perform?
- What are your preconceived thoughts and opinions about each character? Consider what you know about their social, cultural, and political affiliations.
- What is your hypothesis about what you might discover about each character through portraying their interview excerpt(s)?
- What is your hypothesis about what you might learn about the topic of this ethnodrama as a result of working on this project?

I devised these preinvestigation prompts for ethnoactors, but they can work for other creative team members with a few adjustments. For example, rather than asking a question about a specific character, other creative team members, such as a director or designer, might complete a survey that includes these prompts:

- What do you currently know and understand about the topic of this ethnodrama?
- What was the most memorable moment from your initial reading of the script? Why was that moment memorable for you?
- Which character is the most memorable for you from your initial reading of the script? Why is that character memorable for you?
- What is your hypothesis about what you might learn about the topic of this ethnodrama as a result of working on this project?

The lead artist-researcher on the project should administer these preinvestigation surveys to team members before they have invested too much time or work into the creative process. For ethnoactors, I recommend distributing the survey at the beginning of the rehearsal process after the initial read-through of the script. For all other creative team members, I recommend that they complete this survey after reading the script for the first time and before completing all of their initial preparatory work on the project.

All creative team members should complete the postinvestigation analysis survey within a week of the project's final performance. The postinvestigation analysis survey questions should mirror those on the preinvestigation survey so that there is a clear relationship between the baseline data collected and the data collected after the process. With that in mind, some potential postinvestigation analysis survey prompts for ethnoactors could include the following:

- What have you learned about the topic of this ethnodrama through your participation in this project?
- What discoveries have you made about each character you have investigated and performed for this project?
- How do these discoveries affect your perception of each character?
- How does your learning affect your understanding of the topic of the ethnodrama?
- What has surprised you about your participation in this project?
- What new questions do you have as you complete your work on this project?

Some of these questions directly mirror the preinvestigation analysis survey questions. Others take a broader approach to measure how the entire ethnodramatic process might have affected the ethnoactor. These questions can be particularly revealing when an ethnoactor participates in a process like this for the first time. An artist-researcher should also adjust the postperformance analysis survey questions to reflect the preinvestigation questions used with other creative team members.

Beyond surveying, an artist-researcher can use focus groups as a form of evaluation with creative team members. Convening focus groups can sometimes present more complications because of scheduling an entire team to come together at the end of a long process. Still, a group conversation allows team members to hear about the experiences of others and to respond in the moment to a comment that might resonate with them and relate to their own experience. Some examples of prompts for a focus group at the end of a project could be the following:

- What were your expectations coming into this project?
- What did you know about the topic area before working on this project?
- What do you know about the topic area after working on this project?
- What did you learn from your work on this project?
- What surprises did you experience working on this project?
- What new questions do you have after working on this project?

The focus group and the surveying processes with the creative team may also provide an opportunity to gain invaluable feedback about the team's collaboration on the project. Production processes often include debriefing conversations to evaluate how a team worked together and to look for ways to improve the process in the future. When facilitated with care, these conversations can help the artist-researcher to deepen their understanding of the research and creative processes and present helpful information for future projects.

Analyzing the Feedback

Once the artist-researcher has gathered feedback from the audience, research partici-pants, and creative team members, they can analyze it for answers to the evaluation ques-tions. A coding process to identify recurring patterns in the feedback data can be helpful. Depending on who participated in the feedback process, the artist-researcher can con-sider separating the coding process by the various groups who provided feedback, or they can code the feedback as a single dataset. Whatever the choice, the artist-research should articulate why they chose to make it for their project.

I return to each of the five evaluation questions below and suggest where responses might emerge from audiences, research participants, and creative team members.

How has the ethnodrama answered the project's research question(s)? Feedback from audiences, research participants, and creative team members can all offer insights into how the ethnodrama addressed the project's research question(s). Audience feedback comes with the most distance from the project's development process, so it may have more reliability and less bias attached. However, research participants can offer invalu-able feedback based on their proximity to the topic of the ethnodrama, and creative team members will have the most familiarity with the material overall. Each group brings its unique perspective to the evaluation process because of their level of participation and when they enter the overall process.

What observations have emerged about the aesthetics of the ethnodrama from read-ing the script and experiencing it in performance? Given their proximity to the aesthetics of the ethnodrama and its ethnotheatrical performance, creative team members may be the least objective when it comes to this evaluation question. If a creative member partici-pates in an ethnodrama process for the first time, their feedback around aesthetics may be more reliable than that of others who have participated in multiple ethnodramas.

The audience and the research participants offer the most reliable feedback about aesthetics because they are more distant from the creative process. Research participants may have some expectations about what they might experience based on information they received during the consenting process, but unless they receive a copy of the script to review in advance or attend a rehearsal, their experience of the script in performance will catalyze a similar level of feedback that an audience member with no connections to the project can offer.

What is the ethical orientation of the ethnodrama? Ideally, an ethnodrama and eth-notheatrical production should demonstrate explicitly and implicitly its ethical orienta-tion. An audience reading the ethnodrama or viewing the ethnotheatrical production should understand how the artist-researcher and creative team navigated the ethical con-cerns inherent in qualitative data collection, analysis, and dissemination. The audience's awareness of these considerations may emerge through comments and questions about the process and observations about particular moments of content in the ethnodrama. For example, suppose audience feedback reveals recurring questions about how or why spe-cific interview excerpts appeared in the script or performance. In that case, these ques-tions potentially point to the need for more transparent rules of engagement about data analysis in the ethnodrama and its performance.

Feedback from research participants can provide an artist-researcher with informa-tion about whether an ethnodrama's ethical orientation created a sense of care throughout the process. A participant may see a performance and respond positively to their portrayal. Conversely, a participant could question their portrayal or feel upset by some part of the process. These responses provide information that can inform an artist-researcher's future approaches to ethnoactor coaching, consenting processes, and scripting choices.

While creative team members can provide feedback on a project's ethical orientation, their viewpoints come from inside the process and have contributed in varying ways to how it unfolded. The director and the designers may have greater distance from the research participants than the ethnoactors. Given how closely the ethnoactors work with the material contributed by the research participants, their discoveries through investigation and portrayal can offer important insights about how a participant experienced the interviewing process, which links closely to the ethical orientation of a project.

How does the ethnodrama consider a diversity of viewpoints and perspectives? This evaluation question offers space for feedback from anyone who has interacted with the ethnodrama at any point in the process. Audiences may report feeling represented by the characters in the ethnodrama or express a desire for representation of other perspectives. Research participants who do not appear in an ethnodrama may question why they were not included. In contrast, those who appear in the script and performance as characters may express gratitude and report feeling seen. Creative team members may offer critiques of a script's limitations that only become clear after seeing it fully realized in performance and hearing audience responses. While some of this feedback may create discomfort or disappointment, the artist-researcher should work to receive it with as much openness as possible and consider it part of their reflective practice. Lessons learned from one project can be applied to the next project, ensuring that the artist-researcher's methodology continues to grow and deepen with each new investigation.

What learning has occurred from the ethnodrama and its creation process? This fifth evaluation question provides perhaps the most essential measure of an ethnodrama's effectiveness. If an ethnodrama has offered new insights about its research topic, audiences, research participants, and creative team members will reflect on learning moments through their experiences. Audiences and research participants may speak specifically about what the script and performance reveal about the topic and the research question(s), and creative team members may offer moments of learning from the creation process. The content of the learning moments may overlap from one group to the next, but the pathways to those learnings may differ. Similarly, the level of involvement and length of time with material may also affect the depth of learning. An audience member may see a performance and identify that they discovered something specific they did not know before, and a creative team member may cite a similar discovery but speak in more depth because they have spent more time with the data. In either case, the evaluation question offers the opportunity to assess what and how learning occurs, depending on the individual's relationship to the ethnodrama and its performance.

The evaluation process and resulting dataset represent yet another possibility of dissemination for the artist-researcher and their work. The data collected through the evaluation process may illustrate the efficacy of ethnodrama, or the data might also reveal there is more work to do. A successful evaluation process will yield discoveries that affirm and simultaneously question the ethnodrama and its processes. These affirmations and questions can guide the artist-researcher to iterative and exciting new pathways of investigation.

ACTIVITIES

Creative Collection

Collecting written feedback from an audience following a performance can be a dry undertaking. To lighten and liven up this process, think about how a data collection instrument might relate to the world of the play or a theme from the play. Based on the example of a costume tag mentioned in the audience feedback model for *Of a Certain Age*, consider the different ethnodrama topics listed below. How might a data collection instrument for these examples take a more creative format beyond paper and pencil?

- An ethnodrama exploring the effects of standardized testing on the college application process
- An ethnodrama exploring the impacts of discrimination in health care delivery
- An ethnodrama exploring how social media affect dating in the 21st century

Leveraging Social Media

Since social media platforms like Instagram allow you to conduct polls and solicit feedback, consider how these tools might help evaluate an ethnodrama. If you have an Instagram account, experiment with the polling feature and combine it with a Story and a Reel. Which of these formats receives more polling participation? Does the polling illuminate helpful information about the question you posed? How can you move the polling beyond your followers through a hashtag? Revisit the ethnodrama topics in the first activity. What hashtags could you use for each one alongside your polling question?

NOTES

1. Analytics courtesy of Nora Lambert, NYU-TV.

2. Thanks to Martina Novakova and Yuqing Zhao for their analysis of audience responses and word clouds.

Conclusion

As we arrive at the final pages of this book, I hope you feel inspired and ready to embark on your own journey with ethnodrama. It's crucial to reiterate that the approach I've outlined is one of many. I encourage you to delve into the works of other ethnodramatists and discover a process that resonates with you. I conclude with some final thoughts for your consideration.

Because of its nature as a qualitative, ABR methodology, ethnodrama encourages multiple interpretations, which can lead to contradictions and tensions. As a result, finding a definitive answer to a research question is often elusive. However, the informed artist-researcher deliberately chooses ethnodrama, understanding that their aim is not to arrive at a conclusive answer but to provide a rich, detailed description of a phenomenon that incorporates diverse voices and perspectives. I have learned to embrace multiple interpretations, contradictions, and tensions in my work because they ultimately lead to conversations. Those conversations are not always easy, but I want to have them. If you wish to pursue a particular topic using ethnodrama but feel uncomfortable or unprepared to navigate the challenging discussions that might emerge, think carefully before pursuing it. I consciously use ethnodrama because of its capacity to evoke, provoke, and disrupt (Leavy, 2020b). However, when something provokes, chances increase for strong feelings, including upset and anger. Those responses can create discomfort for me as the lead artist-researcher and for the creative team members who work with me. In particular, the ethnoactors, as public-facing disseminators of the findings, are the most vulnerable, as they embody those findings before an audience. Because of this potential for provocation, an artist-researcher needs to enter the process with eyes wide open to this possibility and is responsible for ensuring those working with them understand that possibility as well. I prepare ethnoactors through conversations during rehearsal and before we open a performance. I have learned that I can rarely predict how an audience will respond to an ethnodrama's discoveries. I have hypothesized around those responses and been wrong more times than I can count, so much so that I now take great pleasure in being wrong. I expect and embrace it, using it to gain a deeper understanding of why I wanted to investigate a topic in the first place. Art making and research are not about "being right." They are about discovery and sharing those discoveries. What comes from sharing is most often out of our control.

In a similar vein, McNiff (2025) reminds us that "a fundamental premise of artistic inquiry is that the end cannot be known at the beginning" (p. 33), and this premise also applies to research. Ethnodrama uncovers answers to the artist-researcher's questions and relies on the artist-researcher to accept the answers that emerge. On many occasions, I have wanted the data I collected to align with my opinion, yet they revealed the exact opposite. Rather than searching for participants who might mirror my opinion, I embraced what the dataset revealed and allowed an audience to engage with it on their terms. *We cannot force a dataset to say something that it doesn't say.* If you take nothing else from this book, please remember that statement. If we want ethnodrama to be taken seriously as a research methodology, we must avoid manipulating our analysis and dissemination to reflect our desired interpretation of the data. I have emphasized ethics and care throughout this book for this very reason. The stronger our attention to the ethical orientation of ethnodrama, the more trustworthiness we build into our process, findings, and dissemination.

And a final consideration about the future. Once you identify a current topic and a research question to investigate and collect data, you have a dataset that represents a snapshot of viewpoints on this topic at a particular moment. You collected that dataset, and it exists. The data only goes away if you choose to let it go. Given its existence, you can revisit it at any moment in the future. Your evaluation process after an ethnodrama's performance might signal a direction for another immediate analysis of the same dataset. Or you could continue working in this particular topic area, and 10 years later, you decide to analyze the dataset again and collect a new dataset to compare moments in time. As an artist-researcher and ethnodramatist, I encourage you to remain open to these exciting, inspiring, and endless possibilities.

Glossary

Aria: A term used in opera to describe a piece of music sung by a solo voice. Arias are essential to an opera's story and require a virtuosic singer. An aria in an ethnodrama is a longer monologue, usually from a character that only appears once in a multicharacter ethnodrama. The character's single contribution addresses the overarching research question in a unique and theatrically compelling way.

Artist-researcher: A hyphenated identity that acknowledges the duality of skills, techniques, and knowledge required by someone who uses an arts-based research methodology such as ethnodrama. Artist-researchers often work at the hyphen, the intersection of the artist and researcher identities.

Artists' literacies: A framework coined by Andrew Freiband (2023) that characterizes art-making as a "unique way of knowing" and a form of "deeply insightful social research." Artists' literacies yield knowledge that can then be applied to create systemic change. For more, see *www.artistsliteracies.org*.

Arts-based research (ABR): A set of methodological research practices that leverages various art-making processes to generate and analyze data and to disseminate research findings (Barone & Eisner, 2012; Chilton & Leavy, 2020; Kara, 2020; Leavy, 2020b; McNiff, 2014). ABR can use various methodological tools grounded in fiction writing, poetry, music, dance, theatre, film, and the visual arts (Leavy, 2020b).

Blocking: The physical movements of actors on stage during a performance.

Bounce: The conversational quality between characters' voices that an ethnodramatist arranges in multicharacter scripting conventions such as duets, trios, quartets, montages, and choral pieces.

Bump: In lighting design, when lighting changes abruptly from one look to another. Turning a light on or off with a switch is an everyday example of a bump.

Cadence: The rhythmic pauses and tempo of how a person speaks.

Closed question: A type of interview prompt that elicits either a "yes" or "no," one-word, or short-phrase response.

Code: "A short word or phrase that symbolically assigns a summative, salient, essence-capturing, and/or evocative attribute" (Saldaña, 2021, p. 5) to a section of a piece of data.

Coding: A process by which a researcher analyzes, organizes, and/or categorizes a textual dataset to identify its emerging meanings. Leavy (2023) describes coding as a way to "reduce and clarify the data generated" (p. 165). In the process outlined in this book, coding happens across three rounds of data analysis: initial, transcribing, and binning.

Coding for speech: Analyzing a speaker's specific speech pattern and cadence and notating those patterns through transcribing. The patterns are noted on a transcript by taking a hard return whenever an individual pauses when speaking. The transcription appears more like poetry on the page rather than prose.

Collaborative coding: A process that utilizes more than one artist-researcher to code for recurring patterns in a dataset. Collaborative coding can happen with a lead artist-researcher and a trusted colleague/collaborator or with an ensemble of artist-researchers.

Composite character: A fictional character in an ethnodrama created by combining thematically related interview excerpts from multiple participants. Creating composite characters can help preserve and protect participants' anonymity, particularly when they come from a small community.

Consent: A participant agrees to participate in research after receiving and reviewing all pertinent information about the project. Securing a participant's consent is one of the most essential steps in any research process: It defines the agreement between the researcher and the participant about what the participant is committing to do and how the researcher will use the results of their participation.

  • **Consent form:** a formal written document that outlines all necessary information about a research project, including its purpose, information about who will conduct the project, the researcher's affiliation if applicable, the data collection/interviewing process, the dissemination plan, information about the potential risks and benefits of participation, and a clause allowing participants to withdraw their permission to use the data from their interview. Participants sign a consent form indicating they consent to participate in a project and agree to all its outlined parameters.

  • **Release form:** a formal written document outlining the same information as a consent form, with additional legally binding language that protects the artist-researcher's creative process. When a participant signs a release form, they relinquish any legal rights to their interview, including how the artist-researcher uses it. The participant cannot exercise any control over artistic and aesthetic choices made in the production process.

Dataset: The results of a data collection process. For the process outlined in this book, the dataset includes the following pieces for each participant: a signed consent/release form; an audio or video recording of the interview; field notes from the interview via the Participant Characteristics and Physical Surroundings Survey; any additional notes or correspondence from the interviewing process. If a research project uses a preexisting dataset, the dataset may contain similar or different elements from the ones described here.

Deep listening: The type of listening used by an artist-researcher to create a scored, raw transcript and by an ethnoactor to rehearse and perform in an ethnotheatrical production. Deep listening requires concentration, focus, patience, and an openness to discovering something new and unexpected.

Dénouement: The circumstances and actions that unfold to resolve the protagonist's central conflict in a traditionally structured play. More generally, how a play unwinds and comes to an end.

Differentiated dissemination: Using various textures in addition to ethnoactors speaking text to share the research findings of an ethnodrama in an ethnotheatrical production. These textures can include movement and design elements that provide multiple points of connection to the research findings. The pedagogical concept of differentiated instruction inspires the technique.

Director's concept: A unique conceptual orientation to a play that develops from a director's careful analysis of a script. A director uses their concept to inform their choices for a play's production.

Documentary theatre: A genre of theatre that uses various kinds of textual data to create a play and performance. Weiss (1971) identified that the sources for a documentary theatre performance may include materials such as "records, documents, letters, statistics, market-reports, statements by banks and companies, government statements, speeches, interviews, statements by well-known personalities, newspaper and broadcast reports, photos, documentary films, and other contemporary documents" (as cited in Paget, 1987, p. 335). Documentary theatre also has subgenres, listed below.

  ● **Tribunal theatre** uses "edited transcripts . . . of trials, tribunals, and public inquiries" as its source material (Paget, 2011, pp. 233–234).

  ● **Verbatim theatre** uses recordings of interviews with "'ordinary' people, done in the context of research into a particular region, subject area, issue, event, or combination of these things" (Robinson, quoted by Paget, 1987, p. 317). Transcripts of those interviews are edited and arranged to form a script, which actors then perform. Depending on the specific project, the actors may or may not have participated in the data collection (Paget, 1987).

  ● **Verbatim documentary theatre** requires actors to use verbatim performance as their technique for performing a documentary theatre production. See also **verbatim performance.**

Dramaturg: A collaborator in a theatre-making process who specializes in dramaturgy, which includes knowledge of dramatic literature, theatre history, dramatic structure, and play development. In a new play development process, such as creating an ethnodrama, a dramaturg supports the ethnodramatist as the play develops and grows (Trencsényi, 2015).

Ethical orientation: How an artist-researcher integrates ethical practices into creating and presenting an ethnodrama.

Ethics committee: A committee charged with vetting and overseeing research projects involving human subjects conducted under the jurisdiction of an institution or organization. An ethics committee's vetting determines whether a project requires their oversight. If so, the research project must adhere to strict guidelines about the safety and welfare of the human subjects participating in the research process, known as **procedural ethics.** Also known as institutional review boards (IRBs) or research ethics committees (Delamont & Atkinson, 2018). **Relational ethics** refers to principles guiding researchers as they work directly with participants in the field. A researcher must keep ethical considerations alive and at the forefront of their process, as what matters most is what happens in the relationship between the researcher and the participant. Relational ethics are related to **good human beingness.**

Ethnoactor: An actor who uses a specific acting approach to portray a real person in an ethnotheatrical production. The ethnoactor must portray the character with dignity and respect, while allowing themselves to experience new knowledge and understanding about the individual's lived experience. The ethnoactor works to avoid caricature, misrepresentation, or falsehood by finding a way to empathize with the character and perform them truthfully (Burch, 2019).

Ethnodrama: A script created from textual data gathered and/or analyzed by an artist-researcher with the explicit purpose of investigating a research question, performing the investigation's findings for an audience, and collecting and analyzing their responses to those findings.

Ethnodramatist: An artist-researcher who uses textual data to create an ethnodrama.

Ethnographer: A qualitative researcher who uses ethnography as their research methodology to study people, culture, and behavior.

Ethnography: A qualitative research methodology with origins in anthropology that includes studying, describing, and interpreting culture and cultural behavior. Ethnography often contributes to naming and describing a culture or community. It has expanded beyond anthropology to other fields in the social sciences, applied health sciences, education, and cultural studies (Saldaña, 2005).

Ethnotheatre: The theatrical production of an ethnodrama that disseminates the investigation's findings to an audience and then engages them in an additional data collection process to further explore the ethnodrama's research question and assess its impact.

Exposition: Information about events that happen before the action of a play's story begins. This information helps the audience better understand the characters' current state of affairs in a play.

Fade and **crossfade:** Terms in lighting design that refer to when lighting changes gradually from one look to another over time. Changing light from on to off by sliding a dimmer switch or rotating a dial is an everyday example of a fade. A crossfade functions similarly, but the gradual change over time moves from one look to another.

Field notes: The results of a researcher's observations when conducting fieldwork. Field notes emerge from the researcher's perception of what unfolds during field observation, informed by their senses of sight, sound, smell, taste, and touch (Harrison, 2018; Small & Calarco, 2022). In the methodology described in this book, the artist-researcher gathers field notes from their experiences interviewing participants.

Gestural coding: A process wherein an ethnoactor uses a video recording to observe and notate specific gestures and behaviors of an individual they will portray. The ethnoactor notates their gestural coding on a scored transcript that matches the text spoken by the individual in the original recording.

Given circumstances: A term from the writings of Russian theatrical director Konstantin Stanislavski referring to "the plot, the facts, the incidents, the period, the time and place of the action [of the play], the way of life, how . . . actors and directors understand the play, the contributions [they] make, the mise-en-scène, the sets and costumes, the props, the stage dressing, the sound effects, etc., etc., everything which is a given for the

actors as they rehearse" (Stanislavski, 2008, p. 52).

Good human beingness: A colloquial way of thinking, writing, and speaking about the importance of maintaining a strong moral compass when conducting research that involves other human beings. Good human beingness embodies the **relational ethics** necessary for working with others.

Identifier: The preferred name or personal description chosen by an interview participant to identify them in an ethnodramatic script. The identifier can be a participant's real name, a partial name, or a pseudonym.

Interview prompt: An open-ended question or command used in an interview protocol for a data collection process. An interview protocol usually contains a bank of interview prompts that an interviewer offers a participant for their responses. Interview prompts encourage participants to reflect on and discuss their experiences and beliefs related to a project's overarching research question(s).

• **Philosophy-generating prompt:** a prompt in an interview protocol that invites a participant to philosophize or share their viewpoints on a particular topic.

• **Story-generating prompt:** a prompt in an interview protocol that invites a participant to share a personal story related to a particular topic.

Interview protocol: The procedure an interviewer follows when conducting an interview with a participant. The interview protocol begins with introducing the project and reviewing its procedures and potential outcomes. Then, the protocol moves to the series of interview prompts associated with the project. After the interview participant has responded to the interview prompts, the protocol concludes with a review of the procedures and potential outcomes. The participant may also change their identifier; adjust the names of people, places, or things mentioned in the interview; and identify any sections they prefer not to be considered for the project.

Interview theatre: A play constructed from interviews with participants and performed by actors.

In vivo coding: Using the actual words of interview participants to develop codes; also known as verbatim coding (Leavy, 2023; Saldaña, 2021).

Lenses: Refer to theoretical schools of thought used to conduct research and analyze data. Examples of these lenses include critical race theory, feminist theory, Indigenous theory, postcolonial theory, and queer theory, among others.

Literature review: A step in the research process that explores and documents what other scholars have discovered and written about a specific research topic and adjacent topics that might relate. A literature review may also explore how other researchers have used a particular methodology. A literature review may identify a knowledge gap, guiding a researcher to craft a project that can significantly contribute to a field or discipline.

Member checking: A process that allows an interview participant to review their interview, edit what they have said, and request that certain sections not be utilized. Its goal is to protect participants and help them maintain control over how a researcher uses their gathered testimony. Member checking also helps to disrupt the power differential between a researcher and a participant. Member checking can happen at various stages of a research project following data collection.

Participant Characteristics and Physical Surroundings Survey: An instrument used to collect field notes following an interview. The survey begins with the interviewer's name, the participant's chosen identifier, and the date and time of the interview. The survey then asks for brief, detailed observations perceived using the five senses for the following four sections: physical description of the participant, description of the participant's physical behavior, description of the specific location where the interview takes place, description of the geographical location where the interview takes place.

Participant population: The group of people a researcher would like to engage during data collection for a particular research project.

Performed ethnography: "The dramatic scenarios, public staging, crafted theatricality, and improvisational enactments of fieldwork and ethnographic data that will *be*, that have *been*, and that are *being* performed" (Madison, 2018, p. xvii, author's original emphasis). Madison distinguishes between performed ethnography and performance ethnography (see below), and I appreciate this nuance.

Performance ethnography: "The local and symbolic enactments of performances within the field and on the ground of social life and processes" (Madison, 2018, p. xix). As an example, Denzin (2018) identified that an interview is performative in nature, a "site where meaning is created and performed" (p. 163), implying that when a researcher conducts an interview as part of their fieldwork, the interview participant's responses are a performance.

Performance phenomenology: The relationship between the audience, the performers, and the material being performed. This relationship helps define and maintain the world of a play as a performance unfolds (Olf, 1997).

Point-of-view statement: A written space where the artist-researcher takes a *subjective* position in their project. This statement typically dismisses the artist-researcher's neutrality by focusing on their biases, beliefs, and the points of view from which they come at the research. The point-of-view statement is similar to the stance of the researcher statement used with more traditional research approaches.

Portraying across identity: A performance style in which an ethnoactor portrays someone of another race, ethnicity, gender, gender identity, age, ability, or orientation different from their own (Salvatore, 2023; Vachon & Salvatore, 2023). When a director selects ethnoactors for this performance style, they are **casting across identity**. Ethnotheatrical productions can intentionally use this performance style to reinforce an audience's critical engagement with and analysis of research findings.

Procedural ethics: See **Ethics committee.**

Project need analysis: Similar to a literature review, this analysis states the importance of investigating a proposed topic based on understanding what other researchers have discovered about it (or topics adjacent to it).

Props: Elements that the actors handle and carry in a theatrical production.

Qualitative research: "An umbrella term for a wide variety of approaches to and methods for the study of natural social life. The information or data collected and analyzed is primarily (but not exclusively) nonquantitative in character" (Saldana, 2011b, p. 3). Qualitative research relies primarily on textual data as source material to describe a situation or phenomenon that is more open to interpretation.

Quantitative research: A variety of methodologies "characterized by deductive approaches to the research process aimed at proving, disproving, or lending credence to existing theories" (Leavy, 2023, p. 9). Quantitative research relies primarily on numerical data to "[achieve] objectivity, control, and precise measurement" (Leavy, 2023, p. 99).

Reader's theatre: A common method of presenting an ethnodrama to an audience. In reader's theatre, actors do not memorize their lines. Instead, they read the play aloud using vocal inflection to bring the play to life. Reader's theatre does not usually incorporate staging or design choices.

Relational ethics: See **Ethics committee.**

Repertory lighting plot: A fixed lighting package provided by a theatre. The lighting plot provides basic lighting coverage for all areas of the stage. All productions in that theatre use that same plot. A lighting designer works within the confines of that fixed plot without changing the lighting instruments' positions or colors.

Research paradigm: A specific framework used for conducting research (Leavy, 2023).

Research question: The main question that guides a research project (Leavy, 2023). The research question for an ethnodrama should signal that it will explore, describe, or explain a complex situation or phenomenon, rather than declare a concrete finding or work to prove or disprove a hypothesis (Rubin & Rubin, 2012.

Research-based theatre (RbT): A method of inquiry grounded in theatre-making, arts-based, and qualitative research methodologies while simultaneously being "a more inclusive term to describe the multiple ways of integrating theatre throughout the research process" (Belliveau & Lea, 2016, p. 6).

Rules of engagement: Information presented early in an ethnodrama and an ethnotheatrical performance that prepares an audience to engage with the research findings as critical thinkers rather than cathartic responders. The rules of engagement help an audience for ethnodrama and ethnotheatre to understand they are experiencing a play based on collected and analyzed data. The rules of engagement in ethnodrama are similar to the **exposition** in a traditional play.

Sample: The pool of individuals recruited for a research project whose participation yields data for the project.

Sampling: The process of recruiting and selecting participants for a research project.

- **Convenience sampling:** recruiting and selecting participants because they are easily accessible.

- **Purposeful sampling:** intentionally recruiting and selecting participants based on a particular strategic approach (Leavy, 2023) or a particular characteristic, identity, or experience of the participant.

- **Snowball sampling:** recruiting and selecting participants based on referrals from other participants.

Saturation: The point at which data collection ceases to reveal new insights (Leavy, 2023).

Scenic elements: Large structural elements, including furniture pieces, that help define the playing space and physical world of the play in a theatrical production.

Scripting conventions: The various ways an ethnodramatist can arrange interview excerpts in an ethnodrama: monologue, duet, trio, quartet, montage, choral piece. These terms most accurately represent what happens structurally in the ethnodrama and ethnotheatrical performance (Salvatore, 2020b, 2025).

- **Monologue:** a continuous section of an interview transcript from one character performed by one ethnoactor.

- **Duet:** two related interview excerpts from two characters come together in a conversation to illuminate a particular topic or idea from different perspectives and drive home a point revealed during the data analysis. A different ethnoactor performs each character.

- **Trio:** similar to a duet but uses interview excerpts from three characters.

- **Quartet:** similar to the duet and trio but uses interview excerpts from four characters.

- **Montage:** functions similarly to a trio or quartet but features more bounce because the spoken excerpts from each character are usually shorter. Additionally, it can feature more than four characters, and ethnoactors can portray more than one character if needed. Montages usually only feature characters who appear elsewhere in the ethnodrama.

- **Choral piece:** similar to a montage but features even shorter snippets or single lines of text pulled from transcripts and then arranged to simulate a chorus of voices. Choral pieces usually only include voices from characters who appear elsewhere in the ethnodrama. However, an exception to this could be using other participants from a dataset that have not become characters in the script in any other way.

Stage directions: Descriptions that a playwright uses throughout a script to notate how they imagine the play's setting and how its action might unfold.

Staged reading: A step in the script development process in which actors perform the play while carrying scripts and executing minimal blocking. Staged readings do not include design elements such as scenery, lighting, props, sound effects, or projections. A staged reading helps a playwright to begin seeing their play come to life on stage, allowing the next round of edits to occur.

Staging: How a director presents a play to an audience and, more specifically, how the play's production looks, moves, and sounds.

Statement to participants: A statement shared with potential participants that provides relevant information about a research project and allows them to assess whether they wish to move forward with participation.

Talisman: A costume piece or hand prop used by an ethnoactor in performance to represent each different character they perform. A costume designer sources a character's talisman from the field notes collected and recorded on the interview participant's Participant Characteristics and Physical Surroundings Survey during data collection.

Talkback: A facilitated conversation with an audience after a performance. A talkback can take various formats, depending on its purpose.

Textual data: The source material for qualitative research; the data are textual rather than numerical and can also include audio and visual materials. See Table 1.1 in Chapter 1 (p. 6) for examples of textual data.

Textures: Additional ways of sharing research findings in an ethnotheatrical performance alongside ethnoactors performing the data. Textures can provide audiences with multiple connection points to the research findings. Textures include movement, scenic elements, costuming, lighting, projections, and sound.

Theatrically compelling coding: Selecting excerpts of a participant's interview for an ethnodrama based on whether the excerpt would be dramatically interesting in performance and includes information that an audience must hear. In the initial coding process, artist-researchers should listen for "complete stories, unique explanations, surprising declarations, and struggles for meaning," as these ways of sharing information could be theatrically compelling in performance (Salvatore, 2025, p. 268). A theatrically compelling excerpt must also answer a project's overarching research question.

Thematic bins: Symbolic containers that hold and categorize related pieces of data (Anzul, Downing, Ely, & Vinz, 1997). Thematic bins represent codes that emerge during the binning round of the analysis process as the artist-researcher reviews and analyzes the data and decides what to include in the ethnodrama. Thematic bins can also play an organizational role in an ethnodrama's scripting process.

Transcribe: To document the words spoken in a conversation, interview, or media artifact. As an artist-researcher transcribes a recording, they create transcription on the page.

Transcript: The written record of the audio of a conversation, interview, or media artifact that reflects as accurately as possible what was spoken. When an artist-researcher listens to a recording, they transcribe what they hear to the page.

   • **Flat transcript:** a transcript that presents buffed transcription as prose on the page. A flat transcript provides information about the content of what a speaker said but little or no information about how the speaker delivered the content.

   • **Scored transcript:** a transcript that presents raw transcription in a specific and nuanced way, notating a speaker's cadence by taking a hard return while typing each time a speaker pauses. The transcription appears more like poetry on the page, illustrating visually how someone spoke.

Transcription: The written notation of language that results from transcribing.

   • **Buffed transcription:** transcription that has been edited and polished during the transcribing process to remove a speaker's pauses, filler words, disfluencies, and repeated words or phrases. Buffed transcription typically appears in a flat transcript.

   • **Raw transcription:** transcription that notates what a speaker says verbatim, including all filler words such as "ums" and "aahs," verbal stumbles, and disfluencies. Raw transcription typically appears in a scored transcript.

Unity of time: In general theatrical terms, the amount of time that unfolds onstage in a play's fictional world is equal to the amount of time that unfolds offstage in reality. For ethnodrama using verbatim performance, an ethnoactor's performance of an interview excerpt should unfold across the same amount of time it took for the participant to speak it in the original interview.

Verbatim performance: The precise portrayal of an actual person using their exact speech and gestural patterns as a data source for investigation, literally word for word and gesture for gesture (Salvatore, 2023; Vachon & Salvatore, 2023).

Verbatim Performance Lab (VPL): VPL creates ethnodrama and documentary theatre performances and investigates the results with actors and audiences. The ethnoactors of VPL perform words and gestures collected from found media artifacts and interview-based data. Through these investigations and performances, VPL aims to disrupt assumptions, biases, and intolerances across a spectrum of political, social, and cultural narratives. VPL is a project of the Program in Educational Theatre in the Department of Music and Performing Arts Professions at New York University's Steinhardt School of Culture, Education, and Human Development. For more, see *http://steinhardt.nyu. edu/verbatimperformancelab*.

Verfremdung: A term coined by the 20th-century German playwright and director Bertolt Brecht that describes several theatrical techniques he used in plays and productions to raise an audience's critical awareness. *Verfremdung* has no English equivalent but is typically translated to "alienation." I prefer Meg Mumford's (2018) translation to "defamiliarization," as she believes that word "conveys more clearly the fact that Brecht regarded *Verfremdung* as political intervention into the (blindingly) familiar" (pp. 60–61).

Witness: A staging technique used in ethnotheatre that serves as a visual metaphor for the interviewer in the original interaction between the artist-researcher and an interview participant. The ethnoactor serving as the witness should direct their full attention to whoever is speaking onstage. They may also announce a character's identifier when they speak for the first time in a production.

World of the play: The context within which a play and its performance occur; the historical, social, and cultural contexts of the play and its characters; it can also impact how the characters who inhabit the play interact with each other and with the audience.

Additional Resources

The scholars and artists I have cited throughout this book warrant deeper examination to unearth the full scope of their knowledge and techniques. In most cases, as is usually the case when writing about an expansive topic, I have shared only snippets of their extensive bodies of work. Aspiring artist-researchers should explore the references list in greater detail, and I have provided additional resources here to assist you further.

As this book outlines my specific process for creating ethnodrama, I wanted to offer examples of other ways of working. Some projects mentioned below use techniques similar to my process, while others take an entirely different approach. The list of academic publications below covers various topics and methods for creating ethnodrama and is only a beginning. Just from reading the titles of the articles and journals, you can see the breadth and scope of ethnodrama's applications for academic research. Select the titles and topics that appeal to you, read those projects, and then continue exploring based on your interests.

Ahmed, S., Quinlan, E., McMullen, L., Thomas, R., Fichtner, P., & Block, J. (2015). Ethnodrama: An innovative knowledge translation tool in the management of lymphedema. *Journal of Cancer, 6*(9), 859–865.

Appadoo-Ramsamy, W., Samuel, M. A., & Ankiah-Gangadeen, A. (2022). Representing teachers' voices: An ethnodrama of Mauritian teachers under times of curriculum reform. *Journal of Education, 1*(86), 40–63.

Baur, V., Abma, T., & Baart, I. (2014). "I stand alone": An ethnodrama about the (dis)connections between a client and professionals in a residential care home. *Health Care Analysis, 22*(3), 272–291.

Davis, C. A. (2014). Unraveled, untold stories: An ethnodrama. *Adult Education Quarterly, 64*(3), 240–259.

Dell'Angelo, T. (2021). Down the rabbit hole: An ethnodrama to explore a fantastical first year of teaching. *Qualitative Inquiry, 27*(1), 77–84.

Dellenborg, L., & Lepp, M. (2018). The development of ethnographic drama to support healthcare professionals. *Anthropology in Action, 25*(1), 1–14.

Domínguez, A. D. (2024). The other black box: Compiling, co-constructing and composing ethnodrama inside a Zoom screen with Latina/x youth artivist-researchers. *Ethnography and Education, 19*(2), 152–174.

Eaton, J., Cheek-O'Donnell, S., Johnson, E., & Clark, L. (2022). Using ethnodrama to support parents in sense-making after prenatal or neonatal diagnosis of a child's disabling condition. *Journal of Applied Research in Intellectual Disabilities, 35*(1), 261–270.

Eaton, J., & Donaldson, G. (2016). Altering nursing student and older adult attitudes through a possible selves ethnodrama. *Journal of Professional Nursing, 32*(2), 141–151.

Hadley Dunn, A. (2023). The day after: An ethnodrama about teachers' decision-making amid silencing school policies. *Qualitative Inquiry, 29*(8–9), 928–940.

Hart, C. M., Ford, N. M., Hoffler, U., Reese-Durham, N., Singleton, D., Livingston, J. N. (2022). The use of the ethno-drama experience to increase knowledge and promote cervical cancer health related behavior among people of color. *Journal of Cervical Cancer Research, 4*(1), 318–326.

Hradsky, D. (2024). Composing cultural connections: Exploring tensions of creating composite ethnodramatic characters. *Qualitative Inquiry, 30*(10), 858–871.

Humphrie, J., and Lesnick, E. S. (2019). How we GLOW. *ArtsPraxis, 5*(1), 76–135.

Lewis, C., Miller, E., & Pike, S. (2023). Writing research-based theatre on aged care: The ethnodrama, After Aleppo. *Culture and Organization, 30*(3), 305–322.

Malhotra, N., & Hotton, V. (2018). Contemplating personalities: An ethnodrama. *Journal of General Education, 67*(1–2), 152–171.

McMahon, J., McGannon, K. R., & Zehntner, C. (2017). Slim to win: An ethnodrama of three elite swimmers' "presentation of self" in relation to a dominant cultural ideology. *Sociology of Sport Journal, 34*(2), 108–123.

Moore, C. E. & Whorton, R. T. (2019). My other job. *ArtsPraxis, 5*(1), 136–189.

Murray, T. (2019). The right of way. *ArtsPraxis, 5*(1), 38–80.

Nimmon, L. E. (2007). ESL-speaking immigrant women's disillusions: Voices of health care in Canada: An ethnodrama. *Health Care for Women International, 28*(4), 381–396.

Randolph, A. W., & Weems, M. E. (2010). Speak truth and shame the devil: An ethnodrama in response to racism in the academy. *Qualitative Inquiry, 16*(5), 310–313.

Rhoades, R. (2021). Ethnodrama of projectivity as hopeful pedagogy in envisioning non-dystopic futures with youth. *Research in Drama Education: The Journal of Applied Theatre and Performance, 26*(2), 335–351.

Rowe, K. (2021). Tangled: Black hair and texturism in ethnodrama. *Cultural Studies ↔ Critical Methodologies, 22*(4), 1–12.

Sánchez, R. M. (2020). Performing school failure: Using verbatim theatre to explore school grading policies. *LEARNing Landscapes, 13*(1), 203–217.

Sangha, J. K., Slade, B., Mirchandani, K., Maitra, S., & Shan, H. (2012). An ethnodrama on work-related learning in precarious jobs: Racialization and resistance. *Qualitative Inquiry, 18*(3), 286–296.

Shu, J. (2023). Facets of human conditions: Some artistic records and ethnotheatrical interpretations of ex-gambling addicts. *Applied Theatre Research, 11*(1), 57–70.

Smith, M., & Arthur, C. (2021). Understanding the coach–athlete conflict: An ethnodrama to illustrate conflict in sport. *Qualitative Research in Sport, Exercise and Health, 14*(3), 474–492.

Smith, M., Robert, C., Wagstaff, D., & Szedlak, C. (2022). Conflict between a captain and star player: An ethnodrama of interpersonal conflict experiences. *Journal of Applied Sport Psychology, 35*(4), 598–624.

Speechley, M., DeForge, R. T., Ward-Griffin, C., Marlatt, N. M., & Gutmanis, I. (2015). Creating an ethnodrama to catalyze dialogue in home-based dementia care. *Qualitative Health Research, 25*(11), 1551–1559.

Sweet, J. D., & Carlson, D. L. (2018). A story of becoming: Trans* equity as ethnodrama. *Qualitative Inquiry, 24*(3), 183–193.

Țîțtea, I. (2021). "Ain't I also a migrant?": An ethnodrama of weaving knowledges otherwise in Finnish migration research. *Nordic Journal of Studies in Educational Policy, 7*(3), 136–147.

Vanover, C. (2016). Listening to the silences: A teacher's first year in words and music. *Art/Research International: A Transdisciplinary Journal, 1*(1), 174–207.

Williams, S. P., Bush, A., & Baker, C. (2024, March). Supporting the professional sports coach in the workplace: Presenting the pedagogue as the missing scientist. *Sports Coaching Review*, pp. 1–30.

Yanko, M., & Lee, H. (2023). Resisting heteronormative traditions to stage the possible: An ethnodrama. *Departures in Critical Qualitative Research, 12*(4), 53–76.

As an arts-based research methodology, ethnodrama has a close relationship and shared lineage with theatrical forms such as documentary theatre, tribunal theatre, and verbatim theatre. I share a list of contemporary theatre artists and companies working internationally and creating theatre using various forms of textual data as their source materials. This list is a sampling for your consideration and is far from exhaustive. Also, inclusion on this list is not an endorsement but an invitation to explore the variety of approaches and their results. You should search for these theatre makers and others, read and experience their work, and use whatever you learn to inspire your own projects.

Hassan Abdulrazzak
- *The Special Relationship*

Emily Ackerman and K. J. Sanchez
- *Reentry*

Mojisola Adebayo
- *The Interrogation of Sandra Bland*

Dustin Lance Black
- *8*

Jessica Blank and Eric Jensen
- *The Exonerated*
- *Aftermath*
- *Coal Country*

Alecky Blythe and Recorded Delivery
- *London Road*
- *The Girlfriend Experience*

Gregory Burke
- *Black Watch*

José Casas
- *14*

The Civilians
- *The Unbelieving*
- *The Undertaking*
- *Pretty Filthy*

Eve Ensler
- *The Vagina Monologues*

Nadia Fall
- *Home*

David Hare
- *Stuff Happens*

Lucas Hnath
- *Dana H*

Moisés Kaufman and Tectonic Theater Project
- *The Laramie Project*
- *Gross Indecency: The Three Trials of Oscar Wilde*

Nicholas Kent
- *All the President's Men?*
- *Srebrenica*

Andrew Kushnir and Project: Humanity
- *Towards Youth: A Play on Radical Hope*

Life Jacket Theatre Company
- *America Is Hard to See*

Emily Mann

- *Execution of Justice*
- *Greensboro (A Requiem)*

Lucía Miranda and The Cross Border Project

- *Fiesta, Fiesta, Fiesta*

Arian Moayed

- *The Courtroom*

Richard Norton-Taylor

- *The Colour of Justice*

Roslyn Oades

- *I'm Your Man*

Dael Orlandersmith

- *Until the Flood*

Ping Chong + Company

- *Undesirable Elements* series

Tina Satter

- *Is This a Room*

Tetsuro Shigematsu

- *Empire of the Sun*
- *1 Hour Photo*

Gillian Slovo

- *Grenfell: in the words of survivors*
- *Guantanamo: "Honor Bound to Defend Freedom"* (with Victoria Brittain)

Anna Deavere Smith

- *Fires in the Mirror*
- *Twilight: Los Angeles, 1992*
- *Let Me Down Easy*
- *Notes from the Field*

Robin Soans

- *Talking to Terrorists*

University of Denver Prison Arts Initiative

- *If Light Closed Its Eyes*

Verbatim Performance Lab

- *Guess the Candidate*
- *If Just the Rights of People Were Considered*
- *Dare I Use the Word*
- *The Kavanaugh Files*
- *The Serena Williams Project*
- *We're Not There Yet*
- *Veterans Story Collecting Project*
- *The Grab 'Em Tapes*

Waltzing Mechanics

- *EL Stories*
- *A Chip on Her Shoulder* by Kristin Rose Kelly

Doug Wright

- *I Am My Own Wife*

References

Ackroyd, J., & O'Toole, J. (Eds.). (2010). *Performing research: Tensions, triumphs and trade-offs of ethnodrama*. Trentham Books.

Adams, T. E., & Boylorn, R. M. (2019). Public ethnography. In P. Leavy (Ed.), *The Oxford handbook of methods for public scholarship* (pp. 269–288). Oxford University Press.

American Academy of Arts & Sciences. (2019, November 6). *In Conversation with Anna Deavere Smith—Annual David M. Rubenstein Lecture* [Video]. YouTube. www.youtube.com/watch?v=R8orTcppRvg.

American Speech–Language–Hearing Association. (2024, June 29). Stuttering. www.asha.org/public/speech/disorders/stuttering.

Anzul, A., Downing, M., Ely, M., & Vinz, R. (1997). *On writing qualitative research: Living by words*. Routledge.

Aspen Institute. (2020, July 8). *Aspen Ideas Festival 2020: Bill Gates, Madeleine Albright, Anna Deavere Smith, and Yuval Sharon* [Video]. YouTube. www.youtube.com/watch?v=YlvzAZA6M2w.

Barnett, D. (2015). *Brecht in practice: Theatre, theory and performance*. Methuen Drama.

Barone, T., & Eisner, E. (2012). *Arts based research*. Sage.

Belliveau, G., & Lea, G. W. (Eds.). (2016). *Research-based theatre: An artistic methodology*. Intellect.

Boal, A. (1985). *Theatre of the oppressed* (C. A. Leal McBride & M. Leal McBride, Trans.) Theatre Communications Group. (Original work published 1979)

Bogart, A. (2001). *A director prepares: Seven essays on art and theatre*. Routledge.

Bram, J. (1953). Section of anthropology: The application of psychodrama to research in social anthropology. *Transactions of the New York Academy of Sciences, 15*, 253–257.

Brecht, B. (1992). *Brecht on theatre: The development of an aesthetic* (J. Willet, Trans.). Hill & Wang.

Brown, L. I. (2015). *New play development: Facilitating creativity for dramaturgs, playwrights, and everyone else*. Focus.

Burch, D. (2019). The ethno-actor: Encompassing the intricacies and challenges of character creation in ethnotheatre. *ArtsPraxis, 5*(1), 24–37.

Chilton, G., & Leavy, P. (2020). Arts-based research: Merging social research and the creative arts. In P. Leavy (Ed.), *Oxford handbook of qualitative research* (2nd ed., pp. 601–632). Oxford University Press.

Costa, A. L., & Kallick, B. (1993). Through the lens of a critical friend. *Educational Leadership, 51*, 49–51.

Cox, S., & Belliveau, G. (2019). Health theatre: Embodying research. In P. Leavy (Ed.), *The*

Oxford handbook of methods for public scholarship (pp. 335–357). Oxford University Press.

Delamont, S., & Atkinson, P. (2018). The ethics of ethnography. In R. Iphofen & M. Tolich (Eds.), *The SAGE handbook of qualitative research ethics* (pp. 119–132). Sage.

Denzin, N. K. (2003). *Performance ethnography: Critical pedagogy and the politics of culture.* Sage.

Denzin, N. (2018). *Performance autoethnography: Critical pedagogy and the politics of culture* (2nd ed.). Routledge.

Dominus, S. (2009, September 30). The health care monologues. *New York Times.* www.nytimes.com/2009/10/04/magazine/04smith-t.html.

Faris, R., & Felmlee, D. (2011). Status struggles: Network centrality and gender segregation in same- and cross-gender aggression. *American Sociological Review, 76*(1), 48–73.

Fisher, A. S. (2020). *Performing the testimonial: Rethinking verbatim dramaturgies.* Manchester University Press.

Fisher, T. (2014). *Post-show discussions in new play development.* Palgrave Pivot.

Freiband, A. (2023). *What are artists' literacies?* Artists' Literacies Institute. https://www.artistsliteracies.org/about-us.

Garson, C. (2021). *Beyond documentary realism: Aesthetic transgressions in British verbatim theatre.* De Gruyter.

Gee, J. P. (2014). *Introduction to discourse analysis?: Theory and method* (4th ed.). Routledge.

Guadalupe, M., & Salvatore, J. (Eds.). (2017). *Her opponent.* Unpublished script.

Hammond, W., & Steward, D. (Eds.). (2008). *Verbatim, verbatim: Contemporary documentary theatre.* Oberon Books.

Harrison, A. K. (2018). *Ethnography.* Oxford University Press.

Haus, H.-U. (1991). Experiment in mass appeal: Theatre of the Weimar republic. In *Classics in Context Louisville.* Actors Theatre of Louisville.

Howland, R. (2022). "Yet through such connection . . .": Building anti-racist and culturally responsive drama programs in rural communities. *ArtsPraxis, 9*(2), 80–95.

Huff, K. R., & Salvatore, J. (2023). *That's not supposed to be happening.* Unpublished script.

Irmer, T. (2006). A search for new realities: Documentary theatre in Germany. *Drama Review, 50*(3), 16–28.

Janesick, V. J. (2020). Oral history interviewing with purpose and critical awareness. In P. Leavy (Ed.), *The Oxford handbook of qualitative research* (2nd ed., pp. 457–479). Oxford University Press.

Kara, H. (2020). *Creative research methods: A practical guide* (2nd ed.). Policy Press.

Klein, E. (2020). *Why we're polarized.* Avid Reader Press.

Kronenberg, D., & Ricardo, L. (2022). The blended audition: An open invitation to all students. *Theatre Topics, 32*(2), 73–82.

LaBonte, M., Mosley, T. W., Hamilton, A. L., Forbes, C., & McKinnie, D. (2023). *If Light Closed Its Eyes.* LuxLit Press.

Leavy, P. (2020a). A changing terrain: Qualitative research in the age of transdisciplinarity and public scholarship. In P. Leavy (Ed.), *Oxford handbook of qualitative research* (2nd ed., pp. 1183–1195). Oxford University Press.

Leavy, P. (2020b). *Method meets art: Arts-based research practice* (3rd ed.). Guilford Press.

Leavy, P. (2023). *Research design: Quantitative, qualitative, mixed methods, arts-based, and community-based participatory research approaches* (2nd ed.). Guilford Press.

Lerman, L., & Borstel, J. (2022). *Critique is creative: The critical response process in theory and action.* Wesleyan University Press.

Madison, D. S. (2018). *Performed ethnography and communication: Improvisation and embodied performance.* Routledge.

Marcus, E. (1992). *Making history: The struggle for gay and lesbian equal rights, 1945–1990, an oral history.* HarperCollins.

Marcus, E. (2002). *Making gay history: The half-century fight for gay and lesbian equal rights.* Harper.

Marcus, E. (Host). (2018, January 4). *J. J. Belanger* (Season 3, Episode 4) [Audio podcast episode]. *Making Gay History.* https://makinggayhistory.org/podcast/j-j-belanger.

McNiff, S. (2014). Art speaking for itself: Evidence that inspires and convinces. *Journal of Applied Arts and Health, 5*(2), 252–262.

McNiff, S. (2025). Philosophical and practical foundations of artistic inquiry: Creating paradigms, methods, and presentations based in art. In P. Leavy (Ed.), *Handbook of arts-based research* (2nd ed., pp. 23–36). Guilford Press.

McVarish, J., & Milne, C. (2014). A model of action for self-assessment and self-evaluation: The nuts and bolts of getting started. In J. McVarish & C. Milne (Eds.), *Teacher educators rethink self-assessment in higher education* (pp. 29–46). Peter Lang.

Meyers, C. (2021). Divided we stand. *ArtsPraxis, 8*(1), 1–63.

Meyers, C. (2023). Two truths and a lie: An ethnodramatic exploration of resistance and relationships between women in our current political and social climate. *Qualitative Inquiry, 29*(5), 598–609.

Mienczakowski, J. (1995). The theater of ethnography: The reconstruction of ethnography into theater with emancipatory potential. *Qualitative Inquiry, 1*(3), 360–375.

Mienczakowski, J. (2001). Ethnodrama: performed research—limitations and potential. In P. Atkinson, A. Coffey, S. Delamont, J. Lofland, & L. Lofland (Eds.), *Handbook of ethnography* (pp. 468–476). Sage.

Mienczakowski, J. (2019). Ethnodrama and ethnofiction. In P. Atkinson, S. Delamont, A. Cernat, J. W. Sakshaug, & R. A. Williams (Eds.), *SAGE research methods foundations.* Sage. https://methods.sagepub.com/foundations/ethnodrama-and-ethnofiction.

Mienczakowski, J., & Moore, T. (2008). Performing data with notions of responsibility. In J. G. Knowles & A. L. Cole (Eds.), *Handbook of the arts in qualitative research* (pp. 451–458). Sage.

Mumford, M. (2018). *Bertolt Brecht.* Routledge.

National Geographic Society. (2009). *United States regions.* National Geographic Education. https://education.nationalgeographic.org/resource/united-states-regions.

Nichols, J., Cox, S. M., Cook, C., Lea, G. W., & Belliveau, G. (2022). Research-based theatre about veterans transitioning home: A mixed-methods evaluation of audience impacts. *Social Science and Medicine, 292,* Article 114578.

Olf, J. M. (1997). Reading the dramatic text for production. *Theatre Topics, 7*(2), 153–169.

Paget, D. (1987). "Verbatim theatre": Oral history and documentary techniques. *New Theatre Quarterly, 3*(12), 317–336.

Paget, D. (2011). *No other way to tell it: Docudrama on film and television* (2nd ed.). Manchester University Press.

Parenteau, A. (2017, August 22). *How do you solve a problem like documentary theatre?* American Theatre. www.americantheatre.org/2017/08/22/how-do-you-solve-a-problem-like-documentary-theatre.

Parker, C., Scott, S., & Geddes, A., (2019). Snowball sampling. In P. Atkinson, S. Delamont, A. Cernat, J. W. Sakshaug, & R. A. Williams (Eds.), *SAGE research methods foundations.* https://methods.sagepub.com/foundations/snowball-sampling.

Pinson, K. S. (1966). *Modern Germany: Its history and civilization* (2nd ed.). Macmillan.

Rosenberg, J. M. (1962). Ethnodrama as a research method in anthropology. *Group Psychotherapy, 15*(3), 236–243.

Rubin, H. J., & Rubin, I. S. (2012). *Qualitative interviewing: The art of hearing data* (3rd ed.). Sage.

Sajnani, N., Sallis, R., & Salvatore, J. (2019). Three arts based researchers walk into a forum: A conversation on the opportunities and challenges in embodied and performed research. In P. Duffy, C. Hatton, & R. Sallis (Eds.), *Drama research methods: Provocations of practice* (pp. 77–96). Sense.

Saldaña, J. (2005). (Ed.). *Ethnodrama: An anthology of reality theatre.* AltaMira Press.

Saldaña, J. (2010). Reflections on an ethnotheatre aesthetic. *ArtsPraxis, 2*(1), 1–14.

Saldaña, J. (2011a). *Ethnotheatre: Research from page to stage.* Routledge.

Saldaña, J. (2011b). *Fundamentals of qualitative research.* Oxford University Press.

Saldaña, J. (2021). *The coding manual for qualitative researchers* (4th ed.). Sage.

Salvatore, J. (2008). *The class project.* Unpublished script.

Salvatore, J. (2010). *open heart.* Unpublished script.

Salvatore, J. (2014). *Towards the fear.* Unpublished script.

Salvatore, J. (2018). *Of a certain age.* Unpublished script.

Salvatore, J. (2020a). *Making gay history: Before Stonewall.* Unpublished script.

Salvatore, J. (2020b). Scripting the ethnodrama. In P. Leavy (Ed.), *Oxford handbook of qualitative research* (2nd ed., pp. 1045–1083). Oxford University Press.

Salvatore, J. (2023). Verbatim performance and its possibilities. *ArtsPraxis, 10*(1), 1–20.

Salvatore, J. (2025). Ethnodrama and ethnotheatre. In P. Leavy (Ed.), *Handbook of arts-based research* (2nd ed., pp. 260–280). Guilford Press.

Salvatore, J., & Huff, K. R. (2022). *Whatever you are, be a good one.* Unpublished script.

Shigematsu, T., Cook, C., Belliveau, G., & Lea, G. W. (2021). Research-based theatre across disciplines: A relational approach to inquiry. *Applied Theatre Research, 9*(1), 55–72.

Small, M. L. (2019, April 6). *Rhetoric and social science in a polarized society* [Lecture]. American Educational Research Association Spencer Lecture, Toronto. www.spencer.org/news/aera-2019.

Small, M. L., & Calarco, J. M. (2022). *Qualitative literacy: A guide to evaluating ethnographic and interview research.* University of California Press.

Smith, A. D. (1993). *Fires in the mirror.* Anchor Books.

Smith, A. D. (1994). *Twilight: Los Angeles, 1992.* Anchor Books.

Smith, A. D. (2000). *Talk to me: Travels in media and politics.* Anchor Books.

Smith, A. D. (2018). *Let me down easy.* Theatre Communications Group.

Smith, A. D. (2019). *Notes from the field.* Anchor Books.

Snow, S. (2022). *Ethnodramatherapy: Integrating research, therapy, theatre, and social activism into one method.* Routledge.

Snow, S., Segalowitz, N., D'Amico, M., & Mongerson, E. (2023), The audience impact of an ethnodrama based on the lived experiences of family caregivers of loved ones with a mental illness. *Drama Therapy Review, 9*(2), 239–257.

Soloski, A. (2013). What's up, doc?: The ethics of fact and fabulation in documentary performance: A forum. *Theater, 43*(1), 9–39.

Stanislavski, K. (2008). *An actor's work* (J. Benedetti, Trans.). Routledge.

Summerskill, C. (2021). *Creating verbatim theatre from oral histories.* Routledge.

Trencsényi, K. (2015). *Dramaturgy in the making: A user's guide for theatre practitioners.* Bloomsbury Methuen Drama.

U.S. Department of Health and Human Services. (2023, January 30). *Office of Human Research Protections.* www.hhs.gov/ohrp/regulations-and-policy/regulations/45-cfr-46/index.html.

Vachon, W., Hossain, R., Ramsay, N., Moore, M., Milo, M. (2019). Frictions and actions: The actor's role in ethnodrama. *Qualitative Inquiry, 25*(2), 118–129.

Vachon, W., & Salvatore, J. (2023). Wading the quagmire: Aesthetics and ethics in verbatim theatre: Act 1. *Qualitative Inquiry, 29*(2), 383–392.

Vanover, C., & Mihas, P. (2022). Data and conceptual options. In C. Vanover, P. Mihas, & J. Saldaña (Eds.), *Analyzing and interpreting qualitative research: After the interview* (pp. 1–5). Sage.

Verbatim Performance Lab. (2021). *Portraits US: Covid-19.* https://wp.nyu.edu/verbatimperformancelab/portraits-us-covid-19/.

Wallace, A. J. (Host). (2021, May 28). The Violet Protest (No. 6) [Audio podcast episode]. In *State of the Arts Arizona.* https://heararizona.org/state-arts-arizona/episode-6-violet-protest.

Watt, D. (2009). Local knowledges, memories, and community: From oral history to performance. In S. C. Haedicke, D. Heddon, A. Oz, & E. J. Westlake (Eds.), *Political performances: Theory and practice* (pp. 189–212). Brill.

Weiss, P. (1971). The material and the models: Notes towards a definition of documentary theatre. *Theatre Quarterly, 1,* 41.

Young, S. (2017). The ethics of the representation of the real people and their stories in verbatim theatre. In E. O'Toole, A. P. Kristić, & S. Young (Eds.), *Ethical exchanges in translation, adaptation and dramaturgy* (pp. 21–42). Brill.

Index

Note. f, n, or *t* following a page number indicates a figure, note, or table; boldface page numbers indicate glossary terms.

About the Author

Joe Salvatore, MFA, is Clinical Professor of Educational Theatre at the Steinhardt School of Culture, Education, and Human Development at New York University (NYU), where he teaches courses in ethnodrama, verbatim performance, community-engaged theatre, and new play development. In 2017, Mr. Salvatore founded the Verbatim Performance Lab, which, under his direction, has created over 25 video and live performance projects, and he has facilitated outreach and education programs throughout the United States. He is a recipient of honors including the Johnny Saldaña Outstanding Professor of Theatre Education Award from the American Alliance for Theatre and Education, the Dr. Martin Luther King, Jr. Faculty Award from NYU, the Teaching Excellence Award and the Champions of Equity: Gender and Trans Justice Award from the Steinhardt School, and the Dedication to Education Award from the NYU LGBTQ+ Center. Mr. Salvatore is a cluster member of the University of British Columbia's Research-Based Theatre Collaborative, a collaborating faculty member with Arts & Health @ NYU, an advisory board member for Artists' Literacies Institute, an alumnus of the Lincoln Center Directors Lab, and a member of the Dramatists Guild of America. His website is *www.joesalvatore.com*.